Life After High School

of related interest

Developing College Skills in Students with Autism and Asperger's Syndrome
Sarita Freedman
ISBN 978 1 84310 917 4

Job Success for Persons with Developmental Disabilities
David B. Wiegan
ISBN 978 1 84310 922 8

Guiding Your Teenager with Special Needs through the Transition from School to Adult Life
Tools for Parents
Mary Korpi
ISBN 978 1 84310 874 0

Life After High School

A Guide for Students with Disabilities and Their Families

Susan Yellin and Christina Cacioppo Bertsch

Jessica Kingsley Publishers
London and Philadelphia

First published in 2010
by Jessica Kingsley Publishers
116 Pentonville Road
London N1 9JB, UK
and
400 Market Street, Suite 400
Philadelphia, PA 19106, USA
www.jkp.com

Library of Congress Cataloging in Publication Data

Yellin, Susan.
Life after high school : a guide for students with disabilities and their families / Susan Yellin and Christina Cacioppo Bertsch.
p. cm.
Includes bibliographical references and index.
ISBN 978-1-84905-828-5 (alk. paper)
1. People with disabilities--Vocational guidance. 2. Students with disabilities--Vocational guidance. I. Bertsch, Christina Cacioppo. II. Title.
HV1568.5.Y45 2010
646.70087--dc22
2010004298

British Library Cataloguing in Publication Data
A CIP catalogue record for this book is available from the British Library

ISBN 978 1 84905 828 5

Printed and bound in the United States by
Thomson-Shore, Inc.

Dedicated to our families—

Paul, David, Matthew, and Benjamin Yellin

and James, Sophia, and Audrey Bertsch

with thanks for your love and support

Acknowledgments

A number of people helped us bring this book to life and we want to take this opportunity to thank them.

We are particularly grateful to Jo Anne Simon, Esq., who lent her nationally recognized expertise in disability law and high-stakes testing to Chapters 1 and 5, and we are most appreciative for her insights, information, and editorial assistance with these chapters.

Dr. Paul Yellin, Susan's husband, served as our medical consultant, and James Bertsch, Christina's husband, shared his knowledge as an educator and school administrator to give us a look into the real workings of high school guidance offices.

Our readers included Matthew and David Yellin, and Danielle and Maureen Cacioppo. David, particularly, assisted with technical editing and we are grateful for his expertise in legal citation format.

Christina's parents, Maureen and Paul Cacioppo, and Catherine Smith spent countless hours babysitting Christina's daughters, making it possible for Christina to actually sit down and write.

All of those who contributed their knowledge and assistance have made this book better. To the extent that if there are any errors or omissions, the fault is entirely ours, not theirs.

Our acknowledgments would not be complete without thanking the students and families who shared their stories with us. We hope that their experiences will help and inspire families and other students who are moving beyond high school to college, the workplace, and adulthood.

S.Y. and C.C.B.

Contents

Introduction

If you are reading this book, you are probably a high school student with a disability, or the parent, counselor, or teacher of such a student. High school may be going well, or may be a constant struggle, but you have recognized that it will eventually come to an end and you have been thinking about what comes next and how to get there.

We've written this book to help answer the many questions that students, families, and their advisors have asked us over the years. We hope that our experience can help you better understand students' rights, responsibilities, and options as they move on to further education or the workplace—and help provide the tools they will need to succeed once they get there.

Our desks are piled high with books about attention deficit and learning disabilities, and we will certainly address these issues throughout this book. But we recognize that there are many other kinds of disabilities—including physical, psychiatric, and neurological—that students and their families have dealt with throughout elementary and high school and that continue to be an issue as students move beyond the secondary level. And we are mindful that students are complex individuals, many of whom deal with more than one kind of disability, which our medical colleagues refer to as comorbidities.

We hope to give you a unique perspective on transitioning to life after high school. This multi-year journey begins no later than the beginning of high school and continues well into the early years of college, vocational training, or the workplace. We'll set out what we believe to be the best time to start each step, but will help bring you up to speed if you haven't started until later. We believe that the path to adulthood is a partnership between students and their parents, and we have tried to make this book relevant to both of you. Too many of the books we have encountered are highly academic or extremely simplistic. It's easier to take the necessary steps from dependence to adulthood, and from high school to college or the workplace, when all members of the family are literally on the same page.

We also know that each student and each family is different. For some students, high school has gone relatively smoothly with appropriate accommodations. For these students, college has always been a definite goal, and their academic performance has not been seriously diminished by their disability. For other students, whose disabilities are related to learning or attention, high school performance has been problematic, and even with an appropriate learning plan and accommodations, scores on standardized tests and grade point averages have been affected by their disability.

By looking at the transition process through the experiences of real students we have met and with whom we have worked, we hope to raise important issues and provide all of our readers with information they can apply to their own circumstances. As importantly, we aim to make this book a good reading experience. Buying this book and having it sit on a shelf unread is not going to be helpful to anyone. We believe that sharing stories, and avoiding lists and charts, will help make this an enjoyable read.

What qualifies us to write this book? Christina has worked with high school and college students and their families as both Director of Disability Services at Fordham University and as a college counselor to students with a wide range of disabilities. As the founder of CCB Educational Consulting Corp., she helps to identify supportive college settings and assist with standardized test accommodations, applications, and advocacy training to enable students to work successfully with colleges and professors. She has experienced the impact of a disability in a college setting first hand, watching her younger sister struggle with a disability and ultimately leave college without a degree. Christina is also the parent of two young daughters.

Susan has been an attorney for more than 25 years, and was prompted by her own experiences as a parent to create the nonprofit Center for Learning Differences and its annual Life After High School Conferences, which have been attended by hundreds of students, families, and counselors. She also serves as Director of Advocacy and Transition Services at the Yellin Center for Student Success, where her husband, pediatrician Dr. Paul Yellin, and his team use an interdisciplinary model to evaluate struggling students of all ages. Susan has dealt with the college selection and application process with all three of her sons, one of whom has complex medical and learning issues.

We do want to point out a couple of logistical matters. First, all of the students and families we mention by name here are real or composites of real students; however, we have respected their privacy by changing their names and certain identifying details. Second, we have tried to avoid the awkward he/she problem by alternating the pronouns we use by chapter. So our general references to students will be male or female in alternating chapters.

We make mention of a number of organizations, books, and websites throughout the chapters that follow and in our Resources chapter at the end of this book. We provide this information to assist our readers, but cannot be responsible for the accuracy of information set forth in websites or books nor for the services provided by individuals or organizations.

Finally, we thrive on feedback and both believe that the world is made better by networking. Please visit our website at www.lifeafterhsbook.com and reach out to us with your questions and comments at lifeafterhs@gmail.com. We'd love to hear from you.

Susan and Christina

Chapter 1

The Legal Landscape

Nobody likes to read about legal stuff. Laws and legal decisions can quickly put anyone to sleep. But you really do need to know about the bowl of legal alphabet soup we are serving up here—laws such as the IDEA, 504, ADA, FERPA, and HIPAA. So, we'll make a deal with you. Skip this chapter if you must, but realize that the material we discuss here will better help you to understand every other chapter in this book. We've tried to make this background information interesting and to explain why these laws are fundamental to so many aspects of life for students with disabilities, especially as they move beyond high school to college and the workplace. We think you'll be glad if you stick with it.

In the beginning

The Individuals with Disabilities Education Act,[1] universally referred to as the IDEA, is the most important law governing special education services for students from preschool through high school. The impetus for the IDEA and its predecessor legislation, the 1975 Education for All Handicapped Children Act,[2] grew out of a series of court cases which followed the Constitutional arguments made in the landmark 1954 case Brown v. Board of Education of Topeka, Kansas,[3] and sought to expand the reach of these arguments. The Brown case dealt with the segregation of schools by race, and attorneys who argued on behalf of Linda Brown and almost 200 other students included future Supreme Court Justice Thurmond Marshall, the first African-American to serve on the nation's highest court. The Supreme Court decision in the Brown case determined that "separate but equal" education based upon race was a violation of the Constitution—establishing the principle that access to public education is a right that must be made available to all on equal terms. The eventual impact of this decision went far beyond declaring the illegality of excluding students from schools because of their race. Court cases that followed went on to look at students who were excluded from public education because of their disabilities. For example, in Washington, DC, Michael Williams, a 16-year-old who was initially excluded from school because of health problems, and eight-year-old George Liddell, Jr., who was denied admission to attend the local elementary school because he would require a special class, were just two of many students permitted to attend public schools because of these subsequent decisions.[4]

Adding to the public awareness raised by the local cases that followed Brown were revelations by a young television journalist, Geraldo Rivera (yes, *that* Geraldo Rivera) of horrific conditions at the Willowbrook State School in New York. Rivera's 1972 award winning exposé featured hidden cameras showing how more than 6000 developmentally disabled children and adults lived in a facility designed for 4000. By using the power and reach of television, the Willowbrook story helped bring to the attention of the American public the issue of how individuals with profound disabilities were denied decent care—let alone education.

In the mid-1970s, when Congress began looking at how the nation's eight million children with disabilities were being educated, they found that more than half were not receiving appropriate educational services and at least one million were excluded from school completely. Students with emotional disabilities were among the most affected; Congress found that 82 percent of students with these disabilities did not have their educational needs met.[5]

It was against this backdrop that the legislation that became the IDEA was first created. It contains several fundamental principles—FAPE (Free Appropriate Public Education), LRE (Least Restrictive Environment), IEP (Individual Education Program)—which, taken together, have shaped the rights and services provided to students in elementary and high schools for more than a generation.

* The IDEA was preceded by the court decisions and laws of the civil rights movement, which found equal access to education to be a fundamental right under the Constitution.

The IDEA

The Education for All Handicapped Children Act was revised by Congress and renamed IDEA in 1991;[6] it was most recently reauthorized in 2004.[7] Like many other laws, it is essentially a funding statute; it applies to every state because every state takes federal funding for education. There are some minor differences from state to state in how the IDEA is implemented because each state can establish its own laws and regulations, as long as these provide at least the level of rights and services of the federal law.

We need to begin by recognizing that the IDEA was never designed to help all students. It only applies to those students who meet the definitions it sets out for specific disabilities. These specific disabilities include hearing impairments (including deafness), speech or language impairments, visual impairments (including blindness), serious emotional disturbance, orthopedic impairments, autism, traumatic brain injury, mental retardation, specific learning disabilities, and a category called "other health impairments." A student must not only have one or more of these specified types of disabilities, but that student must also need special education services because of such disability. There are a number of court cases that discuss which kinds of disabilities require special educational services and which do not, but the general rule is that if a student is doing well in school and can access—both physically and intellectually—the material in a regular classroom, despite his disability and without educational supports or supplemental services, he will not qualify for services under the IDEA.[8] If his disability interferes with him obtaining the benefits of a regular education, he falls within the group of students the IDEA was designed to serve.

So Luisa, a student with food allergies, would not be entitled to IDEA services based on her allergies, since they do not interfere with her performance in a regular classroom. But Patrick, who has serious learning disabilities, does qualify for IDEA services since his disability has a substantial impact on his ability to handle the curriculum in a regular classroom. But what about Luisa's food allergies? Doesn't the school need to be aware of this medical condition and have a plan in place to handle an allergic reaction? Students with allergies or other medical conditions who don't necessarily need special education services, but who still need to have their disabilities recognized and accommodated by their school, are covered by another federal law we will examine later in this chapter, commonly referred to as Section 504. They are also covered by the Americans with Disabilities Act of 1990, the ADA, which was most recently amended and expanded effective January 1, 2009.[9]

The most basic requirement of the IDEA is that every student who qualifies for services as defined in the law is entitled to FAPE—a Free Appropriate Public Education. Free means just that—there is to be no cost for education in the public schools and, if the public schools cannot offer an appropriate education, then students will be entitled to a publicly funded education in a nonpublic school. The meaning of appropriate has been much discussed over the years, but it is generally still held to be the standard set forth in 1982 by the US Supreme Court in what is known as the Rowley case.[10] Amy Rowley was deaf, with minimal residual hearing. Her elementary school decided that she did not require a sign language interpreter in her classroom since Amy was very bright and was skilled at reading lips. Her parents sued the school, arguing that even though Amy was getting passing grades and progressing from grade to grade, she was missing a portion of what was going on in the classroom and was therefore being denied FAPE. The Supreme Court found that Amy was not entitled to a sign language interpreter. The Justices set out a narrow view of what constitutes FAPE, and stated that to meet that standard an education under the special education law must merely provide:

> personalized instruction with sufficient support services to permit the child to benefit educationally from that instruction… must meet the State's educational standards, must approximate the grade levels used in the State's regular education…and should be reasonably calculated to enable the child to achieve passing marks and advance from grade to grade.[11]

In short, the Court found that FAPE fell far short of requiring excellence; it only required that academic progress be made. In the years since the Rowley case was decided, there have been changes in the law and much commentary that raises the question of whether the minimal Rowley standards still apply.[12] However, Rowley has not explicitly been overturned, by the Supreme Court or by newer versions of the IDEA, and parents who expect that their child will be receiving the very highest level of instruction under the IDEA, to fully maximize his potential, are often disappointed.

In addition to FAPE, the IDEA requires that students be educated in what is called the Least Restrictive Environment, or LRE. That means that to the extent possible, every student should be educated in a regular class in a regular school. Of course, many students need more intensive services or a more specialized setting than can be provided by a regular classroom, or even a regular public school, but each step away from that standard must be justified by the student's educational needs. So, for example, if a student will be in a regular class for part of the day, but will be in a smaller, specialized class for certain academic subjects, the school must explain why it has moved away from the preferred setting of all-day placement in a regular class. For students who need all-day placement in a specialized class, or even placement in a specialized school, the same requirement applies; the school must consider and reject less restrictive placements before it can place the student in a more restrictive environment.

The plan for each student's education under the IDEA—the roadmap to be followed for each academic year—is the Individual Educational Program, the IEP. The law provides that this is to be developed individually for each student and that it should set out the goals for the year and how that student is going to achieve them.

The IDEA also imposes an obligation on school districts that is called "child find." Schools cannot wait until a parent or student comes to them and asks for special education services. School districts must implement programs to determine which students in their community and their school may be in need of such services. The obligation is on the school to see to it that these children are identified and provided with services. We will see that this is very different from what happens in college or the workplace.

Complaints under the IDEA are initially handled by State Departments of Education, which are required to have a system in place that allows parents and school districts to bring disputes before a hearing officer. If matters are not resolved on that level, a lawsuit may be filed in federal or state court. Since the section of the IDEA that gives the federal courts jurisdiction in IDEA cases also provides for an award of attorneys' fees to the "prevailing party,"[13] attorneys will almost always bring lawsuits to enforce the IDEA in federal court rather than in state courts that do not provide attorneys' fees. These cases can move as high as the US Supreme Court, which has ruled on a number of IDEA cases over the years.[14]

By now, many readers who have dealt with the real-world implementation of the IDEA are shaking their heads. We know that the IDEA can be an enormous benefit to students and that the services provided under its auspices can make the difference between a meaningful education and academic failure for many students. But we also know that the failure to identify or properly evaluate students, inadequate IEPs or IEPs that are not followed, and the failure or inability of schools to provide the kind of educational and related services that the IDEA requires are common problems faced by students with disabilities and their families in every part of the country. Still, for all of its flaws, the IDEA is a familiar system and one that many families have worked with for a dozen years or more by the time high school comes to an end. It can be a real shock for students and their families to learn that the IDEA and its rights and protections no longer apply to almost all students who have graduated from high school.

---

* The IDEA puts the obligation on the K–12 school to identify and reach out to students with disabilities. Families need to recognize that this will not be the case after high school.

* The IDEA only applies to students who fall within one of its classifications. For the IDEA to apply to a student who falls within one of the listed classifications, he must ALSO require special education services. We will see that this focus on needing special educational services is unique to the IDEA.

The end of the IDEA

Imagine you are taking a trip by car. You have a plan for your trip and have packed maps and maybe a GPS to guide you. You have decided where you want to go and where you hope to stop along the way, and you have some information about the sights you will be seeing and the highways and side roads you will be traveling. Even if you are going to a new destination, your travel routine is a familiar one and you pretty much know what to expect from your journey. You know how to find gas, food, and whom to call for help if your car breaks down. Then imagine that you are told you can no longer travel by car. All travel must be by air or train. Each of these modes of transport has its own rules—there are restrictions on what you can bring with you, and fares can be expensive and difficult to calculate. In addition, both air and train travel have specific schedules and you can only travel when these schedules allow and to specific destinations. Frustrating? Confusing? Absolutely. This is what many families of students with disabilities feel when they leave behind the legal protections and procedures of high school.

Who continues to be covered by the IDEA after graduation? One group is those students who are awarded a certificate that is not an actual high school diploma, but really just signifies that the student with a disability has met the goals set forth in his IEP. Different states have different names for this certificate of completion, indicating that the student (usually someone with significant learning difficulties) has completed the goals set out in his IEP, but has not met the state or local standards that would enable him to receive a state or local diploma. We'll use a term that some states use for these certificates—an IEP diploma. Students who receive an IEP diploma can continue to receive services under the IDEA through the cut-off age set by their state, usually age 21. Some students use this time to work on completing state requirements so they can eventually receive a state or local diploma. Others work towards mastering independent living or basic life skills that will allow them to move on to adulthood and adult service agencies at a higher functional level.

Another group of students who continue to be eligible for IDEA services after obtaining a diploma from their local school district or state are those students who receive a General Educational Development (GED) diploma, sometimes called a high school equivalency diploma. A GED diploma is given to students who have left school before graduation but are able to pass certain competency tests which demonstrate a level of knowledge equivalent to a high school education. Many GED students are adults and have aged out of IDEA eligibility under state law. But those who have not done so remain eligible to obtain IDEA services until they receive a regular state or local diploma or reach the age at which their eligibility ends. For everyone else—and that includes just about all students who plan to attend college—the IDEA ends with high school graduation. The car ride is over for these students and they need to hop on a train or plane to get where they are going.

---

* Families need to understand the implications of graduation with an IEP diploma, which is the term we will use when students receive a certificate that means only that the student has mastered the goals set out in his IEP. They should be aware of the student's right to continue his education through the year he turns 21, which can provide several more crucial years of free education. They should also be aware that an IEP diploma will limit a student's future options, as we will explore later in this book.

* Most colleges and many student loan programs will not consider students with IEP diplomas. Students who need just a bit more time to get a regular diploma may want to use their extra years of eligibility for services to work towards that higher-level diploma.

Section 504

Some students have always traveled by a different mode of transport. For these students, for a variety of reasons, the help they have needed in high school came not from the IDEA but from Section 504 of the Rehabilitation Act of 1973—generally referred to simply as Section 504.[15] Section 504 is a civil rights law that prohibits discrimination against a student whose "physical or mental disability substantially limits one or more major life activities, such as...seeing, breathing, learning, and walking." It also provides that such students are entitled to receive accommodations so that they can have access to all school programs and activities. Section 504 is sometimes referred to as being designed to level the playing field for individuals with disabilities. A student does not have to need special education services to be covered by Section 504. So we can see why it would be the law that would protect Luisa, the student with food allergies, whom we met earlier in this chapter.

The most important difference between Section 504 and the IDEA for our readers is that Section 504 extends beyond high school. It is not focused specifically on education but on providing equal access and barring discrimination, and it covers not just elementary and secondary schools but also colleges and employers who receive federal government funds. As a practical matter, it includes all colleges and universities except for a very few schools, generally religious in orientation, that decline federal funds. The requirements of Section 504 are not the same for individuals in college or the workplace as they are for students in elementary and secondary schools; there is a separate section of the law that deals specifically with these younger students and coordinates with the IDEA. This section includes the same child find provision that we find in the IDEA and which places the obligation to identify students who might be covered by Section 504 upon the school, not the student or his family. This child find obligation does not extend beyond high school. As we will look at in more depth in later chapters, colleges and employers have no obligation under Section 504 to seek out students who may need accommodations.

There is much overlap between the IDEA and Section 504 for students who have not yet graduated from high school. Some students have medical conditions that are covered by both laws. Other students have specific learning issues that can be covered by the IDEA and also by Section 504, such as dyslexia or attention difficulties. A student who qualifies for IDEA services should be able to have all of his needs met under his IEP and will not require a 504 plan. On the other hand, students who have 504 plans will not necessarily have all their academic issues addressed. However, for students who choose not to be classified as learning disabled under the IDEA, or who are doing well in school because they are putting in extraordinary effort, Section 504 may allow them to receive the accommodations they require without having to receive a label and even if the school does not believe they require special education services. Section 504 accommodations are determined by a

504 coordinator or 504 team, which the law requires to be in place in each school, and are put in place by means of a written 504 plan.

What kinds of accommodations are available to students under Section 504? One common accommodation for elementary or secondary students is receiving medication or medical tests during the school day. This would include dispensing of attention medication or checking blood glucose levels for a student with diabetes. It would also include having an EpiPen® available to deal with allergic reactions and an inhaler available for a student with asthma. For students with physical disabilities, Section 504 accommodations may include using the elevator or a special entrance to the school. Allergic or asthmatic students might have classrooms where allergens or dust are controlled. For students with a specific reading disability, such as dyslexia, accommodations may include extra time for tests or the use of a reader to read test questions aloud.

Parents should be aware that private elementary and secondary schools do not generally offer Section 504 accommodations, but that these schools are subject to the Americans with Disabilities Act (ADA) which would provide the same protections and accommodations. Only schools that accept federal funds, such as public schools and most colleges, are required to comply with Section 504. In private schools the term "504 plan" is often used nevertheless because it is a term with which educators are generally more familiar. Section 504 isn't the answer for every student, but it is one tool which parents may be able to use to help provide their child with a better school experience.

It is important to keep in mind that even though Section 504 applies to colleges, this does not mean that a student who has been receiving accommodations in high school under Section 504 will automatically receive those same accommodations—or, indeed, any accommodations—in college. We will look at the procedures for applying for accommodations in Chapter 4 and see that although the kinds of accommodations a student was receiving in high school may be relevant to the college disability officer, they are in no way binding upon the college. Each institution will review the student's disability documentation and will have its own ideas and procedures for if and how his disabilities may be accommodated. Conversely, even if a student had not needed or received accommodations in high school, college is very different and a student may indeed need accommodations in that setting. This is an individualized determination and one that is best made by the student discussing his needs with the college disability services counselor.

Complaints of violations of Section 504 may be brought to the Office of Civil Rights of the US Department of Education (DOE) or in federal or state court. As we will see later, this is the same way that complaints can be brought under the ADA, the Americans with Disabilities Act, which we will discuss below. Complaints can also be brought by individuals in federal court, where attorneys' fees may be awarded. Unlike the IDEA, there is no formal procedure that must be followed. Take a look at our Resources chapter for more information about where to file complaints with federal agencies.

One final point about Section 504: for young people in post-secondary programs or in the workplace, it is almost identical to the ADA. In fact, the ADA was written to codify the provisions and case law of Section 504 and the new amendments to the ADA are specifically incorporated in Section 504.[16] So, for the practical considerations that our readers require, don't spend too much energy trying to figure out which law covers a particular situation. Chances are that they both do.

---

* Although Section 504 applies to students both before and after high school graduation, younger students are actually covered under a different section of the law. This is intended to provide coordination with the IDEA and IDEA-related services (which include such things as transportation, speech and language therapy, occupational and physical therapy, and counseling services) for those students who might be eligible for them. Post-secondary students and individuals in the workplace, for example, do not have the child find protections that Section 504 extends to younger students.

The ADA

The law that will have the most impact on students with disabilities after high school graduation, along with Section 504, is the Americans with Disabilities Act of 1990, the ADA.[17]

Like Section 504, the ADA is a civil rights law and it clearly prohibits discrimination against individuals with "a physical or mental impairment that substantially limits one or more major life activities of such individual"[18] and states that "major life activities include, but are not limited to, caring for oneself, performing manual tasks, seeing, hearing, eating, sleeping, walking, standing, bending, speaking, breathing, learning, reading, concentrating, thinking, communicating, and working."[19] A separate section also includes within the list of disabilities those that affect "...the immune system,...digestive, bowel, bladder, neurological, brain, respiratory, circulatory, endocrine, and reproductive functions."[20]

Also protected from discrimination under the ADA are individuals who are *perceived* as having a disability. For example, if Tom had a respiratory condition that was mistakenly believed by his college to be contagious, and was not permitted to reside in the dorms because of this perception, he would be covered by the ADA to the extent that he was discriminated against because of a perceived disability. However, unless Tom's breathing was actually impacted by his respiratory condition (which would then be a physical impairment of a major life activity) he would not be entitled to accommodations, such as a room with better ventilation.

One way in which the ADA differs from Section 504 is that it covers any business with more than 15 employees, as well as most private institutions and state and local governments. A school or company does not have to take federal money to be subject to the ADA. However, you should note that the ADA exempts the US government from its terms, which means that the US Armed Forces do not have to comply with the ADA in their recruitment and retention of military personnel, which we will look at in more detail in Chapter 9. In addition, religious schools are not subject to the ADA, but if that institution receives federal financial assistance, such as students paying tuition via the guaranteed student loan program, they will be subject to Section 504. When all is said and done, the protections are virtually the same.

Although the ADA applies to most schools, including preschools and daycare programs, it does not contain a child find obligation. It does, however, include specific requirements for how all the institutions it covers need to make their facilities and services accessible to individuals with disabilities, which is different from the more general language of Section 504. The regulations under the ADA govern the specifics of how buildings, streets, and public transportation need to be accessible to individuals in wheelchairs and to those with other disabilities. Although there are exceptions for cases of undue financial hardship when creating accessible places and services, the scope of the ADA requirements is very broad.

The language of the ADA regarding enforcement also refers back to the language of Section 504 and states that the enforcement procedures shall be the same as those provided for Section 504.[21]

---

* The Americans with Disabilities Act provides very broad protections for individuals with disabilities or who are perceived to have disabilities. It applies to virtually every school and most workplaces.

Congress strikes back

The 2008 Amendments to the ADA are of key importance to students with disabilities who will be relying on the ADA and Section 504 as the basis of their accommodations in college, postgraduate education and in the workplace. They were put into place as a clear rebuke to the US Supreme Court, which had made a number of decisions interpreting the earlier 1990 version of the law. These decisions gave the ADA a very narrow interpretation, contrary to what Congress had intended when it had first passed the ADA.

For example, in 1999 the Supreme Court decided that twin sisters, Karen Sutton and Kimberly Hinton, who were both highly qualified FAA-certified pilots and were turned down for jobs by United Airlines because they were nearsighted, were not covered by the ADA.[22] Why? Because they were able to correct their vision with glasses to 20/20 or better. The Court explained its reasoning by stating, "…if a person is taking measures to correct for, or mitigate, a physical or mental impairment, the effects of those measures—both positive and negative—must be taken into account when judging whether that person is 'substantially limited' in a major life activity and thus 'disabled' under the Act."[23]

In a similar vein, in 2002, when considering the case of Ella Williams, an employee at a Toyota plant in Kentucky, the Supreme Court found that she was not disabled within the meaning of the ADA because she could still perform tasks such as personal hygiene and household chores, even though she had been diagnosed with carpal tunnel syndrome and was unable to grip the tools needed to perform her job or to do repetitive work with her hands and arms extended upward for an extended period.[24] Although the trend in the lower courts had been to limit protections, once the Supreme Court agreed with these limit interpretations of the ADA in the Williams and Sutton cases, lower courts began applying this limited view of ADA protections across a broad swath of other cases. These included an Alabama case where the US Court of Appeals determined that a man with mental retardation was not necessarily disabled and was not protected by the ADA.[25]

Congress was not happy. As the US Senate noted in its discussion of the 2008 Amendments:

> ...some 18 years later we are faced with a situation in which physical or mental impairments that would previously have been found to constitute disabilities are not considered disabilities under the Supreme Court's narrower standard. These can include individuals with impairments such as amputation, intellectual disabilities, epilepsy, multiple sclerosis, diabetes, muscular dystrophy, and cancer. The resulting court decisions contribute to a legal environment in which individuals must demonstrate an inappropriately high degree of functional limitation in order to be protected from discrimination under the ADA.

The Senate report goes on to explain that:

> By retaining the essential elements of the definition of disability including the key term "substantially limits" we reaffirm that not every individual with a physical or mental impairment is covered by the first prong of the definition of disability in the ADA. An impairment that does not substantially limit a major life activity is not a disability under this prong. That will not change after enactment of the ADA Amendments Act, nor will the necessity of making this determination on an individual basis. What will change is the standard required for making this determination. This bill lowers the standard for determining

> whether an impairment constitutes a disability and reaffirms the intent of Congress that the definition of disability in the ADA is to be interpreted broadly and inclusively.

In addition, the Senators stress that they "…reject the Supreme Court's holding that mitigating measures must be considered when determining whether an impairment constitutes a disability. With the exception of ordinary eyeglasses and contact lenses, impairments must be examined in their unmitigated state."[26]

Because, according to the Supreme Court, using corrective measures could remove someone from the definition of disabled, all sorts of individuals with serious disabilities were losing their protection under the law. And if someone was unable to do the work required in his job because of his disability but could do other tasks, how would that help him in the workplace? Congress took action the only way it could. It passed a revised version of the ADA (the ADA Amendments Act or ADAAA) which very specifically rejected these Supreme Court cases and explicitly set out just what standards it intended to have applied in any consideration of the ADA.

Some of the highlights of the amended version of the ADA provide that:

- the ADA should be interpreted broadly, in favor of providing protections to individuals
- when determining if someone is disabled under the ADA, he can be disabled in one major life activity without being disabled in all activities (so that someone can have difficulty with work tasks and qualify as disabled, even if he can handle home tasks)
- use of mitigating measures, such as medications, mobility devices, prosthetics, hearing aids and cochlear implants do not disqualify someone for protection under the ADA (but ordinary eyeglasses or contact lenses are not covered by this section)
- other measures, such as use of assistive technology, reasonable accommodations, auxiliary aids or services (such as a sign language interpreter) or learned behavioral or adaptive modifications also don't interfere with protection under the ADA

- individuals with episodic conditions, such as epilepsy, diabetes, or multiple sclerosis, are protected, if in their "active" state, their impairment would be disabling.

---

* The impact of the ADA reaches every aspect of daily lives. From the curb cuts on city sidewalks, to the Braille letters in elevators and on public restroom signs, to the availability of TTY (teletypewriter) devices in commerce, the impact of the ADA is evident to all individuals, whether or not they have disabilities.

* The ADA provides rights and protections when the IDEA is no longer available. This is the law that provides much of the protection to college students and adults in the workplace.

* Congress has made it clear that ADA coverage is to be applied broadly. It rejected a narrow line of Supreme Court cases and has declared that ADA protection shall not be denied even if the impact of a disability is lessened by use of medication, technology, or otherwise.

Accommodations versus modifications

Let's take a moment to look at two terms that are used frequently when discussing disabilities—accommodations and modifications. Each of these terms is used by schools, organizations such as the College Board, and by employers in generally the same way. What is important to understand is that the laws we have just reviewed do not use this same terminology. For example, the regulations that implement the ADA and Section 504 use the language "academic adjustments," "auxiliary aids and services," and "modifications," but not accommodations.[27]

In casual parlance, accommodations is the term used to describe ways to ensure accessibility. Zoey uses a wheelchair in her high school. She needs access to an elevator and ramps for entering and exiting the building. She uses a disabled-accessible restroom. These accommodations give her equal access to the school building and its classes. In addition to these accommodations, Zoey does not take a physical education class. This change from the standard curriculum is a modification of the general requirements for graduation. Modifications are changes to curriculum or programs that change the requirements, going beyond simply providing equal access.

Marco has a learning disability that impacts how quickly he processes information. He may be given additional time to complete a test, but the test itself is the same as that given to the other students in the class, and Marco has been responsible for the same material as his other classmates. In that case he would be receiving an accommodation. However, if Marco was only responsible for learning part of the material, or if he was given an easier test because he had trouble learning the same material as the rest of the class, he would be receiving a modification to the general curriculum.

These casual usages of the terms "modifications" and "accommodations" will crop up in a number of situations, and individuals with disabilities and their families should be aware of their differences. But it is crucial that you also understand the technical and correct terms for the kinds of services, supports, and changes available under the law, so that you can properly seek those to which you are entitled.

Students should be aware that although it is not unusual for K–12 schools to modify their curriculum for students who cannot manage the standard academic program, this is not something that is done in colleges. As we saw in our discussion of the IDEA, public schools are required to provide an appropriate education for students with disabilities; they cannot refuse to educate a student (although they can place him in a specialized school or setting) because he cannot manage the curriculum. Colleges have no such constraints. If you can't do the work (with appropriate accommodations), you are always welcome to leave, and if you do not perform in keeping with the college's minimum requirements, you may be subject to academic dismissal. They won't give you different work to make things easier for you. Students should also know that just because you were admitted to a college, that doesn't mean that they have to keep you. You may need accommodations to do so, and that's fine, but you must be able to perform.

Under the ADA, many public places require physical modifications to their design or structure that are really ways of accommodating the physical needs of individuals with disabilities and of providing access for individuals who would otherwise find it difficult or impossible to use buildings, transportation, and even the streets and sidewalks of their home town. Here, modifications may be changes from the way a building would otherwise be built, but the purpose of these changes is strictly to level the playing field, sometimes quite literally.

---

* Accommodations and modifications are two terms that are not always used correctly. In common usage, accommodations provide a different way of getting access to the same material or doing the same task, and modifications are changes to the task itself, so that an individual is doing a different assignment or learning different material.

* It is important to be aware that the ADA and Section 504 do not follow this common usage. These laws refer, instead, to academic adjustments, auxiliary aids, and modifications.

FERPA and HIPAA

Two other federal laws that are particularly relevant to students with disabilities and their families are the Family Educational Rights and Privacy Act (FERPA)[28] and the Health Insurance Portability and Accountability Act (HIPAA).[29] FERPA was enacted and became effective in 1974 and was designed to make educational records accessible to parents and students and to give parents and students some control over how and to whom educational records were to be released. FERPA also provides that the right to a student's records transfers from the parent to the student when the student turns 18 or enrolls in college, whichever comes first. This can be particularly difficult for a parent of a student with a disability, who may have been even more involved in school matters than parents of students without such special concerns.

However, even parents of college students still have access to their child's school records in certain circumstances. Most broadly, FERPA permits high schools (for high school students who have turned 18) and colleges to provide information to parents if the student is a dependent on his parents' tax returns. In addition, disclosure to a student's parents is permitted when necessary to protect the health and safety of the student or other individuals, and parents of college students who have not yet turned 21 can be informed if the student has broken any law, or violated any rule or policy of the college restricting use or possession of alcohol or drugs. It should be stressed that nothing in these rights FERPA extends to parents requires that a school provide parental notification. It simply allows the school to do so if they decide it is appropriate without running afoul of federal laws. In addition, FERPA allows for access to disability-related information if it is within a faculty or administration member's educational need to know.

HIPAA covers a wide range of medical and insurance issues, but the part that impacts families is the 1996 Privacy Rule, which is much like FERPA in its approach. This section of HIPAA covers how and when personal health information (PHI) may be released by a medical professional or hospital. It also includes a provision that transfers the right to PHI from parent to child at age 18. This means that your 18- or 19-year-old son's doctor *cannot* speak to you without your son's written consent. Student consent can also be used to override the restrictions on information imposed by FERPA. Students who work with the college Office of Disability Services can sign a release allowing their parents the right to converse via phone, email, or in person with a disability services officer regarding their progress. We will look at the impact of both of these laws in later chapters and discuss ways to manage their rules for the benefit of young people and their parents.

---

* Students are entitled to privacy about their academic and health information. This is not an absolute right, however, and parents still have the right to be told by a school about serious matters impacting health and safety.

By now you must be tired of all these laws, their details, and their nicknames, but at least we can all move ahead with a common body of knowledge about the legal rights that students with disabilities have available to them as they move beyond high school and on to college and the workplace. We will refer to these laws in many places in this book and hope that setting them out for you right from the start makes it easier to understand the chapters that follow.

Chapter 2

Getting Started

Emily shifted uncomfortably in her chair. We were meeting with her and her mother at the beginning of Emily's junior year in high school to discuss the college application process. Emily has a form of epilepsy called absence seizures, which causes her to lose focus for short periods, usually only ten or fifteen seconds at a time. She's had this condition for as long as she can remember, although it took a while before it was properly diagnosed. In the early years of elementary school, her teachers thought she simply wasn't paying attention and told her parents she most likely had an attention disorder. Fortunately, by the third grade, she was seen by a pediatric neurologist who ran a series of tests that determined the true cause of her inattention, and Emily began taking medication that greatly reduced the frequency of her seizures. Still, every once in a while, Emily will get a blank look on her face for a few seconds and lose track of what's going on around her.

Emily's seizure disorder has not affected her intelligence or any other aspect of her intellectual functioning. She is bright and a good student and hopes to attend a campus of her state university to pursue her dream of becoming a high school teacher. She has received accommodations in school since first being diagnosed, including extra time on exams and a set of class notes from the teacher, in case she missed any of the class material. The only difference between her curriculum and that of her friends is that she doesn't take drivers' education, since there are state legal requirements that bar individuals with seizure disorders from operating motor vehicles. Emily is very upset about this, but knows that her form of seizure disorder often disappears by age 20 or so, and she holds out hope that she will eventually be able to drive.

We had just asked Emily whether she had an IEP or a 504 plan. She had no idea. (We hope you remember at least some of the abbreviations and laws we discussed in the last chapter, since we will be using them here as well.) Emily's mom, Mrs. Wilson, promptly volunteered that Emily got her accommodations under a 504 plan. "She's pulling mostly As, with a few Bs," she said. "The school told us that unless she was having problems with her school work because of the seizures, she should be covered by 504." As you may recall, in order to be entitled to an IEP (Individual Education Program) which describes the services a student will receive and the goals she is working towards under the Individuals with Disabilities Education Act (IDEA), a student needs to both have a disability and require special education services because of such disability.

Emily admitted that she had not met with her school's 504 team or participated in any of the meetings setting up her accommodations. Her mom took care of all that and did a fine job. Emily made it clear that she wanted to spend as little time focusing on these issues as she could.

Mrs. Wilson is extremely knowledgeable about what the high school needs to do to help her daughter. She is in close touch with the school nurse who has Emily's medication on hand in the event she needs to take an additional dose during the school day, and has spoken to Emily's teachers at the beginning of every school year to explain about her condition and how they can help her deal with it. Mrs. Wilson has been an effective advocate for her daughter's needs and now plans to continue her role as Emily moves on to college.

In addition to being a good student, Emily is very social and has lots of friends. She participates in several clubs and plays the flute in the school orchestra. But she has not been an active participant in an important part of her high school experience—managing her disability.

We had a similar experience with Scott and his family. Scott has a learning disability that was diagnosed in sixth grade and has been receiving special education services under the IDEA since that time. When we met with his family to discuss post-high school options, both his mother and father were familiar with the specific provisions of Scott's IEP. Scott, however, was silent. When we spoke to him directly, we learned that he hadn't been to any of the meetings of his IEP team. He knows that he has problems with writing and that he gets to use a computer in class and to take essay tests, but he hasn't wanted to become involved in setting up the classroom strategies and goals that his classroom teachers refer to in their work with him. He figures his parents and his teachers have done an okay job with these and he'd prefer not to have to sit through meetings where his disabilities are discussed so frankly.

Scott and Emily are typical of many students we see. They have disabilities that have been addressed in high school, or in some cases throughout their entire school career, but have preferred to ignore these as much as possible and concentrate on other aspects of their lives which don't make them feel different from their classmates. Although we recognize that some young people have physical, emotional, or cognitive impairments that make it difficult or impossible for them to participate in their own educational planning and services, we believe that our readers—who are considering college, vocational education, or the workplace—are able to and need to be involved in their educational and disability issues from the very earliest stages. But, if you are a student who has been more like Scott or Emily than you want to admit—or a parent who has taken over the management of your child's disability, whether actively or by default—it's not too late to establish an effective partnership so that each student becomes involved in managing decisions about her own life.

There is a saying that is used in the disability community: "Nothing about me, without me." It sums up what students in high school should insist upon from their teachers, schools, and even parents. These people are not going to follow you to college or the workplace. Even if you continue to live at home for a while after high school, we suspect that neither parents nor students will be happy with this arrangement for the long term. At some point you, the student, will be dealing with college administrators, professors, and employers. The sooner you understand the issues that qualify you for disability services and are able to advocate for yourself, the sooner you will be ready to accept the rights—and obligations—of adulthood.

---

* Some students want to avoid dealing with the disability services they receive from their school. It is sometimes more comfortable for these students to let their parents handle the details of their disability accommodations and plans.

Different paths to transition: Section 504 and informal arrangements

Before we can look at what students and their families can expect from their high school to assist in the process of transition to college or the workplace, it's first important to know the legal basis for the accommodations and supports a student receives. There are three ways that schools can offer educational supports to a student with a disability: under the IDEA, under Section 504, or, less often, in some sort of informal arrangement.

Students who receive their high school services under the IDEA are entitled to an array of services and support as they move beyond high school, which the IDEA defines as "transition." There is no right to transition services under Section 504 or where a school has informally offered accommodations.[1] This is one of a number of areas where the protections of the IDEA are stronger than those of Section 504. Not all students have a choice of which law applies to them, but for those who do, we urge you to use the IDEA whenever possible. We'll see in a moment what transition services under the IDEA look like, and it will become clear why these can be valuable to students. What about where schools have put supports or accommodations in place without a formal legal plan, bypassing both the IDEA and 504? Nope, no right to any special transition services here either. That doesn't mean that transition planning shouldn't be done for all students, and may not be done by some schools, but just that there is no legal obligation for the school system to provide this service except under the IDEA. Students who aren't entitled to IDEA services need to work with their guidance counselors, parents, and outside resources to make sure they are prepared to transition from high school to college or the workplace. We'll see later in this chapter how this should be done.

---

* Schools have no legal obligation to provide transition services to students with disabilities who are not covered by the IDEA. Section 504 does not require that high schools provide transition services to students facing graduation.

Transition under the IDEA

The IDEA recognizes the importance of planning for higher education and adulthood and Congress made a special point of focusing on these issues when it updated the IDEA in 2004. In fact, in the introduction to its revised version of the law, it noted that "As the graduation rates for children with disabilities continue to climb, providing effective transition services to promote successful post-school employment or education is an important measure of accountability for children with disabilities."[2] When Congress goes to the trouble of mentioning a topic at the beginning of a law, it's a pretty good sign that this is a subject they take seriously.

Transition planning under the IDEA is intended to be part of the same process that determines a student's IEP and generally occurs as part of an annual meeting that includes a consideration of current goals and issues, although it can also be handled in a separate meeting or meetings, especially for students with complicated needs or as graduation approaches. The notice of the meeting sent by the school to the family should clearly state that the meeting will include a discussion of transition issues. The IEP team for a student whose post-high school goals are being considered includes the same individuals as at any IEP meeting—regular and special education teachers, representatives of the district, and an individual qualified to interpret evaluation results, usually a school psychologist. However, although a student of any age may attend a regular IEP meeting "where appropriate," when transition issues will be discussed, the student must be invited to attend and if she does not, the school is required to take steps "to ensure that the child's preferences and interests are considered."[3] The school should also invite any agency that will be involved in providing or paying for transition services, as long as the parents or student (depending upon the student's age) consent.[4] For example, if the State Department of Vocational Rehabilitation (which we will discuss at length in Chapter 9) will be providing economic support, job training, or technical assistance (such as a laptop computer), they should be included in the transition meeting.

The IDEA goes on to describe carefully what it means by "transition services," focusing on a number of different aspects of this process which, taken together, are designed to provide effective help to students with all kinds of disabilities who are moving beyond high school.

The simplest way of understanding what this process involves is to focus on some key terms that appear in the law. For example, transition is described in the IDEA as "a coordinated set of activities," where the different players in the transition planning process are supposed to put their heads together to work out a transition plan. In practice, this can mean working with the student's guidance counselor to make sure her coursework includes sufficient state-level courses to enable her to graduate with a regular diploma, so she can qualify for financial aid or admission to a post-secondary program. Or it can involve working with the Department of Vocational Rehabilitation to arrange driving lessons for a student who will need to be able to drive to a local community college.

The IDEA goes on to say that transition from high school should "be within a results-oriented process." All too often schools focus on the results part of this mandate to the exclusion of the process. When we look at the IEPs of many of the students with whom we work, we see the word "college" written in the section asking about student goals. It may be that most of these students do plan to go to college, but too often that one word statement is really the school's way of saying that they don't need to worry about this kid, because she's got the next few years covered. When we see that, we know that the school is not doing their job.

By dismissing college-bound students from the transition process, some high schools are ignoring the essence of what IDEA transition is supposed to be about: "…improving the academic and functional achievement of the child with a disability to facilitate the child's movement from school to post-school activities…" Those post-school activities are defined to include a wide range of possibilities, from post-secondary education and vocational education to supported employment and independent living options for students whose disabilities are more extensive. They also specifically include activities which will extend into adulthood, including adult education and adult services.[5]

One example of the kind of academic achievement that should be considered during a meaningful transition process for a student who is planning to attend college is a review of her foreign language courses. We discuss this elsewhere, but it is an important part of transition planning. It is not uncommon for a student with a language-based learning disability to have an IEP that exempts her from taking a foreign language even when that would ordinarily be a requirement in her high school. That may help her get through her secondary program more easily, but, as we will see in Chapter 8, it may prevent her from being admitted to a school she considers one of her top choices. Although it is the responsibility of the high school to include this kind of consideration as part of the transition process, we urge both students and parents to be aware of this issue and others we will mention later on, and not to assume that your high school has considered every topic.

We have encountered high schools that do a great job with transition, even more so lately since the IDEA expanded and improved its transition requirements, but there are still far too many schools that just pay lip service to their obligations to provide transition support, and families often find out that they received wrong or woefully insufficient advice when it is too late to do anything about it. There are court cases that have provided compensation, usually extra years of educational support, where school districts have failed to provide appropriate transition support, but they are not common and almost always involve students who have not yet graduated. Because, as we mentioned in Chapter 1, the IDEA ends with high school graduation, a high school would have to have very seriously shortchanged a student for there to be any compensation for inadequate transition services once she has graduated.[6]

The IDEA provides that transition planning should be "based on the individual child's needs, taking into account the child's strengths, preferences, and interests."[7] We've seen this done very well—and very poorly. In one school district we've encountered, a student with an interest in cooking was not only sent to a local culinary program, but was permitted to apply a cooking course he took on a trip to Italy towards his graduation requirements. It would surprise no one that this young man went on to overcome his learning difficulties and become a successful chef.

We've also had the disappointing experience of meeting with a school district transition director to discuss a student with learning disabilities who wanted to work in theatre production. Despite his learning disability, this student read plays and spent a good deal of his free time learning about theatre direction. The transition director managed to upset and alienate the student by suggesting that he see if the local movie theatre was hiring people at the refreshment stand or ticket office. The student explained to us afterwards, "I felt like he couldn't take my interests seriously, because I have a learning disability.

I'm not stupid and I'm certainly not ready to give up on my goal and serve popcorn and soda."

We've also seen too many instances where schools fail to consider "instruction, related services, community experiences, the development of employment and other post-school adult living objectives, and, when appropriate, acquisition of daily living skills and functional vocational evaluation,"[8] as the IDEA requires. Schools have to think about what a student will be doing in the future, not just right after graduation but into adulthood. The transition team needs to view the totality of what a student needs to know and the skills she needs to acquire to function in our complex world.

We'll talk about some of these skills in later chapters, but we cannot emphasize too strongly that they are not only permissible to include in a transition plan under IDEA, but are a necessary part of such a plan. They are crucial to future success. For instance, has a student who uses a wheelchair been given training in using public transportation? Has a student taken a class in disability law? Does she know what the ADA is and how it applies to her? Have all the students handled by that transition team received instruction in money management? Do they know how to handle credit and a bank account? What about instructions in social interactions, and what to do in sexual situations? You're saying, "Wait a minute. What does that have to do with their disability? And what about students without disabilities, shouldn't they learn this stuff too?" Of course every student should have this kind of instruction, and more, to help them function in college, the workplace, and in the adult world. But except when these subjects are set forth in state curriculums, students without disabilities aren't covered by a law that requires that they receive such instruction. On the other hand, the IDEA mandates that those individuals whom it covers be provided with meaningful transition services that are designed to do all of these things. Make sure you take advantage of this. Any school or teacher who says this isn't part of transition doesn't understand the broad scope of transition services required by the IDEA.

---

* The IDEA defines transition broadly and states that it is a coordinated set of activities and can include a number of agencies. These can include state programs that can offer funding or training, even for college-bound students.

* IDEA transition is designed to be a results-oriented process. Declaring that a student will be attending college is not sufficient to provide the kinds of support the law requires.

* The mandate that IDEA transition improve a student's movement beyond high school should be looked at with a view towards what the student will need to know to be successful as she moves on to college, the workplace, and adulthood. Life skills of all kinds should be acquired as part of the transition process.

Timing

We said in the Introduction to this book that we'd set out the timing of the steps you need to take to move beyond high school and that we'd help you catch up if you were behind schedule. Let's start by looking at when school-based transition is supposed to begin. The IDEA provides that consideration of transition issues should begin at the IEP meeting that will cover the period when the student turns 16. So, we are looking at beginning this formal transition process when the student is 15, which means she will be in ninth or tenth grade.

Although the process of transition formally ends when the IDEA no longer applies to a student, there is an important limitation on services available to students who are about to graduate. For those students, schools need only provide a document called a "Summary of Performance"[9] which sets out, in an abbreviated form, the student's "academic achievement and functional performance," but does not need to include any formal testing. This can be a problem for students who need updated test results to obtain accommodations from a college or to take their SAT or ACT exams, as we will discuss at length in Chapter 5.

While we are on the subject of SAT and ACT exams, it is important to make a consideration of these tests, including whether they will be taken and when, part of an effective transition plan. College Offices of Disability Services have different requirements for how recent testing or evaluations need to be to support a student's request for accommodations or special services. But both the ACT Program and College Board, which owns the SAT exams and decides how they will be administered, require that testing be not more than five years old, and even newer when certain mental or emotional disabilities are involved. Armed with that information and with the knowledge that even the broad transition requirements of the IDEA do not require a high school to do testing just before graduation, families and guidance counselors can work together to make sure that the tests needed to support disability accommodations on the SAT and ACT exams, and their pre-tests, are done at times to maximize their usefulness.

For example, where possible, a student with a learning disability who is covered by the IDEA might try to arrange for a full evaluation (called a triennial review since it is generally done every three years) in eighth grade, which would be timely when she applies for disability accommodations on the PSATs in the summer before her junior year. She could then be retested in the beginning of eleventh grade, which would generally be sufficient for obtaining accommodations on the college level. As we will see, some high schools are more flexible than others and some do such inadequate testing, even as part of a triennial review, that it won't be accepted by the testing organizations or colleges. Still, it is a subject worth exploring with guidance counselors or as part of a transition meeting.

---

* It is important to think ahead to the requirements of the standardized testing organizations and college disability accommodations when arranging testing during high school.

* The IDEA does not require high schools to provide testing to students who are about to graduate. These students only need to receive a Summary of Performance.

When IDEA transition doesn't apply

We've seen that formal transition planning is only provided for students who are covered by the IDEA and that even these students are often left without meaningful transition by their schools. So, what can students and parents do to get everything they can from their schools, and what can and should they be doing outside their schools to get ready for when high school is over?

If you take only one step to move ahead to prepare for life after high school, it would be to begin as a family to transfer management of your student's disability from parent to child. No student should reach her junior year like Emily or Scott, without an understanding of the services she has been receiving from her school. Every student needs to begin in elementary school, or as soon as she has been diagnosed, to understand her diagnosis. That is clearly going to be easier for some students than for others. Some students will have a single problem—an orthopedic impairment, a visual limitation, or asthma. Others will have several problems that impact one another—a learning disability and attention deficit hyperactivity disorder (ADHD)—or maybe an anxiety disorder and depression. Some conditions are physical and obvious; others are subtle and harder to explain, although they are every bit as significant. We'll talk a great deal about understanding your disability in later chapters, but families should begin by using clear, direct language, even with young children. Children should be given age-appropriate books with information about their disability. Students with disabilities should be encouraged to participate in asking questions of their doctors, therapists, and others who work with them. In fact, by the time they are in high school they should be experts on their conditions and be able to describe them accurately.

Next, students need to understand what works and what doesn't work for them. We've had even the youngest students tell their teacher that they will need to leave the classroom in a hurry because they have Crohn's disease and need to use the bathroom. Elementary school students may encounter adults—substitute teachers, cafeteria workers, and bus drivers, for example—who don't necessarily have information about the student's disability. It can make a big difference if the student can articulate her needs and explain her situation, even in the simplest terms. In her regular classroom, a student should know if she does better sitting in the front of the classroom, or if she needs large-grid paper to do her homework. This kind of understanding often goes beyond what is written in an IEP and includes those minor classroom modifications or accommodations that almost every teacher will implement, if a student is able to explain her needs.

We firmly believe that every student who is able to do so should attend her IEP or 504 meeting. We saw earlier that schools must invite students to attend IEP meetings dealing with transition issues. For younger students, the IDEA states that the student should attend "whenever appropriate,"[10] but schools vary greatly in encouraging or welcoming students. To be honest, they often aren't comfortable discussing certain topics in front of parents either. We have sat through countless IEP meetings as team members where the IEP team discussed sensitive issues, such as the fact that parents were divorced, or that the parents were difficult to work with, before they invited the parents in from the waiting area to start the meeting that had actually already begun. Of course, none of these pre-meeting comments ever showed up in the minutes of the meeting. It is up to the parents, then, to decide when and to what extent their child is ready to be a part of her own IEP meeting. It may take some pressure from the parents to get the school on board with this idea.

The other side of this equation is that students have to be willing to show up for these meetings. We saw that Scott and Emily were uncomfortable with dealing with their disabilities and were all too willing to take a passive role in their IEP and 504 processes. If Emily's parents had been in touch with their local branch of the Epilepsy Foundation and found a support group for young people with seizures, it is possible that Emily would be more comfortable with her medical condition. Similarly, Scott's parents should have had no problem finding one of the excellent books for children about learning disabilities, some of which we list in our Resources chapter, and educating him about both his areas of difficulty and his many strengths. We know there is no magic wand that can make a student willing to attend a meeting where her disability and special school needs will be discussed by adults, some of whom she may not know. But parents can take a number of steps to help make their child more comfortable with her disability and increase the likelihood that she will be interested in being involved in decisions about her life. They can provide opportunities for their child to meet with other young people who have similar disabilities. They can use a vocabulary that is clear, accurate, and non-judgmental in its description of their child's condition. And they can involve the student early on in discussions and decisions about her disability and school needs. Families should also begin early to inform their child about the legal rights she has as a student with a disability. That means that parents need to take the lead and make sure that they themselves are knowledgable. This can happen in lots of ways, and will differ depending upon the nature of their child's disability and the comfort level of parents with what we have been calling the legal landscape. Many school districts have a separate arm of their parent organization that is called a Special Education Parent Teacher Association (SEPTA). This group can be a good source of information and support for families, and can be particularly helpful in navigating the specific issues that arise in a local school district. Other parents' experiences with a particular school psychologist or the district director of guidance may make a real difference in deciding what strategies to take in advocating for services.

Another way parents can become knowledgable is by attending a program run by a disability organization or by a commercial or nonprofit group that conducts parent trainings. There are also books and websites that deal with the legal issues relating to special education and disability. It's always interesting to see how many lawyers who attend special education classes or conferences are also parents of a student with a disability. But you should be assured that parents certainly don't need a legal background to understand the basics of the law and to share the vocabulary and knowledge they gain with their child. We've included information on legal education in the Resources chapter at the end of this book.

Even elementary school students who have IEPs or 504 plans should know that they have a plan to help them with their learning or their medical condition and have at least some idea of what that plan contains. Especially where a 504 plan is created for conditions that can include medical emergencies, the student needs to know who has her medication, where she should go in case she feels ill, and what precautions the school is supposed to be taking. A second grader with a food allergy needs to know where her EpiPen is located and who she should tell if she thinks she may have eaten something that is triggering an allergic reaction. Students are also the most reliable reporters of problems with compliance with their IEP or 504 plan. Unless Tim knows that he is supposed to take his tests in a "quiet room," it may take a while for his parents to figure out that his classroom teacher isn't permitting this for all tests.

One problem that arises more than occasionally is that teachers have no clue about what is in a student's IEP or 504 plan because the document is kept locked in the guidance office or the principal's filing cabinet and is never shared with the staff charged with implementing it. It seems so ridiculous as to be impossible, but we can assure you that some schools still do this, either out of misplaced concern for the privacy and security of these educational records, or in an attempt to avoid having to provide every one of a student's several teachers with a copy of her educational or medical plan. So, parents and older students need to make sure that the faculty and staff charged with implementing their plan have actually seen it, no matter where in the school building it is stored.

---

* Families need to begin early to include students in discussions about their disabilities and their legal rights to accommodations and services. Age-appropriate education about the nature of a disability and a student's educational needs will make the student more at ease with her disability and help her to better advocate for herself.

* Students need to attend their IEP or 504 meetings. This will allow the student to become comfortable with discussions of her needs and allow her to share her perspective with the adults who set up her educational program and accommodations.

What kind of diploma?

We mentioned in Chapter 1 that when students with significant learning or related disabilities reach the end of high school without completing the requirements for a standard diploma, they may be awarded a certificate that is not an actual high school diploma but really just signifies that the student with a disability has met the goals set forth in her IEP. It's a reasonable way for students with significant learning limitations to "graduate" with their classmates and allows them to remain eligible for IDEA services and to work towards a regular diploma until they age out of eligibility for special education services under state law, usually at age 21. It is also a way for students who clearly will not be able to complete the work for a regular diploma, even with additional years of schooling, to mark the conclusion of their high school study. As we noted, this kind of certificate is called by different names in different states, but we will use the term "IEP diploma." Students and families should be aware that an IEP diploma will not be accepted by colleges but may allow a student time to do the extra work to receive a regular high school diploma. Where an IEP diploma is a possibility, there should be careful consideration of the opportunities and limitations this can create.

Other diploma-related issues are also an important part of the transition process. Students need to be sure they are taking the appropriate courses to allow them to graduate on time with the correct number of credits. Students whose medical conditions have involved substantial absences for hospitalizations or other treatments may need to make up work or courses in order to graduate with their class. Students who are interested in technical vocations may benefit from internships or courses of study not given in their home school. If a student is covered by the IDEA, then her transition meetings are the place to discuss these issues. For those students who will not be involved in IDEA transition, these issues need to be addressed with parents and guidance counselors.

---

* Students and parents need to be aware of what kind of diploma will be earned and whether the student is on track to meet the requirements of such a diploma.

Unsung heroes

No discussion of transition from high school can be considered complete without looking at the role that guidance counselors and case managers play in this process. For students who receive transition services under the IDEA, it is often the guidance counselor or case manager who leads the process, who knows how many credits a student has earned, and whether she needs certain courses to graduate. Case managers are usually special education teachers who work with a number of different students, keeping track of their accommodations and any modifications to their program. For students who get services or accommodations under Section 504 or through some informal arrangement and who are not entitled to IDEA transition, the guidance counselor often serves as a one-person transition team, keeping the student aware of requirements, talking to worried parents, and suggesting post-high school options and accommodations.

We've heard stories about amazing guidance counselors and case managers who have gone out of their way to help their students succeed, and we have also been privy to stories about counselors who, because of an impossible caseload, inexperience, burnout, or other reason, do little or nothing to help a student through the transition process. In our experience, these professionals can be of enormous assistance, and students and parents should get to know their counselor or case manager early on in high school and consider her an important part of their transition team.

---

* Whether your accommodations and services are managed by a guidance counselor or case manager, this individual can be an important part of successful transition.

Envisioning the future

"What do you want to be when you grow up?" may be the question most frequently asked of young people by well-meaning adults. All kids, even those with serious physical or cognitive disabilities, have dreams of careers in which they have exciting jobs or achieve fame and fortune. It's a rare young person whose imagination takes flight and envisions a career as an accountant (with apologies to all the accountants we know, like, and depend upon). An important part of the transition to adulthood for all students, but especially students with disabilities, is to understand their strengths as well as their areas of difficulty, and to build on their strengths and affinities to help focus their life goals. There are a number of things that students and their parents can do to help make high school an effective first step to further education and life as an adult.

Students should be given opportunities to try on careers. Sometimes this can be done through a school program or with help from someone a parent might know. It can take the form of joining an organization or participating in a school activity, such as an orchestra or drama group. Part-time or summer jobs can help focus a student's interest—or rule out a career. One young man we know was fascinated by the Food Network on television and was considering a career as a chef, until he spent a summer working as an assistant in a restaurant kitchen. He literally couldn't take the heat, not to mention that the hours were long and his feet hurt all the time. He built on his experiences to become an excellent amateur cook but left the restaurant business to others.

Aimee, who attended a specialized high school for students with learning disabilities, had serious difficulties with dyslexia. Even with extensive remedial work with the most effective programs for dyslexia, reading remained a struggle and took her longer than most people. But she loved acting. She was the star of her school drama productions from the ninth grade on, with roles that traditionally went to juniors or seniors. She had enormous amounts of dialogue to learn but worked with her mother and a drama coach to get through the reading and commit her lines to memory. Outside of school she was involved in youth theatre groups and amateur productions. We asked Aimee how she managed auditions outside of school, where actors are often asked to read something they are handed on the spot. "I always prepare something ahead of time, something well known that is appropriate to the kind of production I'm trying for," she explained. "I tell the director or whoever is running the audition that I have dyslexia and can't really do a sight reading, but that I have no trouble learning dialogue when I have the time to study it. I offer to read what I have prepared, so they get some sense of my abilities, and when I finish they usually suggest I prepare their material and come back the next day to complete my audition." Aimee knows it is hard to succeed at acting, but when she graduated from high school she went on to study drama at a college that would support her reading difficulties and had a strong acting program. We won't be surprised to find that she beats the odds and makes it to Broadway.

Another way students and parents can work towards a more effective transition to life after high school is to start to think about colleges long before it is time to put together a list of schools to consider. We'll discuss visiting colleges at length in Chapter 8, but students in the early years of high school who have older siblings can, where appropriate, visit them at college. The college sibling needs to be sufficiently responsible to make this work (and to keep their younger sister or brother from inappropriate situations!), but this is one way to give younger students at least some sense of what it is like to go away to college. This kind of visit is even more effective if parents debrief the visiting student afterward, pointing out the skills that she will need to master the situations she observed. Another way to think ahead to college is to attend local college fairs, which feature speakers and information about a number of different schools. These can be sponsored by high schools or local organizations, and will sometimes feature colleges that offer supports for students with special learning needs.

---

* Students need to think about their goals and need to be given exposure to careers and educational settings to help them make decisions about their futures. Opportunities to try out careers or to visit colleges can be useful experiences.

There is no single correct path for an effective transition, but the steps we have outlined can make the process smoother and can land students at their next destination with the skills and knowledge to be successful.

Chapter 3

What's a Disability?

A young woman who is depressed. A young man with attention issues. Do these individuals have disabilities? The answer is sometimes not clear. Since the existence of a legally recognized disability is fundamental to the rights provided by the Americans with Disabilities Act (ADA) and Section 504 of the Rehabilitation Act of 1973 (Section 504), we're going to take some time to look at various conditions and situations and explain why the individuals involved have—or don't have—disabilities which entitle them to accommodations under the law.

We'll start by reminding you that just because you can't see someone's disability doesn't mean they don't have one. Hidden disabilities may include learning disabilities, psychological disabilities, and some chronic illnesses. Medications can mitigate the symptoms of certain conditions, making the disability less noticeable. Some disabilities, such as multiple sclerosis and cancer, have a changing nature—when a flare-up or recurrence occurs, the disability is obvious; when there is a remission, it's hard to tell if there is a disability present. Certain conditions are temporary. Just how long does a student with a broken bone have to be on crutches before he is qualified as having a disability for the purposes of the law? In Chapter 1 we discussed a number of types of disabilities. Let's look a bit further and see whether certain conditions would be considered disabilities under the ADA and whether students would receive accommodations for these.

Does it rise to the level of a disability?

First things first. Not every medical or psychological condition or impairment is automatically a disability. Rather, it must rise to the level of a disability. How does an impairment or condition rise to the level of a disability? Simple—it must impact a major life activity such as walking, eating, sleeping, learning, concentrating, and so on and so forth. If it does, then it is not merely an impairment but a disability that offers the individual protection under the law.

> A diagnosis of impairment alone does not establish that an individual has a disability within the meaning of...[the law]... Rather, the impairment must substantially limit a major life activity, or the individual must have a record of such an impairment or be regarded as having such an impairment. A diagnosis from a treating physician, along with information about how the disability affects the student, may suffice.[1]

Let's look at Rachel, who is a senior in college. Throughout the past four years she has struggled academically to stay in school. Socially, she has loved every minute and has made numerous friends. Part of her struggle is that her social life seems to get in the way of her academics; she finds herself at a party most nights of the week. She has been drinking alcohol more than usual lately in order to calm her worries about her grades. She has also been arguing with her roommates, who are her best friends. This has been worrying her too, and as a result she hasn't been sleeping well, leaving her exhausted each day. When midterm time arrives she panics because she doesn't want to flunk out of college, especially when she is so close to graduating. She has become desperate and her anxiety level has risen so much that she decides to try some of her friend's pills which promise to help her focus and stay awake long enough to complete her studies. Shortly after taking the pills, Rachel sees her Resident Assistant (RA), Danielle, in the hallway of her dorm. Having previously confided in Danielle about boy trouble, Rachel felt comfortable with her and could not help herself when she broke down into tears. Danielle was stunned to see Rachel emotionally unraveling before her eyes. Listening to Rachel and sensing what bad shape she was in, Danielle brought her to the college's Counseling Center. There, Rachel met with staff psychologist Dr. Gorman, who explained that Rachel had been self-medicating with alcohol, hiding her head in the sand regarding her worries about her schoolwork by partying too much, and taking out her stress on her roommates. Underlying all her troubles, was a common link—Rachel's anxiety.

The doctor diagnosed Rachel with an anxiety disorder, explaining that the anxiety she experienced on a daily basis was interfering with her relationships and everyday functions such as her schoolwork and sleep. Because it interfered with her functioning, Rachael's anxiety disorder rose to the level of a disability, according to Dr. Gorman, and so she would qualify for academic accommodations through the Office of Disability Services. Suggested accommodations included an alternative location for testing and extended testing time (1.5 times). The doctor further suggested that Rachel learn anxiety-reducing techniques, meet for weekly therapy sessions, and consider taking medication to address the anxiety disorder. Over time, Rachel discovered there was a history of anxiety in her family.

Pierre is a young man we worked with a few years back. When he was six years old he was diagnosed with Lyme disease. At the time of diagnosis he had no symptoms of the disease except for the bull's eye rash on his arm, which was the site of the tick bite. Yearly, as a matter of caution, Pierre met with a doctor who specialized in Lyme disease. Thankfully, Pierre had been receiving a clean bill of health since age six. During his freshman year in college, Pierre began experiencing intense joint pain and was tired all the time. A visit to the Lyme specialist and updated blood tests confirmed that these were symptoms of the Lyme disease, now in full bloom. Although it had been in hibernation for years, the Lyme disease was now having an impact on him. Pierre's ability to learn and complete his schoolwork, sleep, and physically move around was severely compromised. The Lyme disease now rose to the level of a disability and upon submitting the necessary documentation to his college's Office of Disability Services, Pierre received accommodations. He qualified for a reduced course load as well as an extension on papers, projects, and exams when flare-ups occurred and he couldn't get out of bed.

Carlos was diagnosed with attention deficit hyperactivity disorder (ADHD) in elementary school. Because he was young and still growing, his parents decided not to place him on medication for the ADHD. Instead, they had him classified under the Individuals with Disabilities Education Act (IDEA) as a student with a disability and sought every available support for him. In addition to the resource room and special education teachers Carlos had in school, he had tutors, a therapist, and a learning specialist outside of school. This support network served him well throughout his elementary and secondary school years, and he learned many helpful compensatory strategies along the way. These strategies assisted him in his transition to college, his academic work, and in his relationships with friends and family. But it was not enough.

Although he was trying as hard as he could, Carlos could not keep his act together. Sophomore year in college things began going downhill for him. He was disorganized, couldn't concentrate in class, and his reading assignments took forever to complete because he had difficulty focusing. Carlos decided to meet with a psychiatrist, who eventually prescribed medication to address the ADHD and the interference it caused in Carlos's day-to-day life. Over the next few months and with the help of the medication, Carlos was pleasantly surprised that he was able to pick up the pieces of his life. This was the best he had felt in a long time. The psychiatrist explained to Carlos that even though the ADHD medication had mitigated the symptoms of his disability, so that he was able to function productively, he still qualified under the law as having a disability. He strongly suggested that Carlos meet with someone from the Office of Disability Services to set up academic accommodations. Carlos did not have to use the accommodations on a regular basis if the medication was helping, but the accommodations would be there in case he needed them. Such a scenario may cause students and parents concern. They may wonder if Carlos doesn't use his accommodations, might they be denied in the future? Unlike the College Board that likes to see a long and established history of a student using his accommodations in high school and even earlier, college Disability Services personnel, in our experience, do not set such a condition. Additionally, they do not have the interest or staff to monitor whether students use their accommodations regularly after securing them. Instead, it is left up to the student to make a good decision regarding his education; he is the adult here.

---

* A condition or impairment is not automatically a disability. If a condition impacts a major life activity such as walking, eating, sleeping, learning, or concentrating, then it rises to the level of a disability. The individual is then eligible for protection under the law. You should be aware that although college disability personnel often use the term "condition," the law

refers to "impairment;" we use both terms in this chapter interchangeably.

* One person, one diagnosis, but only sometimes a disability. A person with a specific diagnosis may have a disability at one time in his life, but not at another. Certain disabilities, such as Lyme disease, or some psychological disabilities such as depression, have a changing rather than static nature. When the condition fluctuates and begins to impact a major life activity such as sleeping, walking, eating, and learning, then it has risen to the level of a disability.

* Pharmaceutical treatment–Some disabilities are so positively impacted by medicine that the symptoms of the disability are almost completely mitigated. Even with such effective treatment, the person will still qualify as a having a disability under the law if without taking the medication the disability impacts at least one of his daily major functions.

History of an impairment and being regarded as having an impairment

There are three general sets of circumstances that can result in an individual qualifying as someone with a disability and thereby entitling him to the protection of the applicable laws. As we discussed earlier, a person whose condition or impairment substantially limits a major life activity qualifies as having a disability. In addition, an individual with a history of an impairment that rises to the level of a disability is covered by the ADA. Finally, someone who is perceived to have a disability is also protected under the ADA. The exception in all of these three instances is an individual who is an active drug user. Interestingly, a former drug user or person currently in a rehabilitation program *is* covered by the law and qualifies as having a disability, but not someone whose disability is caused by current drug use.

After high school, Shana is seeking a job as an office receptionist. She has a history of cancer and decides to disclose her medical history on a job interview. Because she missed a year of high school for treatment, it took her five years to achieve her diploma. Rather than a prospective employer assuming a lack of intelligence or motivation as the reason for her delayed graduation, she preferred to be upfront and honest. Unfortunately, some employers are reluctant to hire someone who might become ill again. Luckily for Shana, because she has a history of a disability, she is protected under the law. As long as she can perform the fundamental duties of the job, with or without accommodations, she is qualified and legally cannot be denied employment because of her medical history.

Let's look at what can happen when an individual is regarded as having a disability. As we just mentioned, a person with a "perceived physical or mental impairment whether or not the impairment limits or is perceived to limit a major life activity" has protection under the law.[2] Lenore is a junior in college. When she was in middle school she narrowly escaped an apartment fire with her life. Fortunately, everyone in her family survived. Lenore suffered third-degree burns and her left arm is severely scarred. In warmer weather when she wears short-sleeve shirts, sleeveless dresses, or even a bathing suit, her scar is very noticeable and it sometimes impacts the way people treat her. When she is out in public she notices people are more willing to hold a door open for her. Although the burn and scarring do not impact a major life activity, others perceive that it does. When the coach of the college volleyball team had concerns about permitting Lenore to play because he was worried about damaging her scarred arm, Lenore asked the Office of Disability Services to intercede. Once the coach understood that his conclusion was not only wrong but illegal, Lenore was immediately added to the team.

---

* There are three situations where an individual can be protected as an individual with a disability: a person whose condition or impairment substantially limits a major life activity, an individual with a history of an impairment that rises to the level of a disability, and someone who is regarded as having a disability.

* The ADA does not cover an individual who is an active drug user.

Same diagnosis for both

Interestingly, two people can have the same diagnosis, but one can qualify as having a disability while the other one doesn't. Laurie's depression has made her unable to get out of bed for days at a time. Since Laurie is unable to perform her daily life functions, her depression is a disability that qualifies her for accommodations under the law. Therese has also been diagnosed with depression. Although she often feels sad, she is still able to function and be productive, and therefore is not protected under the law as a person with a disability.

Additionally, two individuals with the same diagnosis can each be impacted differently by the disability, and therefore each exhibits different symptoms and needs different accommodations. Billy and Brian are veterans who were both diagnosed with Post-Traumatic Stress Disorder (PTSD). Both qualify as having a disability under the law. Billy experiences anxiety which interferes with his ability to learn and so needs the accommodation of frequent breaks during class to manage his disability; Brian does not. Brian finds himself frequently distracted and it takes him longer than it should to complete tasks. Given this symptom of his PTSD, he qualifies for the accommodation of extended testing time on exams.

---

* If two people have the same diagnosis, one can qualify as having a disability while the other one doesn't.

* Two individuals with the same diagnosis can be impacted differently by the disability, and therefore exhibit different symptoms and need different accommodations.

Comorbidity

It is common for individuals with disabilities to have more than one diagnosis at the same time. For example, we commonly see students with ADHD and depression, or a learning disability and ADHD. The medical term that refers to this is "comorbidity." There is usually a primary diagnosis and a secondary diagnosis. Our main concern regarding comorbidities is what can happen when a student shares only one of his diagnoses with supporting professionals, instead of discussing all of his areas of difficulty.

Over the years that we have worked with adolescents and young adults, we have come to trust our instincts. While assisting a particular student and family, we have sometimes had a nagging feeling telling us that something was not right. It almost always proves to be the same thing: The student's complete diagnosis has not yet been disclosed to us. Once we begin a series of gentle questions meant to uncover the full diagnosis, everything seems to come together and make sense. Then, and only then, when we know all the information, can we fully serve the family and do what is best for the student.

Candice is a freshman in college who has been granted a leave of absence from her school. In her first weeks on campus she disclosed her learning disability to the Office of Disability Services and received accommodations. She was pretty successful her first semester, until finals hit. The stress of finals and being away from home was just too much for her to handle. Unfortunately, she fell back on bad habits in her time of crisis and lapsed into an eating disorder which she had suffered from throughout high school, but which she had been treated for and beat; or so she thought. If only she had disclosed her full psychological history to the Office of Disability Services, maybe they could have helped her. As Candice later learned, this office could have put more supports in place for her. Accommodations such as extended time on exams and assignments, as well as regular meetings with a counselor on campus, could have helped to relieve her stress.

---

* You need to be open and share all diagnoses with the Office of Disability Services and other appropriate professionals if you want your school to help you.

A temporary disability

Home from college for holiday break, Tommy slipped outside and fell on the ice, leaving him with a fractured leg. His doctor assured him that after a couple of months in a cast, followed by a month of physical therapy, he would be good as new. Fortunately, his insurance covered physical therapy, and he was able to arrange for this on campus through his college's athletic department; one problem solved. The next problem was to find a solution to how he was to get from his dorm to classes until he could walk again. It was winter in the northeast, snow and ice covered the ground, and he was on crutches. He recalled having seen someone with crutches sitting in the back of a golfcart driven by a campus police officer. He contacted the Office of Disability Services, explained his situation, and requested accommodations.

According to the ADA, the law does "not apply to impairments that are transitory and minor. A transitory impairment is an impairment with an actual or expected duration of 6 months or less."[3] In our experience, most colleges will accommodate students with temporary disabilities, although they are not required to do so. According to his doctor, Tommy's injury should heal within a couple of months, thereby qualifying it as temporary. Upon submitting the necessary documentation, his college agreed to arrange for transportation to and from classes and campus activities.

---

* The ADA does not extend to someone with a temporary impairment with a duration of six months or less.

* Most colleges will voluntarily accommodate students with a temporary disability.

Now that we have brought to life many of the types of disabilities we discussed in Chapter 1, we hope you have a working knowledge of the nuances of when a condition or impairment is a disability and when it is not.

Chapter 4

Creating a Paper Trail

If you're a parent, do you have one of those large, brown, accordion-style files that is chock full of papers you've collected since the day your child was diagnosed with a disability? In all likelihood this folder is filled with testing documents, report cards, quarterly progress reports, and Individual Education Programs (IEPs), all ready to be toted along to an IEP meeting or triennial review at a moment's notice. If you have one, you're well on your way to creating a paper trail of disability documentation that will allow your child to be eligible for accommodations in college and even for the standardized tests such as the PSAT, SAT, PLAN, and ACT, which we will discuss in the next chapter.

If you're a student, are you as familiar as your parents are with the papers in your folder? Have you attempted to read your documentation? Do you know the kinds of educational testing you've had, and do you understand the results and what they mean? Can you explain your disability classification, if you have one, and what accommodations help you learn best? No? We're not surprised. We've never met any high school student who has this process and information entirely in hand.

So, whether you are a parent who doesn't have one (or more) of those oversized and overstuffed files, or a student who knows very little about your own disability and the paperwork that has been collected over the years, it's important to realize that it's not too late to begin creating a paper trail and sharing these documents so that both parents and students are all on the same page. No worries, we'll be with you every step of the way. After all, disability documentation is a key to access at college and in the workplace, and there is no way we're going to let you miss out on that!

Why is disability documentation needed?

Remember that we told you in the very first chapter of this book that the laws that governed disability rights would be important to many other topics we would discuss? Well, disability documentation is one of those topics. It's pretty basic, if you think about it. Colleges and most employers are required to comply with the Americans with Disabilities Act (ADA) and often with Section 504 as well. Both of those laws clearly state that they only protect individuals with disabilities, and they go to great lengths to define what a disability is for the purposes of the law. So, colleges and employers need to know whether you have a disability. No disability means no legal protection for your condition. Of course, the question of what is a disability can be so complex that we have devoted the entire previous chapter to answering it!

The way you prove to a college that you have a disability is with documentation. The role of the documentation is to identify a student as a person with a disability and to indicate how this disability impacts her major life functions, which can be things like mobility, vision, or learning. Although the laws set the mandate for documentation, they also permit each college the freedom to decide what kind of documentation they will require. Colleges can also decide how they will inform students of their disability policies. Each college will have written and published guidelines as to what evidence they will require to document specific types of disabilities. These guidelines are generally available on colleges' websites and may be published as a separate document or as part of the official college handbook. When you visit a campus as a prospective student, you should pick up a copy of these guidelines from the Office of Disability Services. You can also call or email and ask that the guidelines be sent to you. Although this sounds fairly straightforward, there can be a number of problems with disability documentation. That's why it is so important to begin the college process early and for both students and parents to be educated about what is required in order to qualify for accommodations in college.

---

* Colleges and employers need to know whether you have a disability in order to offer you legal protection for your condition.

* The golden ticket—Documentation is the way to prove you have a disability.

* Colleges have written guidelines as to what evidence they require to document specific types of disabilities. Guidelines may be available on their website, as part of the official college handbook, or published as a separate document through the Office of Disability Services.

Who is responsible for what?

Madelyn is a high school junior who attends a high-performing suburban public school. She was diagnosed with a reading disorder in the second grade and was classified under the Individuals with Disabilities Education Act (IDEA) as having a learning disability. Shortly after completing her triennial review under the IDEA, during which updated testing is customarily done by the school, Madelyn and her mom went to visit a local college which has a good reputation for their Learning Disabilities (LD) program. She and her parents thought their visit was perfectly timed because all of her documentation would be in place for submitting applications to colleges in the coming weeks. After touring the campus and meeting with the LD Program Director, they were handed a brochure entitled Documentation Guidelines. The Program Director explained to Madelyn and her mom that students with learning disabilities must submit a psychoeducational evaluation including results of IQ and achievement testing administered within the past three years. Mom had a sinking feeling in her stomach as she realized that even though Madelyn had just had her triennial review, the district did not administer any testing this time around because her current educational plan was working out well and her accommodations would stay the same for the remainder of her time in high school. The last time Madelyn had IQ and achievement testing was when the school psychologist had tested her in the fall of eighth grade. Therefore, her testing results were already three years old and would be over the deadline by the time Madelyn applied to the college's LD program. Upon returning home after the college visit, Madelyn's mom immediately placed a call to the Director of Special Education for her district and explained the situation. The Director agreed to set up IQ and achievement testing as soon as possible so that Madelyn's documentation could be updated and she could be considered for the college's LD program.

Stephen is a senior who attends a public high school. He grew up in a working-class community where the school system operated on a particularly tight budget. Stephen is a math wiz, but he has always struggled in school due to his lack of attention and poor organizational skills. In seventh grade he was diagnosed with attention deficit hyperactivity disorder (ADHD) and throughout his secondary schooling he has received accommodations including extended testing time and an alternative location for testing that was quieter and less distracting than his classroom. Stephen is a great self-advocate and has a charming personality; he's not afraid to ask for help and makes fast friends of students and teachers. In February of his senior year Stephen rushed to meet the colleges' application deadlines. Not only did he submit applications to Admissions Offices, but he also submitted a few additional applications for the structured ADHD support programs offered by a select number of the colleges. He was greatly relieved to be done with the bulk of the college process and to have made the deadlines. Then he received notification from the ADHD Program Director at his top choice college. She explained that the disability documentation Stephen had submitted was not sufficient and that he would not be eligible for the program unless he submitted the testing they required. She explained that his high school had used the WASI (Wechsler Abbreviated Scale of Intelligence) which is a shortened version of the IQ test. The college required the full-scale IQ test which is the WAIS (Wechsler Adult Intelligence Scale). The next day Stephen stopped by to speak with the school psychologist at his high school. The psychologist, Dr. Ramos, explained that the district only uses the abbreviated version of the IQ testing. The full-scale test was just too time-consuming given all the students they had to evaluate. Dr. Ramos doubted the district would retest Stephen at this point. He told Stephen that the IDEA no longer requires full testing of students who are about to graduate. It was simply a matter of economics, Dr. Ramos explained. He was truly sorry, but the school just didn't have the resources to run the full battery of tests Stephen needed and they weren't required to do so. He offered to help Stephen find a local center or psychologist who would perform the necessary testing quickly and as cheaply as possible, but Stephen knew that even the least expensive testing would put a financial burden on his family.

Many parents and students approach us completely unaware of what is the proper documentation to receive accommodations in college and how to go about obtaining it. As you can see from the examples above, neither Madelyn nor Stephen knew what type of documentation they needed. They both knew they would need to submit documentation but did not realize that there were detailed specifications as to what type of testing was needed or how recent the testing must be. Stephen clearly lost out due to the lack of resources at his high school which had chosen to use a less expensive testing tool. Madelyn's school had the resources to go beyond what the law required of them and to do the retesting for the purposes of her college accommodations. Wouldn't these students have run into problems earlier with their SAT accommodations? You've gotten a bit ahead of us, but, as you'll see in the next chapter, Madelyn would have been fine because her last round of testing, in eighth grade, would have been recent enough for her to apply for accommodations on the PSATs in the summer before her junior year. Stephen's testing might have been less comprehensive than the College Board, which owns the SATs, would generally like to see, but because he had his accommodations in place for several years and used them regularly, this was sufficient for him to be granted the same accommodations for his PSAT exam.

It is the student, and not the school district, who is responsible for making sure she has the proper documentation to qualify for accommodations in college. High schools, whether public or private, are not legally obligated to offer educational testing for the purpose of college accommodations. We have found that wealthier districts will sometimes do testing solely for the purposes of college, but they are not required to do so by law. In working with families who need to obtain updated or more extensive documentation of a disability, we suggest approaching the high school first to request testing. If a student attends a public high school, she should contact the Director of Special Education for the district. If a student attends a private school, he should contact the Director of Special Education for the school district in the town where the school is located, rather than where the student resides. This reflects a provision in the IDEA which shifts responsibility from the student's home school district to the district where the private school is located. This request for testing can be made by phone, but we suggest following it up in writing and certified mail. If the district refuses to retest, the only option you are left with is to go outside the district for private testing. We offer more detailed information on where to go for private educational testing in our Resources chapter.

Let's take a moment to explain briefly a couple of terms we have been using. You are probably very familiar with IQ testing; these tests are designed to measure that elusive characteristic "intelligence." Whether they do so accurately and whether they should be part of the documentation of a learning disability is a question that has been the subject of entire books. IQ tests look at an individual's performance on a variety of verbal and language sub-tests and on another group of sub-tests that focus on nonverbal skills such as visual organization and problem-solving. The actual score is a combination of the scores from these two kinds of questions. When there is substantial variation among the sub-tests, this may render the total IQ score less reliable and may itself be an indication of certain kinds of learning disabilities. You may be less familiar with the term "neuropsychological testing." This refers to a group of tests that look at an individual's aptitude for certain tasks not covered by IQ tests, such as attention, memory, complex language functions, and executive function. Achievement tests are just what they sound like. They measure the student's level of achievement across a variety of basic academic subjects, including different parts of reading and mathematics.

Some of what we discuss in this chapter will be of use only for individuals whose disabilities are related to learning or attention. Students with physical or medical disabilities, or mental illnesses, may need to submit documentation relating to their specific disability but not necessarily psychoeducational or achievement testing. For some conditions, such as dysgraphia, executive function disorders, and ADHD, schools may accept documentation from a physician without a full IQ and achievement battery, but we usually find this is not the case. We'll talk about the specifics of documentation for physical, medical, and mental disabilities in a moment, but the procedure for submitting these kinds of documentation is the same as for documentation for learning and attention issues.

What about documenting disabilities for employment? Most obvious disabilities—use of a wheelchair, missing limbs, or dwarfism—may not require any documentation. Employers and employees can determine together what will assist the employee to perform her job. Employers of individuals who advise that they have other types of disabilities generally require the employee to provide documentation by a medical professional that sets forth the disabling condition and its duration, how it may limit the employee in the performance of the job, and what specific accommodations the employee or her physician believe will enable the employee to perform the job.

---

* Colleges have detailed specifications as to what type of testing is needed and how recent the testing must be in order for a student to be eligible for accommodations.

* The student, and not the school district, is responsible for making sure she has the proper documentation to qualify for accommodations in college. High schools, whether public or private, are not legally obligated to offer educational testing for the purpose of college accommodations. If the district refuses to retest, you can go outside the district for private testing at a fee.

* IQ tests are designed to measure intelligence and look at an individual's performance on a variety of verbal and language sub-tests and on another group of sub-tests that focus on nonverbal skills such as visual organization and problem-solving. The usefulness of IQ tests is a subject of some debate, but the fact remains that they are required for many kinds of disability documentation.

* Neuropsychological testing refers to a group of tests that look at an individual's aptitude for certain tasks not covered by IQ tests, such as attention, memory, complex language functions, and executive function.

* Achievement tests measure the student's level of achievement across a variety of basic academic subjects, including different parts of reading and mathematics.

IEPs are not enough!

It is essential to remember that just as the IDEA ends with high school graduation, so does a student's IEP. We'll say it one more time because it is so important: IEPs don't qualify a student for accommodations in college. This goes for high school 504 plans too. So, if these don't apply after high school, then what do the colleges want? What should the documentation look like? We're glad you asked.

Most colleges have almost identical general guidelines as to what makes up good documentation. For example, all documentation, regardless of what kind of disability is involved, needs to be from a licensed professional in the appropriate field. A visual impairment may be documented by an ophthalmologist, but not by a licensed psychiatrist. The professional cannot be related to the student. The documentation should be recent. How recent depends on the type of disability and we will offer more detail about this later in this section. A clear diagnosis must be stated and the evaluation method used to diagnose must be described. Documentation needs to be thorough enough to demonstrate how the disability impacts a major life activity such as learning, eating, and sleeping, and to describe the student's current functional limitations. In addition, the most effective documentation includes recommendations for accommodations in college.

One resource that is often used by colleges in deciding what kind of documentation to require for specific disabilities is the guidelines set forth by the Association on Higher Education and Disabilities (AHEAD). "AHEAD is a professional membership organization for individuals involved in the development of policy and in the provision of quality services to meet the needs of persons with disabilities involved in all areas of higher education."[1] The organization was created in 1977 and today has more than 2500 members internationally.

Keep in mind that some colleges are more flexible than others when it comes to what documentation must be presented to qualify for accommodations. The Disability Services personnel at College A may employ a commonsense philosophy, whereas those at College B may not. College A, although preferring recent documentation, may use their "discretion in accepting older documentation for conditions that are [not subject to change]."[2] College A may not require that documentation for a particular disability contain specific words or phrases. On the other hand, College B may only accept documentation for certain disabilities that are very specific and use certain medical terms and no others. Although AHEAD encourages colleges not to elevate "form over substance in documentation guidelines,"[3] at College B you may feel as if you are jumping through hoops to provide exactly the documentation they are looking for. The differences in philosophies at various colleges' Office of Disability Services may simply come down to the Director sitting behind the desk. Maybe the Director of Disability Services at College A has been in the field forever and is very comfortable filling in gaps in documentation by having a conversation with the student and problem-solving together. On the flip side, maybe the Director is a newly hired and less experienced professional who feels she has to follow the documentation guidelines to the letter and to err on the side of being legalistic. We point out these varying philosophies to show you the importance of knowing way in advance what specific documentation you need to present to be eligible for accommodations at a particular college.

* Accommodations a student received in high school under an IEP or 504 plan do not continue in college or the workplace. Although Section 504 applies to both students and adults, the specific accommodations provided in high school won't necessarily be provided in college or the workplace.

* Although the guidelines provided by most colleges for disability documentation are almost identical, there will be variations in how they are implemented.

A learning disability

Let's begin by discussing a student who has a learning disability and the documentation she will need to submit to the Office of Disability Services on campus in order to be eligible for accommodations. Professionals who generally have the most experience in diagnosing LDs and are considered qualified include, but are not limited to, psychologists and neuropsychologists. Diagnostic reports should include the date(s) of testing, names, titles, credentials, and contact information for the evaluator.

Testing may take place over more than one day. Prior to the administration of the test, there is an interview conducted by the clinician to gather background information about the student's academic, developmental, and family history; parent(s) and student are present for this conversation. Information culled from this meeting is included in the first few pages of the final psychoeducational testing report.

The testing report needs to include IQ and achievement testing. If the student is 16 years or older, the preferred IQ testing should be the adult version (the WAIS—Wechsler Adult Intelligence Scale—is most commonly used) rather than the children's version, the Wechsler Intelligence Scale for Children (WISC). Assuming the student is 16 years or older, college disability personnel will usually want to see testing that is normed for adults rather than children. Typically, they are looking for a discrepancy between the student's potential, as reflected by her IQ score, and her performance, as reflected by her achievement scores. Although this standard has come into serious question in recent years, many if not most academic institutions continue to use it when making decisions about accommodations and other supports. It is our hope that, in the near future, the decision-making process will more closely reflect emerging knowledge about how best to diagnose these disabilities, but, for the time being, it is wise to cover your bases and give the colleges what they want. In addition, IQ testing must be the full-scale version rather than the abbreviated form of the test (WASI). As we saw in the case of Stephen, he was not eligible for accommodations in college because his testing included the abbreviated version of IQ testing rather than the full-scale. It is important that all test scores are included in the report, especially the standard scores and percentiles.

Since accommodations are based on the current impact of the learning disability on the student, documentation is usually not accepted by colleges if it's more than three years old. If you are applying to an LD program, it is not uncommon that they may want documentation that is more recent than three years. We've even heard of a college that wants students' documentation to be a year old or less. Be sure to double-check with the Director of the LD program. In the case of Madelyn, she was lucky that her district agreed to readminister IQ and achievement testing for the purpose of receiving college accommodations. As we saw, even though she had recently had her triennial review, her high school had not retested her. This scenario is not uncommon at many high schools and for numerous students across the country.

---

* Students with learning disabilities must submit a psychoeducational evaluation including results of IQ and achievement testing administered within the past three years, or even more recently, depending on the college.

* WASI v. WAIS—Some high schools administer the WASI (Wechsler Abbreviated Scale of Intelligence)—a shortened version of the IQ test. Most colleges require the full-scale IQ test, the WAIS (Wechsler Adult Intelligence Scale), before a student can be eligible for accommodations.

* Just because a student was given a triennial review by her school, don't assume updated testing was done.

ADHD

Away at college for his freshman year, Ryan had received very poor grades and was placed on academic probation. Although he was diagnosed with ADHD in high school and had received accommodations including extended time for tests and a quiet testing location, he was determined to begin college with a clean slate and to use no accommodations. He wanted to prove to himself that he could go it alone. Returning to school for his sophomore year, he again decided not to request accommodations. Come midterm time, realizing how desperate his academic situation had become, Ryan made the decision to disclose his disability to the Office of Disability Services. Knowing that his testing from high school was completely outdated, he contacted his pediatrician and asked that he send proof that Ryan had indeed been diagnosed with ADHD. Upon receiving a letter from his doctor, Ryan submitted it to the Office of Disability Services and requested accommodations. A day or two later he received a phone call from the Director of Disability Services at his college explaining that the diagnosis of ADHD scribbled on a doctor's pad is not an acceptable form of documentation to qualify him as having a disability under the law.

Fortunately, the conversation didn't end there. The Director of Disability Services gave Ryan a documentation guideline listing all the requirements necessary to support a diagnosis of ADHD. He even gave him a list of local professionals who could assist him with completing the documentation. In our experience, it is not at all uncommon for students to submit "documentation" that consists of diagnoses scribbled on doctors' pads, or from pediatricians they haven't seen in several years. An additional problem we often run into, specifically with students requesting accommodations for ADHD, is that their documentation has no differential diagnosis—meaning that no testing was done to rule out other diagnoses. To prove a diagnosis of ADHD, colleges want IQ and achievement testing to be administered to assist in ruling out a learning disability. The college often looks for the diagnostician to include in the report the age that the student was first diagnosed with ADHD. Early onset and a history of such symptoms going back to childhood are a necessary component of diagnosing ADHD. Of course, a clear diagnosis and current symptoms that cause significant impairment of a major life activity must be included as well as any current medication a student may be taking. Dosage, frequency, and side effects of the medication need to be noted. In addition to documentation of the diagnosis, some schools will want documentation indicating how the disorder is affecting performance.

---

* A diagnosis of ADHD (or any other diagnoses) scribbled on a doctor's pad is not an acceptable form of documentation. Rather, early onset and a history of such symptoms going back to childhood are a necessary component of diagnosing ADHD. Current symptoms that cause significant impairment of a major life activity, how the disorder is affecting performance, and current medication a student may be taking, including dosage, frequency, and side effects should all be noted in the documentation.

* ADHD documentation must have a differential diagnosis. Colleges want IQ and achievement testing to be administered to assist in ruling out a learning disability.

Head injury or traumatic brain injury

Towards the end of his senior year in high school, Michael was hospitalized with meningitis. Lucky to be alive, it took months for him to recover. Daily physical therapy and the best doctors and nurses available helped him relearn how to walk, write, and feed himself. Although he had made huge strides, he was still left with cognitive side effects due to the impact of the meningitis on his brain. He had a traumatic brain injury. Having already been accepted to college before he was hospitalized, Michael was doing everything in his power so that he could begin college with his peers come fall. When his doctors conducted post-meningitis educational testing, he discovered that his capacity for memory and recall was significantly diminished compared to before he was sick. As his neurologist explained, Michael would be severely limited in his ability to store the information he learned in college classes and recall it for exams. He would most certainly qualify as a person with a disability under the ADA. Michael's neurologist prepared a comprehensive psychoeducational report with his history, testing scores, and recommendations for accommodations in college. The diagnosis of traumatic brain injury was clearly stated, as was the probable site of lesion.

Over time, and little by little, Michael's brain injury healed. Because of the changing nature of the disability, the Office of Disability Services at Michael's college asked that each year he visit his neurologist for a check-up and provide an updated report illustrating his current symptoms and functional limitations. Freshman year, Michael had qualified for copies of class notes, extended testing time, and a scribe. By senior year Michael had improved so much that he only needed extended testing time as an accommodation.

---

* A neurologist is the most qualified professional to diagnoses a traumatic brain injury and prepare the necessary documentation for college.

* The report should include the student's history, testing scores, recommendations for accommodations in college, and the probable site of lesion.

* Because of the changing nature of this disability, the Office of Disability Services at your college may ask for an updated report each year.

Physical disabilities or systemic illnesses

Documenting a physical disability or systemic illness is often more straightforward than documenting a disability such as a learning disability or ADHD. Medical specialists, with expertise in the area for which accommodations are being requested, are the appropriate professionals to provide evaluation and diagnosis. Of course, documentation needs to include a description of current symptoms that meet the criteria for diagnosis. How recent the documentation must be depends on the changing (or static) nature of the disability.

A psychiatric or psychological disability

When documenting psychiatric or psychological disabilities, the diagnosing psychologist or psychiatrist must include a GAF (Global Assessment of Functioning) score in addition to the general guidelines for documentation. A GAF score of 60 or below indicates the presence of a substantial interference with [AQ]major life functions such as working, learning, establishing and maintaining relationships, and sustained concentration. The date of diagnosis, date of last visit to the therapist, and how often the therapist regularly meets with the student should be included in the documentation. Medication the student may take to address the symptoms of the disability and the side effects of the medication must be part of the doctor's report. Due to the changing nature of some disabilities in this category, it may be necessary to be retested during college or to submit initial documentation that is more recent than three years old.

> It is helpful when documentation provides information on expected changes in the functional impact of the disability over time and context. Information on the cyclical or episodic nature of the disability and known or suspected environmental

triggers to episodes provides opportunities to anticipate and plan for varying functional impacts. If the condition is not stable, information on interventions (including the individual's own strategies) for exacerbations and recommended timelines for re-evaluation are most helpful.[4]

---

* The student's GAF, date of diagnosis, date of last visit to the therapist, and how often the therapist regularly meets with the student should be included in the documentation. Type of medication taken (if at all) and possible side effects should be indicated in the report.

* It may be necessary to be retested during college or to submit initial documentation that is more recent than three years old due to the changing nature of many psychological and psychiatric disabilities.

Timeline of when to get the testing done

In deciding when to get testing done, one needs to be strategic. We work backwards from the dates of the practice standardized exams, PSAT or PLAN. If a student needs testing accommodations for these tests, then we suggest the disability documentation be submitted to the standardized testing organizations four to six months in advance of the test. It usually takes the College Board a couple of months to process the accommodation request. It is common for the request to be kicked back to the high school with a notation that more documentation is needed. If this happens, then by having begun the accommodation request process four to six months before the actual exam, you now have some extra time to resubmit the request. The PSAT is offered once a year in the month of October. Most students take the PSAT exam in October of their junior year. Therefore, disability testing should be completed by the spring of sophomore year and submitted to the PSAT organization then. Accommodations that are granted for the PSAT will automatically carry over to the SAT. You'll read more about this in Chapter 5 on college admissions tests.

Depending on the nature of the disability, the student may need to be retested toward the end of her high school career in order to be eligible for accommodations. This may be the case where changes in the disability—for better or worse—can be expected.

---

* If you need testing accommodations for the practice standardized exams, PSAT or PLAN, then your disability documentation should be submitted to the standardized testing organizations four to six months in advance of the test.

* Most students take the PSAT exam in October of their junior year. It is offered once a year in the month of October. Therefore, disability testing should be completed by the spring of sophomore year and submitted to the PSAT organization then.

* Accommodations that are granted for the PSAT will automatically carry over to the SAT.

Where should I get the testing done?

There are a few options available if you are going to go outside the school district to obtain disability documentation. Many universities with graduate education departments offer educational testing services to the public. Check with universities in your area. This type of testing is most appropriate for a student with a learning disability or ADHD. Universities often offer testing for a reduced fee because masters or doctoral level interns in training are administering the testing rather than licensed professionals. These interns are supervised by professionals in the field with years of experience who must sign off on the final report.

Private clinicians, including but not limited to psychologists and psychiatrists, offer comprehensive educational testing (for students with a learning disability and ADHD) as well as diagnostic reports (for students with a psychological or psychiatric disability). Some clinicians offer sliding-scale fees based on a student's family income. Educational testing is usually not covered by medical insurance, although medical testing and other kinds of testing may be. We suggest checking with your insurer and asking the clinician what insurance plans she may accept. We also suggest contacting the Office of Disability Services at a local college and asking them for referrals for outside testing.

---

* To obtain testing and documentation for a student with a learning disability or ADHD, look to local colleges with graduate education departments that may offer educational testing services to the public, private clinicians, including but not limited to psychologists and psychiatrists, or ask the Office of Disability Services at a local college for referrals.

* Educational testing is usually not covered by medical insurance. Check with your insurer.

Where do I send my documentation and when?

Students, parents, and high school guidance counselors often assume that disability documentation should be sent to a college's Admissions Office. In reality, this is rarely the case. Most often a prospective student's documentation must be sent to the Office of Disability Services. Sending documents by certified mail or by a method that allows tracking of delivery is always a good idea. If the student is applying to a separate and structured LD program, then documentation must be sent to the director of the LD program. Of course, there are exceptions to the rule and once in a while a college does ask that disability documentation be sent to the Admissions Office, but by and large this is not the case. For example, we have spoken with numerous Admissions Officers who attest to the fact that any disability-related testing reports that come across their desk are put into the shredder. Because this information is confidential, they feel they are doing the right thing by destroying it, since they have no use for it. It may leave you shaking your head in dismay, but it is not the norm for Admissions Offices, Disability Services Offices, and LD programs to communicate with each other on a regular basis and have a system worked out to pass on to the correct office any documentation that may be mistakenly sent to the Admissions Office. We suggest that you always read the college website and call the Disability Services Office to double-check where disability documentation should be mailed.

The documentation review process is housed in the Office of Disability Services. Note that there is not one consistent name for this office and various campuses can use different names. It may be called the Office of Student Support Services, Office for Students with Special Needs, or Disabled Student Services. It is helpful to the student and university to have a streamlined documentation practice and guidelines as well as a specific person or office that reviews documentation. This avoids the chaos and lack of consistency that could occur if each professor were offering accommodations individually.

We often hear the question: In order to request accommodations, at what point in the college application process should documentation be sent to the college? We discuss this issue at length in Chapter 12, but we will simply note here that there are two different answers. If you are requesting basic accommodations, meaning that you are not applying to an LD program, then you will need to send your disability documentation to the Office of Disability Services after you are admitted to the college. The summer before you begin your freshmen year is the perfect time to do this and to request a meeting with Disability Services personnel. Do not wait to the last minute to submit documentation. Do it before classes begin.

If you are applying to an LD program, then you need to submit your documentation when you are applying to the program. LD program application deadlines vary by college; they can be as late as February, although we suggest getting the application in by Thanksgiving of senior year.

---

* Most often a prospective student's documentation must be sent to the Office of Disability Services.

* There is not one consistent name for the Office of Disability Services; it varies by college.

* If you are applying to an LD program, then submit your documentation as soon as possible, preferably by Thanksgiving of senior year.

What happens once the documentation is submitted?

We mentioned earlier that all documentation is reviewed on a case-by-case basis. What does this actually mean? Each student who submits documentation of a disability is looked at as an individual, separate from another student who may also have submitted documentation for the same kind of disability. So, two students can both be diagnosed with clinical depression, be impacted differently by the disability, and therefore exhibit different symptoms and need different accommodations.

The service provider reads the student's documentation and then invites the student for an intake interview where they discuss possible and appropriate accommodations. It's important that the determination of accommodations is a conversation with input from the student, rather than a one-sided, closed-book decision. There is no better way to obtain helpful information regarding the impact of the disability and what accommodations may work best than consulting the student. An interview with the student can fill in gaps in the documentation and is tremendously helpful in "substantiating the existence of a disability, understanding its impacts and identifying appropriate accommodations."[5] For example, if the student didn't receive copies of class notes in high school, but upon reading her documentation and discussing this with her, Disability Services personnel feel she'll need to receive notes to access information presented in class, then this accommodation can be offered to her.

Once in a while, when evaluating the documentation of a student requesting accommodations, it may be necessary for the college's Office of Disability Services to obtain a second opinion. This can happen if the college does not believe the student's condition rises to the level of a disability. The second opinion, which comes from an outside and qualified professional, must be obtained by the college at its own expense. Let's look at the example of Brooke, who is a freshman at a large university and is requesting the accommodation of extended testing time. Two years ago her best friend committed suicide, which sent Brooke into a depression. She had been prescribed the medication to help relieve the effects of the depression, which included the inability to sustain concentration. She also met with a psychiatrist a few times a week. As time progressed, she was able to stop the medication and meet with her psychiatrist only once a month. Now, living out of state at college and away from home, she sees her psychiatrist infrequently. According to her documentation, her GAF score, a measure of function of individuals with emotional or mental difficulties, is 70, which illustrates that she is functioning at a higher level than usually indicates a psychological disability. Based on her documentation, the Office of Disability Services at Brooke's college found that she did not qualify as a person with a disability. Brooke did not take this news well; she was academically successful in high school when she received accommodations, and she wanted to receive accommodations in college. The Office of Disability Services sent Brooke's documentation to an outside clinician for a second opinion. It turned out that this psychologist agreed with the college that Brooke's condition had improved over the years and she no longer qualified as a person with a disability. She did not receive accommodations from her college.

---

* Each student who submits documentation of a disability is looked at as an individual, separate from another student who may have also submitted documentation for the same kind of disability; accommodations are on a case-by-case basis.

* The student is invited for an intake interview with the Disability Services provider where they discuss possible and appropriate accommodations.

* If the college questions whether the student's condition rises to the level of a disability, it can obtain a second opinion from an outside professional at its own expense.

What happens if you don't have the correct documentation?

Raj began his freshman year of college without updated documentation. He had presented testing from tenth grade that stated he was diagnosed with clinical depression. His testing report, from the psychologist at his high school, stated the frequency he was seeing his therapist and the medication he had been prescribed. During a conversation with the Assistant Director of Disability Services, Raj explained that he had not seen his therapist in a while and had not refilled his medication since it last ran out a few months ago. Because of the changing nature of some disabilities, such as clinical depression, the Assistant Director requested updated documentation before accommodations could be put in place. So that Raj would not be totally thrown off by having no accommodations in his first semester in college, the Assistant Director did allow him to have provisional accommodations. She explained they would be denied for subsequent semesters if he did not update his testing. The following semester came and Raj again requested accommodations at midterm time, begging that he needed them for exams. But he had not yet set up an appointment with his therapist to obtain updated documentation. His request for accommodations was denied.

Without current documentation, students are ineligible for accommodations. The last thing we want is for a student who has received accommodations her entire academic career to begin college only to be told that she must take classes without them because her documentation is outdated or doesn't include the required testing.

---

* Although colleges are not required to do so, some may offer provisional accommodations for one semester while you are obtaining the correct documentation.

Under lock and key

A student's disability documentation is confidential, as required by our old friends from Chapter 1, HIPAA (for medical information) and

FERPA (for educational records). It is literally kept under lock and key in the Office of Disability Services and purposely stays separate from the student's academic file. Information within the documentation is shared on a need-to-know basis. For example, if a professor speaks with Disability Services personnel and asks what kind of disability the student has, information regarding diagnosis should not be disclosed, even if the professor has the best intentions in mind. Disability Services personnel are trained to disclose only how the disability impacts how the student learns, rather than disclosing her actual disability. Details of a disability are shared if the student signs a release indicating to whom details should be provided. Exceptions are made (and are permitted by law) if the student is feared to be a danger to herself or others.

We once worked with a student whose disability documentation was subpoenaed from her college. She was involved in a court case that had nothing to do with her education, but a court had issued an order to the college requiring them to release her medical and disability records. Since both HIPAA and FERPA have provisions that require the release of records when ordered by a court, the school properly provided copies of these records.

---

* Disability documentation is confidential and shared only on a need-to-know basis or if the student signs a release.

Whether you had that bursting file folder from the beginning of your school career or are just now working to create it, we hope you can fully appreciate its importance. Follow the paper trail and you'll find it's one necessary component that will lead you to success in college and the workplace. You can also understand the need to guard that folder with your life!

Chapter 5

College Admissions Tests

Lyle woke up with a start. It was early on a Saturday morning in May of his junior year of high school, and he had a lot to do. He was glad he had allowed some extra time and had set out his pencils and calculator the night before. But he needed to check his glucose level and to double-check that he had packed glucose-testing equipment, diabetes medication and snacks. Why all the preparation? He was taking his SAT exam this morning. He knew that the stress of taking the test could affect his glucose levels and make it necessary for him to check his blood and possibly to eat or drink something to raise his blood glucose.

Carly was far less prepared than her classmate Lyle. She had started to find her pencils the night before, but got sidetracked by a question her sister had asked and never went back to her task. She could not find her admissions card and looked for her watch in three different places before she located it. She was nervous, which made her even more distracted than usual, and she was hoping she could stay focused and put her attention deficit disorder aside long enough to finish her exam.

Craig, who attended a small private school in the same town, was fast asleep. He had taken the ACT exam in April and was waiting to receive his scores. Craig had been planning to take the SAT exam—until he checked out the College Board website and realized that the SATs contained a mandatory essay section and that he would almost certainly be denied permission to use a computer for that section of the test. Craig was a strong student, but always used a computer in school to prepare written work and to take essay tests. His teachers had told him for years that his handwriting was illegible and he sometimes found that he could not read his own handwritten notes. In fifth grade he got a history paper returned with a big red "F" with the words "I can't read this!" written beneath. That led to a meeting of his parents and teachers, where it was decided that his school would provide him with a computer for his tests and that he would have a laptop to use both in school and at home for regular assignments.

When Craig first met with his school's college advisor, Mr. Kane, in tenth grade, they spoke about the difficulty in getting the right to use a computer for his SAT essay without long-standing formal documentation of Craig's handwriting difficulties and a diagnosis of dysgraphia, neither of which Craig had. "I'd suggest not even trying for this on the SATs," said Mr. Kane. "Why don't you plan to take the standard ACT exam instead? That doesn't have the writing section and you should have no trouble with the short answers. And the colleges you are considering are fine with it." So Craig took the PLAN exam, the practice version of the ACT, in tenth grade, then took this actual ACT exam in April of his junior year—and slept in on the day of the SATs.

We'll see in a bit how each of these students went about dealing with the SAT and ACT tests and what kind of success they had, but let's start by looking at the SAT exam and its competitor, the ACT, to understand how these tests have come to be such a major part of the college application process. Before we even start, we should clear up some common confusion about the names of the organizations and tests we will be mentioning. ETS, formerly Educational Testing Service, develops and administers the SAT test for the College Board, which owns the test and decides how it will be administered (and how accommodations will be given to students who request them). The primary exam offered by the College Board is the SAT, sometimes called the SAT I. Younger students are also familiar with the PSAT, a preliminary version of the SAT, also owned by the College Board. Since, as we will see, the SAT does not focus on specific curriculum areas, the College Board also offers specific SAT subject tests, sometimes called the SAT II tests. We'll use the names SAT and SAT II tests throughout this chapter. The ACT owns and administers the ACT exam and its preliminary version, the PLAN.

In the beginning

It may be of some comfort to our student readers to know that the SAT has been making college-bound students miserable ever since an early version was first tested in 1926. Originally designed to evaluate scholarship applicants to Harvard, the test had the seemingly benevolent goal of allowing students from all kinds of high schools and backgrounds to demonstrate their suitability for college. The thought was that some individuals had an innate ability, sometimes referred to as aptitude, which would make them successful in college even if they came from less prestigious high schools or disadvantaged backgrounds. During World War II the test was used for various purposes by the Army and Navy, and after the war it was put into general use for college admissions.[1] There have been changes in how the SAT is scored and in the component sections of the exam, especially the addition of a writing section in 2005. Additional subject matter tests have been added to the College Board's offerings. But the SAT has remained fundamentally unchanged for decades.

There have been differing views on exactly what the SAT is intended to measure. Some studies have suggested that SAT scores correlate with freshman year college grades, but others dispute this correlation[2] and in 1994 the College Board abandoned its long-standing position that the SAT measured aptitude for college. They dropped the formal name Scholastic Aptitude Test and issued a statement that "...SAT is not [initials]; it does not stand for anything." That may be, but it still stands as a barrier for many students—with and without disabilities—who are applying to college.

The American College Testing Program, now ACT, was established in 1959 to offer students an alternative to the SAT. The ACT was historically used more often in the midwest and south, while the SAT prevailed on the east and west coasts, although these distinctions are becoming far less common. To give some perspective on their usage, the College Board reported that over 1.5 million students took the SAT I exam in 2008; according to the ACT, their test was administered to over 1.4 million students that same year.[3] Most colleges accept either exam for admission purposes and we will look later in this chapter to see if one or the other would better suit the needs of particular students.

* The SAT and ACT tests have been in existence for many years. The SAT was originally designed to measure aptitude or intelligence, but the College Board dropped any such claim by the mid-1990s.

Goodbye to flagging

It is important to keep in mind that both testing programs offer accommodations for students with disabilities because they are legally required to do so, not as a public service. As we discussed in Chapter 1, the Americans with Disabilities Act mandates that individuals with disabilities be afforded access to public accommodations and services. There is no question that the SAT and ACT exams, administered nationwide and used by hundreds of colleges, fall within the kind of services covered by the ADA. Since the ADA requires that accommodations be extended only to individuals who have disabilities, the testing programs begin the accommodation process by determining whether the student applying for accommodations is, indeed, disabled.

One factor that has impacted this process was the decision by the College Board to stop "flagging" tests taken with accommodations. Prior to this change in policy, students who took the SAT with accommodations, such as extra time, had their scores reported with a notation "Non Standard Administration." Some students with disabilities were concerned that this notation would negatively impact how colleges would consider their scores by implying that they had an advantage over other students taking the test. Others, who did not want to disclose their disability during the application process, objected to having to choose between using accommodations they were entitled to by law and having the right to make their own decision about disclosure of their disability. If the College Board was required to accommodate students with disabilities under the ADA, in order to create a level playing field, advocates argued, didn't the step of flagging the scores of students who received accommodations to give them equal access to the test create an inherently uneven playing field?

These concerns led to legal action by several groups and individuals. In 2000, a federal court in California considered a case brought by Mark Breimhorst, who needed to take the GMAT exam (required of applicants to business schools and both developed and administered by the Educational Testing Service) on a computer with a track ball and with additional testing time because he had no hands. In an interim decision on whether Breimhorst had a basis for his lawsuit, Judge William Orrick of the US District Court in Northern California agreed that the flagging policy of the ETS "indentifies [individuals with disabilities] and stigmatizes them against their will, and prevents people with disabilities from competing in the application process on an equal basis with nondisabled people."[4] The lawsuit was resolved before it went to trial and ETS dropped the flag on all the tests it administered. But the SAT was not owned by ETS, so it was not legally bound by the settlement in the Breimhorst case. It was only after the College Board formed an advisory panel in 2001 which recommended removing the flags that the decision to eliminate them on the SAT exams was made, and the change in policy was not effective until October, 2003. The ACT eliminated its flagging system in September of that same year. As the College Board noted in a list of frequently asked questions about the flagging issue that it released in July, 2002,[5] it already had guidelines in place to "aid in separating reasonable from unreasonable requests" and would take "appropriate actions to protect against abuse." What about Mark Breimhorst? According to his personal website,[6] he went on to attend Stanford Graduate School of Business and become a businessman and disability rights advocate, working in positions including Executive Director of the World Institute on Disability, a public policy development and research center.

Our experience and conversations with guidance counselors, college advisors, and parents indicate that there have been several consequences of the decision to drop the flag, none of which is surprising. As students with disabilities are provided with greater opportunities in education, more of them are now taking the SAT and aspiring to a college education.

According to Jo Anne Simon, whose legal practice specializes in helping teens and older students deal with high-stakes standardized tests, such as College Board and ACT exams, postgraduate admissions tests, and professional licensing exams, the proportion of students with disabilities requesting accommodations from the College Board as compared with students without disabilities has remained roughly the same since the 1980s. Although more students with disabilities are taking the SAT, so are more non-disabled students. In anticipation of increased requests for accommodations and the concern that some students without disabilities would seek to manipulate a system that was not intended to help them, the College Board tightened its review of applications for accommodations to the extent that legitimate applicants for accommodations are finding them difficult to obtain. Students who are applying for accommodations need to keep in mind, Ms. Simon notes, that the College Board and other standardized testing organizations assume that you will be trying to "game the system." Because of this, if you take the PSAT without accommodations and do even marginally well, even if not nearly what you should have been able to do with the proper accommodations, you may find that the College Board will assume you do not need accommodations on the harder, longer SAT. These practices are similarly true for the ACT as well.[7]

---

* Beginning in 2003, both the SAT and ACT exams ended the practice of "flagging" tests taken with accommodations, such as extended time or use of a computer.
* The end to flagging allowed students to keep their disabilities private during the application process, but led to stricter scrutiny of requests for accommodations.

Applying for accommodations

Let's go back to our three high school juniors and see what steps—and missteps—they took on their way to their SAT and ACT exams. Lyle, the student with diabetes, had been diagnosed with the disease in third grade, and had a 504 plan in effect since then. Lyle's 504 plan provided several accommodations to make sure that his condition did not unduly impact his school work or regular school exams. He was permitted to take breaks to check his glucose level and to eat and drink when necessary. He was permitted to keep food and juice boxes at his desk at all times and could be excused from class to see the nurse without having to explain himself to his teacher. To the extent that his breaks took time away from his tests, he was allowed extended time to complete them. Lyle didn't use his accommodations all the time at first; most of the time his diabetes was well controlled and he could remain at his desk and finish his work with his classmates. But once Lyle entered middle school, his parents advised him to use the extra time and the right to bring food and medical supplies with him for all his exams. His mother had heard of a student who never used the accommodations the school had given her and who "had them taken away" because they didn't seem necessary. She wanted to make sure that Lyle didn't have the same problem.

Lyle had always been a good student and he planned to take the PSAT exam, the Preliminary SAT, in October of his junior year. He knew that the PSAT was also used as the National Merit Scholarship Qualifying Test, to determine winners of the prestigious National Merit Scholarships and that although only a small number of the scholarships were awarded each year, even students who didn't get scholarship money could be recognized for scoring well on the exam.

Lyle had a terrific guidance counselor, Mrs. Packman, who called him in at the end of tenth grade to ask him if he planned to take the PSAT. Mrs. P. suggested that Lyle apply for the exam at the end of his sophomore year, well in advance of most students, who received a packet early in eleventh grade with their PSAT application form. She showed him that there was an entire section of the PSAT/SAT website for students with disabilities and an extensive procedure for seeking the kinds of accommodations that Lyle had been used to getting under his 504 plan. She stressed that it was important for him to apply for his accommodations early, in case there was additional documentation needed or in the event Lyle was turned down and needed to appeal that decision. She explained that even though all students could bring snacks to eat during the brief breaks in the exam, they had to keep their food out of sight and could not eat or drink during the exam itself or get additional time to complete the exam sections if they were not feeling well. "One good thing," Mrs. P. told Lyle, "once you are approved for accommodations for the PSAT, they will be given to you for the SAT as well."

Lyle and his parents sat down and went through the College Board website section for students with disabilities. He signed up and created a password so he could manage his application process online in the future and learned that the basic requirements for being granted the kinds of accommodations he needed were pretty straightforward. He needed to have a disability that required accommodations. "Okay," he said to himself, "that's my diabetes."

Next, he would need to have documentation on file with his school that showed that he needed the accommodations. This documentation had to meet a number of requirements, and Lyle was beginning to realize that what had seemed simple sure had a lot of conditions attached to it. He took out a pad and pen and started to make a list. The information he needed to provide had to be specific, current, and include his relevant medical history. It needed to describe the kinds of tests used to determine his diagnosis and describe how his disability had an impact on his learning. He would need to describe the specific accommodations he was requesting and show that his doctor was qualified to make the diagnosis of his disability.

Finally, Lyle needed to demonstrate that his school gave him the same kind of accommodations he was requesting from the College Board and that he actually used those accommodations to take his regular school exams. Listening to his parents and actually using the accommodations the school had included in his 504 plan was starting to look like a pretty good idea. The wise Mrs. P. counseled Lyle, "This is the most important part of getting accommodations. Because you have had your 504 plan in place since elementary school and actually need and take the breaks for your high school exams, you stand an excellent chance of getting the same accommodations from the College Board."

All of the information Lyle would need to provide had to be current—not more than five years old—the website stated, and Lyle realized that there would be no problem with this, since he saw his endocrinologist, the specialist who managed his diabetes, regularly, and had just gone to a meeting with his parents to update his 504 plan a few months earlier. Best of all, Lyle realized that the College Board would accept the information that his school kept on file as part of his 504 plan, since it met the College Board guidelines. Otherwise, he would have had to submit a separate student eligibility form and have the College Board determine if it was sufficient, which would be a time-consuming process. Long before school began in September of his junior year, Lyle had received notice that he had been approved for the accommodations he had requested. He took the PSAT that October and drank a box of juice he had brought with him about halfway through the test. He did well and liked that the test results allowed him to see where he had made mistakes.

Lyle decided to take his SAT exam in the spring of his junior year. He didn't need to apply again for accommodations; he simply provided his code number when he registered and received his accommodations with no further action. So, although he wasn't happy about getting up early on a Saturday morning, Lyle was ready in every way to take his exam.

Carly had difficulty with reading and attention issues during elementary school, and by fourth grade her teacher had recommended that Carly be tested so that she could qualify for special education services. Carly's parents were concerned about Carly being labeled "learning disabled" so they decided not to have her tested by the school but instead arranged for her to be tutored three days a week. This helped somewhat and Carly was able to manage with her tutoring support until she reached ninth grade. The increasing demands of high school were just too much for Carly, and she and her parents realized that unless she got some significant support for her reading and attention difficulties she would not be able to pass her ninth grade courses. They requested an evaluation in early October of Carly's ninth grade year and after the evaluation was completed by the school, the district Committee on Special Education met and found Carly to be qualified for services under the IDEA under the category of "learning disabled." They recommended reading support services and other academic supports and determined that Carly was to be entitled to 50 percent additional time on her tests because of her attention deficit disorder. These services and accommodations were listed on her IEP and were put into place by Thanksgiving of ninth grade. By spring, both Carly and her teachers could see that her school performance had improved.

Like Lyle, Carly had a guidance counselor who was aware of which of her students were receiving accommodations on school tests under their IEP or 504 plan. She contacted Carly and reminded her to apply early for extended time for the PSAT exam. Carly and her mom checked the College Board website and put together the materials that the website listed to qualify for extended time on the PSAT. Just before school began, both Carly and her guidance counselor were advised that Carly's request for extended time was denied. Carly's guidance counselor helped her put together an appeal, including statements from Carly's teachers that she had used the extra time consistently since it was granted to her. Several more weeks went by and Carly was getting really concerned.

Finally, five days before the PSAT, the College Board denied her appeal, indicating that Carly had not met the burden of showing that the accommodations she was requesting were long-standing and something she had used during most of her school career. Carly took the PSAT without the additional time she had requested and was disappointed in her score. She was just relieved that it did not get submitted to colleges unless she requested that it be released.

After the PSAT results were made available, Carly and her parents decided to apply again for extended time. This time, Carly's guidance counselor suggested that she might want to consider the ACT test, instead of the SAT, but Carly's parents were not as familiar with the ACT and decided that she should try again with the College Board. Once again Carly's request for extended time was denied, and she took the exam without extended time. As we saw in the beginning of this chapter, she was nervous, but when she sat down to take the exam she found she was more familiar with the format this time around. Carly also realized that the test preparation course she had attended was helpful and she was able to complete most of the sections in the allotted time. When the scores were reported, she didn't do as well as she had hoped but decided that her scores would be sufficient for the less competitive colleges in which she was interested.

---

* It is crucial to apply for accommodations sufficiently in advance to allow time for the testing companies to review your documentation. This will allow you a chance to appeal if your request is denied.

* Having long-standing accommodations in place in high school, and using them regularly, is an important consideration when testing companies determine whether a student will be given accommodations for the SAT or ACT exams.

SAT or ACT?

Craig's decision to take the ACT instead of the SAT was based on his concern that he would be unable to score well on the SAT writing section without the accommodations he was getting in school. But there are a number of differences between the two tests that all students, especially those with disabilities, should consider when deciding which one to take. Start by checking the website and admissions materials for the colleges to which you are interested in applying. Virtually every US college accepts either test, but some may have specific requirements; for example, that students taking the ACT take the newer version of the test, which includes a writing section. Next, consider whether you will need to take SAT II subject tests for the colleges to which you would like to apply. These are offered in the categories of English, history, mathematics, science, and language, with several choices and levels in most categories. Language tests are offered with and without a listening component. Every college website will specify what their requirements are for these, including what subject areas they want to see. Some schools require SAT II tests if you are submitting SATs but not if you are submitting ACT scores, since the ACT exam is based on four distinct subject areas: English, mathematics, reading, and science. Since the SAT II subject tests are administered by the College Board, just like the SAT, the requirements for accommodations are the same. If a student is granted accommodations for the SAT, he will have the same accommodations on the SAT subject tests.

Let's look beyond what specific colleges want to how the tests differ, and what those differences may mean to students who have particular disabilities. For example, as we have seen with our friend Craig, the ACT is strictly multiple choice. There is an optional writing section which some schools require, but the basic test has no writing. This is a substantial difference from the SAT: Although two sections, mathematics and critical reading (formerly "verbal"), are multiple choice, the writing section is part of the basic exam and is not optional. Students for whom the physical act of writing is difficult or whose learning disabilities impact organizing written work might want to stick with the basic ACT exam, especially if they have difficulty obtaining the kinds of test accommodations they would like. Those students with disorders that result in impulsive behaviors may do better on the ACT where their scores will not be lowered if they guess on problems where they are not sure. The SAT deducts a quarter of a point for wrong answers, although there is no deduction for failing to answer a question.

Another difference between the ACT and SAT is the nature of the questions. As we have mentioned, the ACT focuses on subject matter content, so that students can study each area to improve their score. The SAT may have dropped the word "aptitude" from its name, but it still measures general reasoning and problem-solving skills more than specific subject content. Students whose learning issues make them less comfortable with complex reasoning may find they are more comfortable with the ACT, whereas bright students who have not applied themselves to the content of their high school courses might do better on the SAT, where knowledge of specific course content is not as important.

The SAT is longer—three hours and 35 minutes (including the writing section), for those who take it without extended time. The ACT is only two hours and 55 minutes, but will last another 30 minutes if you need to take the optional writing section. Students with poor attention may find that they do better on the standard ACT.

One way of deciding which test works best for you is to try them both. Since this can involve signing up for both tests, applying separately to the College Board and ACT for the accommodations you may require, paying for two different tests, and actually taking them both, a far better way to evaluate which is right for you is to take practice tests. The ACT sells a "Real ACT Guide" in both an online and print version that contains several complete ACT tests that were actually administered to students. The College Board offers a print version of a study guide with practice tests as well as a more expensive online course that contains both practice tests as well as additional materials. We'll look a bit more at test preparation later in this chapter, but these online and print resources are certainly sufficient for the decision about which test would work best for a particular student.

---

* There are real differences between the SAT and ACT that might make one or the other test a better fit for a particular student. Students with disabilities who will require testing accommodations should look at both tests, and possibly take one or more practice tests of each, to determine which test will best meet their needs.

Practical problems with obtaining accommodations

What about the differences in the policies of each organization towards granting test accommodations? In our experience, there is none. Both can be arbitrary or illogical in granting or withholding test accommodations, and students seeking accommodations from either test company should allow plenty of time for the process to be completed. Complicating matters, we have heard complaints of poor or inconsistent communications, such as from one high school guidance director who is his school's Director of Services for Students with Disabilities (SSD, in College Board lingo). Sometimes, he finds that the school will be notified when a student is denied accommodations, but the student will receive no notice. Sometimes, the student will receive the notice, but not the school. And he is still frustrated by the three tries it took to get the College Board to change the contact information for a new student with disabilities so the young man would be eligible to take the SAT in his new district.

A more serious complaint from school representatives with whom we have spoken is the stringent documentation requirements of the testing organizations and their impact on poorer school districts and less affluent families. IQ testing is expensive for school districts, and some of them are willing to use less complex tests than those required by the College Board or ACT. For example, a high school may use a test called the WASI (Wechsler Abbreviated Scale of Intelligence) which is a shorter version of an IQ test. It has fewer sections and provides far less information than the longer form of the test, the WAIS (Wechsler Adult Intelligence Scale), which is the test that the College Board and ACT want students to provide when requesting documentation for disabilities related to cognitive, learning, and attention difficulties. Also, although the IDEA requires a full evaluation of all classified students every three years, many schools are not in full compliance with this requirement. As we have seen in Chapter 2, revisions to the IDEA transition requirements have eliminated the obligation of school districts to provide complete testing for classified students who are about to graduate, and Section 504 has never required such testing. Families may not be aware of what kind of testing the school should be doing, and even those who are don't often complain unless there is a problem with their child's IEP. Until they realize that the testing the school has done will not satisfy the College

Board or ACT, they know of nothing amiss and may have no alternative but to have the student tested privately to meet the requirements of the testing organizations.

---

* Students and parents should insist that school districts provide the kind of testing, in a timely manner, that will enable students to apply for disability accommodations without having to have additional testing done outside the school system.

Score choice

For many years, the College Board did not permit students any flexibility in deciding which SAT exams they wanted to submit to colleges. If a high school student took the SAT exam more than once—for example, in spring of his junior year and then again in the fall of his senior year—the College Board would send the results of both tests to those colleges he listed. Many schools stated in their application materials that they would only consider the higher scores, but students could not be certain that the colleges would not be influenced by the lower scores in some way. This was particularly frustrating for students who had uneven scores—a higher mathematics score on one test date and a higher critical reading and writing score from another.

Beginning in 2009, the College Board instituted a new policy it calls Score Choice, which permits students to select not just test scores from specific test dates, but individual sub-test scores as well. A student can choose to send his mathematics score from one date, his critical reading score from a second date, and a writing score from yet a third date. This would seem to give all students a chance to provide colleges with their highest possible SAT scores, but the reality is nowhere near as simple. The fact is that Score Choice permits students who take the SAT more than once to select from among their scores, but it does not require colleges to agree to this selection process. The College Board website offers elaborate lists of the policies of individual colleges with regard to Score Choice. Many schools simply decline to participate and instruct students to submit all of their SAT scores. Other schools request all scores and indicate that they will only consider the top score in each component test, effectively implementing their own Score Choice process.

All students faced with decisions regarding Score Choice should carefully investigate the policy of each school in which they are interested and make sure they are in compliance with what that school wants to receive. This should not be done via the College Board website but by checking directly with each school in question.

The ACT has long permitted students to select which test dates they wish to have reported to colleges. However, although the ACT calculates the scores of its component sections—English, mathematics, reading, and science—it does not permit students to send only part of the testing from any test date. Nor does it permit students to send or eliminate the writing section from the scores of a particular date. All test information is provided for each test date reported.

---

* Score Choice is one of those innovations that sounds better than it turns out to be. Although it allows students to pick and choose their highest scores to submit to colleges, many colleges decline to participate and require all scores to be submitted, even if they indicate that they will only consider the highest scores they receive.

Choosing and using your accommodations

What kind of accommodations can a student with a disability expect to receive on the SAT or ACT tests? Both testing organizations have extensive lists of the kinds of accommodations they offer on their websites.[8] The College Board divides these by function, and offers lists in four categories: Presentation (accommodations such as large print, Braille, and audio magnification); responding (use of a scribe, large-print answer sheets, and computers with limited features); timing (extended time, multiple breaks, testing over more than one day with or without extended time); and setting (small group or private room, special lighting, and adaptive tools).

The College Board requires that students granted accommodations put those accommodations to use. If a student is approved for extended time, he must use the additional time for each section of the exam and cannot move on until his allotted time is over. Nor can a student with extended time leave the test early. The ACT allows a student who has been granted extended time of 50 percent more than the regular allotted time to pace himself within the total permitted time. For a student requiring more than 50 percent more than the standard time, or who uses extended time only on the optional writing section, the time for each section of the ACT is individually monitored.

The ACT is far less specific about the kinds of accommodations it offers and mirrors the language of the ADA when it notes that students who submit appropriate documentation will be given the accommodations they require, provided the accommodations don't place an 'undue burden' on the ACT or change the nature of what the exam is "designed to measure."[9] Neither testing organization will give a student accommodations that exceed those he has been granted and has used in high school. The goal of the accommodation process for students, schools, and families is to make sure that students don't receive less than they have been used to getting when they take these high-stakes tests.

One other consideration for students is the location where they will be tested. Both the SAT and ACT tests are given in numerous locations on the same date, and where a student is assigned to take the test depends on the extent of his accommodations. Usually, a student with more extensive accommodations, such as use of a scribe, a sign language interpreter for instructions, or 100 percent extended time, will be assigned to the SAT at his own high school, whether or not that school is a regular testing center. Students with accommodations whose home schools are designated testing centers will generally be assigned to a separate room with their own proctors, where they will be tested with students who have been granted similar accommodations. When students are granted the unusual accommodation of 100 percent extended time, they will actually be taking the test over the course of two days.

The ACT breaks down its test centers by the kinds of disability accommodations offered. Test Center #1 is for students who do not have extra time for the test, but who have been granted other accommodations such as a wheelchair-accessible room or a sign language interpreter. Students granted the accommodation of 50 percent extended time are assigned to a national extended time testing center. And students with accommodations not covered by these two testing centers are tested at their home school.[10]

---

* Both the SAT and ACT determine the location of testing by the kinds of accommodations a student will be using.

Test preparation

We are often asked whether it is useful for students to enroll in test preparation courses for the SAT or ACT exams. The major test preparation companies offer a wide variety of classes and individual tutoring designed to help students score as high as possible on these tests. They claim to be able to raise scores of students who take their classes. We have heard countless stories of students who have taken exams a second time with the help of a class and raised their score. We have also heard stories of students in the same situation whose scores dropped.

What we do know for certain is that students who are familiar with the format of the tests and who have taken numerous practice tests are going to be more relaxed on test day. "I took a course," reported Lee, who was very satisfied with his scores on the SATs. "But the most valuable part was becoming familiar with the way the test was set up. I must have taken 20 practice tests, from the ones they gave us in the course to the ones I did on my own at home. I wasn't happy about it at the time, but I have to say that it was helpful. I don't know if it raised my scores, but I felt that going through so many old exams I had a real feel for the timing and kind of material I encountered."

Before you commit to a preparation course, you might want to check out the materials on the test company websites we have listed in our Resources chapter.

* The most valuable part of test preparation courses is becoming familiar with the format of the standardized exams.

Ditching both tests

For some students the SAT and ACT exams are insurmountable barriers to college admission. These students may have anxiety disorders that make high-stakes tests unbearable even with accommodations. They may have processing disorders or memory difficulties that make even the extended time offered to them insufficient to complete the test with meaningful results. Or they may not have any diagnosed disabilities but simply did poorly, despite retaking the tests several times. For these students there is a growing option—simply to opt out of the SAT/ACT testing process and to apply to colleges that do not require either test.

The National Center for Fair and Open Testing (FairTest) is a nonprofit organization that has significant concerns with standardized, high-stakes tests such as the ACT and SAT. They engage in advocacy and research to promote the use of alternatives to these tests in the college admission process to better predict college success and to eliminate cultural, gender, and economic biases in current tests. FairTest believes that by using more effective measures, such as high school performance, in evaluating students for college, educational institutions will become more diverse without diminishing academic standards.[11]

One of the services FairTest offers is a listing on its website of colleges that do not require SAT or ACT tests in their admissions decisions. The over 800 schools listed include some that require these standardized tests of some students, such as foreign students or those with lower class rank. Some of the colleges listed want to see these tests but indicate that they only use them for placement purposes. Many excellent colleges, however, have simply dropped the requirement for standardized tests for all purposes, and any student who believes that SAT or ACT tests will have a negative impact upon their college applications should consider applying to at least some SAT/ACT-optional schools. We urge you to check carefully with each school you are considering. FairTest makes it clear that some of its information comes from secondary sources and every student should do his own investigation of this important information.

---

* An increasing number of colleges do not require the SAT or ACT for admissions purposes.

Whether you are fully prepared with documentation of a long-term disability and have submitted it in plenty of time, like Lyle, or whether you have only recently begun receiving accommodations, like Carly, and are unable to persuade the testing organizations to provide you with the accommodations you believe you need, we hope this chapter lays out some helpful options for you. And if you or your school have been asleep at the wheel, and have not laid the groundwork for the accommodations you require, as happened to Craig, we hope that having two kinds of tests to choose between and knowing about SAT/ACT-optional schools will help salvage the situation and improve your chances of admittance to the school of your choice.

Chapter 6

Selecting a College

There are over 3000 post-secondary institutions in the United States and you eventually have to narrow them down to one. Your options include community colleges, public colleges and universities, private colleges and universities, vocational training programs, and trade schools. If you are like most parents and students we work with, the prospect of such a task is overwhelming. Now, as much as you may want to put your head in the sand, hoping the right college will magically be chosen for you, we suggest a different approach. We believe that if you start with knowing the basic ingredients of how to select a college, you will feel in control of the process; you may even feel excited about the process. Have you ever taken Cooking 101? No? Well, you are about to. Put on your apron and roll up your sleeves; we are the five-star chefs who are about to lead you through the myriad considerations that are essential in finding the best college match for a student with a disability.

An overview of the basic ingredients

Before we go into more detail about each of the basic ingredients, we want to point out that students with disabilities have all the concerns of students without disabilities, plus a number of additional issues they need to consider. Let's look at Amy and Rob, who are both good students heading off to college next year. They attend the same high school and their families have been friends since Amy and Rob were in nursery school. At the beginning of his junior year of high school, Rob went through a period when he struggled with depression and mood shifts. He was hospitalized for several weeks and diagnosed with bipolar disorder. He underwent intensive therapy and was prescribed medication, which has been very helpful but has some side effects.

Rob, his parents, and his doctors decided that Rob would need some classroom accommodations when he returned to school, especially extended time to take tests and a quiet testing location, since his medication sometimes caused him to be tired and distracted. They contacted the school, which set up a 504 plan for Rob that provided these accommodations. Despite Rob's disability, much of his and Amy's college selection process is the same. When figuring out what colleges they want to apply to, they are each considering specific ingredients, such as the retention rate of students, selectivity (including how economic climate may impact application numbers and acceptances at particular colleges), geography, courses of study and majors, large versus small student population, and city versus rural location. We'll examine each of these ingredients in a moment.

In addition to the factors that Rob and Amy are both considering, Rob will need to think about a number of other things that are relevant to him because of his disability. These include the availability of counseling services on and off campus, the college's commitment to students with disabilities, the distance of the college from Rob's home and the parental and psychiatric support available there, and the challenges of dorm living. Students with other kinds of disabilities might want to investigate whether the campus is accessible to someone who uses a wheelchair, the level of academic support offered, whether there is a separate Learning Disabilities or Asperger's program, and whether a foreign language is required for admission or for college graduation.

---

* Although many of the factors that go into selecting a college are the same for a student with a disability as for the general population of students, there are some specific issues that students with disabilities need to consider.

Bye-bye, ostrich! Knowledge is power

There's no need to put your head in the sand and make like an ostrich. If you are a student and have not yet done so, sit down with your parents and figure out your college preferences. Decide, for example, how far from home you'd like the college to be, whether an urban, rural, or suburban campus setting is your style, and if you'd feel more comfortable with a large or small student enrollment. If you haven't been engaged in the college selection process and figure your parents or your guidance counselor will figure it all out and tell you where to apply, you are making a huge mistake. And if you are a parent who has decided, without significant input from your child, where she should apply, you are doing her a disservice. She's the one who will be going there for the next few years and she must be completely involved in the decision. If there are issues that are important to you as parents—perhaps financial constraints, or your child's physical or mental well-being—they need to be put on the table. It's not always easy to do this. Especially when a student has a disability that has required her parents to be even more concerned than they might otherwise be about her health or ability to manage on her own, it can be very difficult for parents to sit down with their child, to be frank about their concerns, and to reach a consensus about what their child's next steps should be. Students need to realize that this can be tough for their parents, and should try to understand that this process is not easy for them either.

If you don't know where to start, in order to figure out what your preferences are, we suggest that you chunk. Chunk? Yes, chunk! The term "chunking" refers to taking a seemingly overwhelming task and breaking it into smaller, more manageable parts. Essentially, we want you to take the college selection process and break it into bite-size pieces. Begin with identifying different categories of criteria—size, location, majors offered, for example. If you learn best using visual materials, you can write each of these categories on an index card and then spread all the cards out on a table. Some students prefer to use a spreadsheet, or even to talk these issues through with a parent or trusted advisor, such as a guidance counselor. Begin with one index card at a time and ask yourself, "Self, what do I want from a school and what will work best for me?" For example, if in considering the location, you quickly figure out that you want to be four hours or less by car from your home, then you already have one criterion decided and will know in which states you will focus your college search.

Ask yourself what major, or majors, you are interested in. Hint, hint: This is code for what comes easily to you. What do you enjoy doing with your time? One way to start narrowing down schools is by making sure the college has the major you are interested in. If you are even just considering a specific major, such as marine biology, you don't want to end up only applying to landlocked schools that don't offer this subject as a major. Once you have gone through a number of different variables, you can then take all your preferences and plug them into a college search website. Many of these websites may even prompt you to answer questions you might not have included in your list to further determine your preferences and criteria regarding colleges. Once you've entered all the information into one of these websites, it will automatically generate a list of schools for you to consider. Just remember that these websites aren't perfect. They don't know your personality and can only provide suggestions for suitable schools if the information you give them is accurate. Many students find that they can get better suggestions from a decidedly low-tech resource—their high school guidance counselor. A good guidance counselor will know the student personally, will know what colleges have looked favorably on graduates of a particular high school in the past, and may be an excellent resource. We have had experience with several different students who applied to particular schools only because their guidance counselor insisted they do so. In each case, this school, which they would not have otherwise considered, was where they ended up enrolling and having a terrific college career.

Websites that allow you to search a large number of colleges can be another very helpful resource for families. It takes mere moments to get on the internet and search for information about a specific college. You can find out how many students attend, if it's a private or public school, what percentage of the enrollment comes from in-state verses out-of-state, and what division sports the college offers. Specific websites are listed in the Resources section of this book. Another wonderful resource is a college readiness survey. It certainly can't hurt to take one, and completing such a survey will only take 15 minutes. Flip to the back of this book and check the Resources section for websites where you can access these surveys. We guarantee that figuring out your preferences will help you become engaged in deciding for yourself which colleges will be the best match for you. This really is a rather exciting task—not a scary one!

* Deciding the basics will help you become engaged in the college selection process. Take it one criterion at a time and chunk!

* There are a number of computerized tools that can help you narrow down your search. And don't forget about your guidance counselor, who may have the added benefit of knowing you personally and knowing which colleges are particularly interested in students from your high school.

University versus college

Throughout this book we predominately use the term "college" to refer to most institutions offering post-secondary education. Although there is no hard and fast rule, colleges generally offer only undergraduate programs of study whereas universities offer both undergraduate and graduate programs. Some schools were named so long ago that the designation of college may not honestly reflect the level of academic programs if, over the years, the college has evolved into a university but has chosen to keep its original name—for example, Boston College, which has a number of graduate programs.

Types of placement: Community colleges and private two-year programs

In addition to colleges and universities, there are all kinds of post-secondary options for education, and each option means something a little different. Not all colleges are designed to grant degrees after four years. There are several kinds of colleges that grant two-year degrees, generally called associate degrees. One kind is the community college, a two-year school that is usually open enrollment. Open enrollment means that all students in a particular community have the right to enroll at this school. Be aware—it is not just show up and matriculate (register to begin work on your degree). You can be required to show that you have a particular scholastic average from high school or you may need to take a competency test in a particular subject area before beginning classes. If you do not fulfill this requirement, you are generally able to take classes but may not be able to enroll in a degree program. Only once you reach a level of competence determined by the community college can you begin work on your associate degree. This degree will usually be accepted by four-year colleges, and many students decide to begin their education at a community college, for financial or logistical reasons which we mention elsewhere in this book. They will then apply to a four-year school to complete their bachelor's degree, and enter the four-year college as a junior, having completed the first two years of their program at the community college. Community colleges are public and are funded by counties and states. They usually do not offer on-campus student housing, but there are a few exceptions to this rule. Community colleges sometimes offer pre-professional certificates, in addition to an associate degree. Certificates may be given to a student who completes a more hands-on, skill-based program—for example, air conditioning repair. A certificate program may also be for a student who, rather than achieving a high school diploma, received what we have been calling an IEP diploma. Because this is not technically a diploma, most colleges will not accept this for matriculation.

There are also two-year private colleges. These schools are generally designed to provide limited curriculums or to offer students with learning or attention difficulties a chance to work on their areas of disability as a way to prepare for attending a more competitive four-year college program. These private schools are operated by a private individual or board of trustees and are generally a good deal more expensive than community colleges.

---

* There are both public and private two-year college options. The community college, funded by a state, city, or county, generally offers open enrollment and a very affordable way to complete the first two years of a four-year degree. These colleges offer an associate degree at the end of two years.

Types of placement: Trade, technical, and vocational programs

The designations for these kinds of post-secondary programs are used interchangeably, but the details of different programs can be significant. A trade or vocational school can be public or private. Many school districts, alone or in combination with other districts in their region, have programs that begin in high school and allow students with particular interests to begin training in their chosen field, while still completing the academic requirements for a high school diploma. Sometimes trade schools are operated by unions, and are designed to train interested individuals for specific union jobs, such as electrician or plumber. Technical schools are sometimes called technical institutes, but should not be confused with colleges that may also call themselves institutes and can offer the highest level of university education, such as the Massachusetts Institute of Technology (MIT) or the California Institute of Technology (Caltech). Students with disabilities should be careful to determine whether a trade, vocational, or technical program will be able to provide the kinds of accommodations they require to succeed in such a program.

* Trade, technical, and vocational programs are other options for post-high school education.

Types of placement: Certificate, gap year, and internship programs

There are growing numbers of alternative programs for students with disabilities—and those who just need some additional time before they are ready to enroll in a college program. These come in a variety of formats. One alternative that has been around for a number of years is the post-high school year offered by some private secondary schools. This used to be utilized primarily by would-be college athletes, who wanted an additional year to raise their grades, or to grow physically, before trying for an athletic scholarship. More recently, especially at private high schools specializing in students with learning disabilities, it is a way for students to have an additional year in a familiar environment that they can use to build academic skills and gain maturity before they apply to college.

There are also programs that call themselves gap year programs. These can involve travel to a foreign country, often combined with work or study. They can provide internships in areas of student interest, often in conjunction with mentoring and enrollment in a community college program. Most of these programs are designed for students who want to take some time off before attending college, and sometimes students will have already been accepted to college and arrange to defer their start date for a year while they have their gap year experience. Although there is no reason for students with disabilities to avoid such programs, we do recommend that you carefully check out the supports they offer, the availability of medical care, and the same kinds of issues we suggest you consider when selecting a college.

A small number of colleges offer self-contained certificate programs. These can range from one to four years in length. The shorter programs are designed to familiarize students who have learning disabilities, attention deficit hyperactivity disorder (ADHD), and Asperger's syndrome with the educational and social aspects of college; the expectation is that students who complete the program will then apply to college as freshmen for the following year. The longer programs are generally designed for students whose cognitive or other disabilities would make it difficult for them to manage college. These programs offer job and social skills training and independent living skills.

---

* Another group of post-secondary programs focus on getting ready for college, providing time for students to mature, or building life skills for students who won't be attending college.

The three different tiers of support

We've spent some time looking at different kinds of post-high school programs, but it's time to turn to what you need to consider when deciding if a particular program or college is right for you. Most people don't know this, but different colleges offer different levels of disability support. It's essential to know what level of support the colleges you are interested in provide. The minimal level, as required by the Americans with Disabilities Act (ADA), is the type of support offered by most colleges. Virtually every college in the country, with the exception of the military academies, must have one person in charge of coordinating accommodations for students with disabilities. When a student submits adequate documentation of a disability, she will then be eligible for accommodations, such as extended testing time. This basic accommodation is the most common example of what is often referred to as tier one level of support.

Magdelena, who is a terrific self-advocate, is very successful in college. Her vision impairment, and, of course, supporting documentation, qualifies her for accommodations. Her college grants her enlarged print and the use of books on CD as accommodations. Magdelena is also permitted to take tests without scantrons, the test sheets on which students mark a "bubble" to correspond with their answer. Many students with visual impairments are unable to follow in line with the test sheet. She is also given access to the computer lab housed in the Office of Disability Services and uses the JAWS software. JAWS is a computer program that converts text to speech by reading aloud to the user what is on the screen. In Magdelena's case, more than these basic technological accommodations is not necessary and she does just fine at a college that offers the most minimal level of disability support.

Colleges that go above and beyond what the law requires offer what is called a tier two level of support. This includes not only basic accommodations to students with documentation of a disability, but also services. Peer tutoring free of charge to a student with a disability and access to meet with an academic coach to work on organization skills are examples of services.

Tier three level of support is the most comprehensive of all. These colleges offer special programs designed to support students with learning disabilities or attention disorders. Nothing will compare to the amount of support offered in high school through the Individuals with

Disabilities Education Act (IDEA), but a tier three program comes the closest. A college that offers students accommodations and services is not offering a program; there is a significant difference. Programs are offered at less than 100 colleges in the country. There is usually a hefty price tag attached to a program and fees vary by college. It is common for a separate application to be required to apply to such a program. These programs look to accept students with language-based learning disabilities and students with average, rather than below average, IQs. Programs offer students private sessions with a learning specialist during the week. For sure, more hand-holding occurs at colleges offering tier three supports than at those offering tiers one and two, but once again it's important to be aware that nothing will compare to the level of support offered in high school.

Andrew has a learning disability and ADHD and has struggled through high school without much confidence in himself when it comes to the classroom. Unfortunately, his self-advocacy skills are virtually non-existent, his mom having advocated for him throughout his school career. What little confidence he does have is gained from his success on the athletic field; he is the star of his high school's soccer team. Andrew also has the reputation among his peers of having a great sense of humor, usually self-deprecating and at his own expense. He enthusiastically told us the story of how he first got his nickname—Pigpen—after the famous Peanuts cartoon character. The scene was from middle school. He was the disheveled kid who, as he ran to make the bus home from school, had a trail of papers, books, pens, and pencils falling out of his backpack. One of the older kids on the bus must have caught a glimpse and the nickname stuck. Now a senior in high school, Andrew has applied to mostly local colleges that offer Learning Disability programs. He is nervous about the workload of college, and is aware enough to know that his lack of self-advocacy skills, organizational skills, and classroom confidence will make him a perfect candidate for a LD program.

Though much more scarce than LD and ADHD programs, there are a few tier three programs of support for students with high-functioning autism/Asperger's syndrome popping up here and there around the country. These may offer social skills training by a professional and peer mentoring from students without a disability. Some programs have fees; others do not.

* Different colleges offer different levels of disability support. Basic accommodations—extended testing time or assistive technology—is referred to as tier one level of support. Tier two level of support goes a bit above and beyond what the law requires and offers services such as peer tutoring free of charge, in addition to accommodations, to a student with a disability. Tier three level of support includes special programs for students with learning disabilities or attention disorders and generally includes an extra fee in addition to tuition, room, and board.

An Academic Resource Center

Some colleges have an Academic Resource Center open to all students, not just students with disabilities. Academic Resource Centers are known to offer tutoring in various subjects as well as workshops on topics such as study skills, note-taking skills, and stress management. We think this is a wonderful model for colleges to have available to students. A centralized location for services, for all students, whose goal is to increase retention and graduation rates—how can you go wrong if your college offers this? In addition, all students are mixed together so there is no division between students with disabilities and students without. This decreases the discomfort factor and the exclusionary feeling some students with disabilities have that they are different from their peers, when, in reality, they have more in common than not.

The quality of tutors offered by an Academic Resource Center varies by college. Some colleges employ peer tutors, who are other students who have a strong background in the subject they are tutoring. Others have graduate level tutors, and still others have professional tutors. Not all tutors are created equal, so it is wise to find out their qualifications and experience. We suggest you inquire if there is a fee for tutoring. Also, how available are tutors, especially at exam time?

The Academic Resource Center is usually separate from the Office of Disability Services that offers accommodations to students with disabilities. The college administrator charged with coordinating accomodations has an office housed in the Academic Resource Center, but usually they are in a separate office elsewhere on campus. Of course, a one-stop shopping model is much more helpful for a student with a disability, especially if it is a physical disability or one that impacts a student's organizational skills. A college whose Academic Resource Center is located separately from its Office of Disability Services doesn't have to be a make-or-break for whether you will enroll there, but it is wise to recognize that it will likely require more organization on your part and a bit more running around.

---

* The Academic Resource Center is open to all students at the college. Subject tutoring as well as study skills, note-taking skills, and stress management workshops are offered. The quality of tutors varies according to whether the college employs peer, graduate level, or professional tutors.

* The Office of Disability Services may be located in the Academic Resource Center, but it is usually separate.

Selectivity

You always want to know how selective a college is. You may know its general reputation, but the numbers do change from year to year. For example, in an economic climate when times are good, public colleges may not be in as high demand as when times are tough. When economic times are tough, the application numbers at public schools, which almost always have lower tuition fees than their private counterparts, may be through the roof and their acceptance rate much lower than just a year or two before. Keep this in mind when you create your list of schools to visit and apply to—you want a mix of private and public schools on there to give you the best chance of being admitted to a number of colleges.

As we'll discuss in our work chapter, college is no longer a place for only the lucky few in our society. Many more students attend college now than in years past, and the sheer numbers of students applying make it much more competitive to get into college. In recent years, there has been a trickle-down effect in terms of school selectivity. As Ivy League colleges receive more and more applications and have to turn down more and more highly qualified students, usually because they literally do not have the room to house them in their dorms and fit them in their classrooms, those top-tier students who are not admitted have to enroll at their second choice schools. This then boosts those second choice schools, making them more selective than in the past. And by the way, for all the hype, the term Ivy League is really just a sports league and students shouldn't exclude many other excellent schools just because they are not Ivies.

How do you find out how selective a particular school may be? Although we sang the praises of internet-based college search engines earlier in the chapter, we do not recommend them as enthusiastically for finding out the number of applicants accepted compared to how many apply. Although a search website may offer you a general picture, you really want to call the college's Admissions Office to obtain the most reliable information. You can speak with an Admissions Officer to ask what the average SAT/ACT scores and grade point averages (GPAs) are for accepted students. Most colleges have these statistics and are happy to share them. Based on the numbers they give you, you can then gauge if you are on target for that school, given your standardized testing scores and high school grades, or if this school is too competitive or too easy for you in terms of admission.

Many of the parents of the students we work with recall applying to one school and one school only when it was time for them to head off to college. Times have changed. We definitely do not recommend this. In fact, this situation brings several very fitting egg proverbs to mind. Don't place all your eggs in one basket and apply to only one or two schools. Admission to a college is never a sure thing. We have seen a number of situations with students who seem like a perfect fit, on paper, for a particular college and for some reason they are not accepted. And definitely don't count your chickens before they hatch! So, how many schools should you apply to? If there isn't a limit from your high school and if application fees aren't a problem, we suggest applying to two or three reach schools, two or three safe schools, and four or five in the middle.

---

* How selective a particular college is may change year to year depending on varying factors including economic climate. Call and speak with an Admissions Officer to ask what the average SAT/ACT scores and grade point averages (GPAs) are for accepted students.

* Getting into most colleges is harder now than it was a generation ago. Don't place all your eggs in one basket and apply to only one or two schools. Rather, we suggest applying to two or three reach schools, two or three safe schools, and four or five in the middle.

Distance, climate, and location

Have you always dreamed of living on the east coast, in the city that never sleeps, or on the west coast, the setting of those endless summers? Well, college may or may not be the time to fulfill this dream, but geography is a consideration when selecting a college. How far do you want to be from home and your family? A car or plane ride away? Do you fare better in cold or warm weather, or do you prefer to experience the four seasons each year? Are you such a surf, ski, or snowboard fanatic that, if in the ideal climate for your sport of choice, you will be tempted to miss class? Are you a city mouse or a country mouse? Have you figured out if you'd thrive in a city, rural, or suburban location? Attending college without a support safety net in place is not a good idea if you are like Alan, a student with ADHD, who traveled far from home and experienced all that Atlanta had to offer (or, rather, was distracted by everything Atlanta had to offer). Alan was asked to leave a top Atlanta school after two semesters because his grades were so abysmal; not surprising given that he only rarely attended class. Maybe it is the best decision to stay local for college and in time transfer to a college away from home, if you are like Megan who has a learning disability and has always struggled with organizational skills. She is currently working with a wonderful therapist, near her home, who is helping her make great strides organizationally and academically.

---

* Geography is a consideration when selecting a college. Do you have the focus and organizational skills to be successful living far away from home? Will your schoolwork suffer when you are tempted to take advantage of the city night life, surf, or snowboard scene?

Challenges of dorm living

Dorm living can be a lot of fun; it can also be very challenging. For students with particular disabilities including Asperger's syndrome, ADHD, allergies, Crohn's disease, those who need a personal aide, or those recovering from drug and alcohol addiction or an eating disorder, dorm living may be especially challenging. Some accommodations may be available to make dorm living possible—for example, a single room, or a room with a bathroom—but students and families have to decide together whether or not living in a dorm will offer the best option for success. Sarah is a recovering alcoholic and has been sober for over three years. We spoke with her as she finished up her freshman year of college and she shared with us her experience of the college selection process. Sarah explained that she decided what colleges to apply to based on the basic ingredients and then one more additional ingredient which was the make-or-break for her. She only chose colleges with dry campuses or schools that had a themed dorm, or floor of a dorm, dedicated to alcohol- and drug-free living. And although Sarah matriculated at a college where she lives in a dorm with students who chose intentionally to live in an alcohol- and drug-free environment, she's realistic in the sense that she knows substances are readily available elsewhere on campus. It is good that her dorm is her safe place, and nearby AA meetings help her to stay sober.

---

* Living on campus in a dorm is not for everyone and that is okay. Some disabilities make it more challenging to be successful while living in a dorm. Discuss the advantages and disadvantages with your family.

Academic classes and professors

Student-to-teacher ratio and average class size are essential components to selecting a college. Lecture style classes with 300 students tend to lose students with disabilities who may not have the best self-advocacy skills. These students, often those with learning or attention issues, usually have more success at smaller colleges where it is less likely that they will fall through the cracks. This being said, there are a select number of colleges in the country whose unique philosophy has created seminar style classes. Although characterized by small class size, this philosophy requires students to be working independently all semester long, culminating in a final project or portfolio. This type of learning environment is likely not the best match for someone who doesn't do well without structure. For example, a student with ADHD who has poor organizational and time-management skills may not know how to be successful in a class where there is one large project that counts for most of her grade.

Many schools, especially larger research universities, utilize teaching assistants (TAs) to teach, or assist in teaching, undergraduate classes. One university's handbook explains that the TA will "participate in the instruction, advising, and evaluation of undergraduates. In many cases, especially in courses with large enrollments, you [the TA] will provide the human contact and personal motivation that can make the difference between success and failure for individual students."[1] We suggest you avoid schools that regularly employ TAs, unless you feel you are a terrific self-advocate. It is preferable that all your courses be taught by a professor who is an expert in her field and has years of experience teaching. In addition, professors at the college you attend should be accessible. They should have regular office hours where you can make an appointment to discuss questions you may have on course material or how you can be most successful in class given your disability. Accessible professors are especially important for a student who is interested in continuing on to graduate school. The opportunity to collaborate with professors on a research project, a paper to be published, or in an independent study course will set you apart from other graduate school applicants. In addition, since most graduate schools will require teacher recommendations, you want to be at a college that allows you access to professors so that you can build academic relationships and professors can get to know you and your capabilities.

* Lecture style classes with 300 students tend to lose students with disabilities who may not have the best self-advocacy skills.
* Colleges which primarily offer seminar style classes, which culminate in a single large project, may not be the best match for a student who has poor organizational and time-management skills.
* We suggest you avoid schools that regularly employ TAs, unless you feel you are a terrific self-advocate. It is preferable that all your courses be taught by a professor who is an expert in her field and has years of experience teaching.
* Professors should be accessible. This is especially important for a student who is interested in continuing on to graduate school.

Vibe on campus

The feel of a campus at a single-sex school will certainly be different than at a co-educational college. A commuter campus will have a different vibe than a college where every freshman is required to live on campus or which guarantees housing to students. Each setting clearly has its pluses and minuses. Some students intentionally seek out a single-sex college based on its academic excellence; others visit and surprise themselves by falling in love with the camaraderie among classmates and the obvious sense of a close-knit community. Single-sex colleges often have a sister or brother school nearby and classes may be co-ed. Some students choose to attend a historically black college based on its rich tradition and community.

Diversity on a college campus can refer to varying factors including ethnic diversity, economic diversity, and sexual diversity. We encourage the young adults we work with to select a college whose students are diverse. This is an important step towards becoming a mature and fully realized person. Meeting new people different from yourself—and learning from them—is a huge part of going to college. Certainly don't decide to attend a school based on where your buddies—or your boyfriend—goes. Four years is a long time and the buddies or boyfriend may not be part of your life in a few months; you can find yourself at a school that doesn't really meet your needs. Of course, visiting will help, but check out the back of this book for resources that may help you evaluate a college's diversity factor.

---

* Vibe on campus is influenced by factors such as diversity, single-sex verses co-ed population, and history of serving a particular racial or ethnic population.

Services on campus

Selecting a college with a quality Career Center, internship placement or co-op program, and alumni network can be very important; if not freshman year, then definitely down the line. Not only do these services enhance a student's educational experience through networking and hands-on opportunities, but they can make it easier for you to gain employment after graduation. Make it a point to stop into the Career Center while visiting campus. Evaluate the activity level—is it empty or are students there waiting to interview with prospective employers or using the online and print resources that the Center offers?

---

* A thriving Career Center, internship placement or co-op program, and alumni network will not only enhance a student's educational experience but can make it easier to gain employment after graduation.

Specific disabilities

Some colleges offer more support services for a student with one type of disability than another. For example, some colleges invest their resources in hiring sign language interpreters as staff members whereas others do not. There are ways to evaluate whether a campus will be welcoming to individuals with specific disabilities. Some institutions are more likely to offer campuses that are more physically accessible than others—with push pads on the doors and curb cuts in the sidewalk. For a student with a psychological disability, find out if the college you are interested in attending has an Active Minds chapter which is "aimed at removing the stigma that surrounds mental health issues."[2] Does the college offer a social skills group or peer mentor for a student with Asperger's syndrome?

---

* In selecting a college, be aware that some schools offer more support services for a student with one type of disability than another.

We'll say it again

There are a few ingredients we will be discussing at length in the coming chapters. Because they are so important they are worth mentioning more than once. These ingredients include the college's commitment to students with disabilities as illustrated by the accessibility of their website and staff, availability of counseling and health services on and off campus, whether a foreign language is required for admission or for college graduation, if the college offers a foreign language or math substitution, and, if not, whether they offer a course in these subjects designed specifically for students with disabilities. Additional factors include single-room policies, cafeteria food options for students with health-related disabilities, test-optional schools, courses of study and majors, and retention rate of students. Chapter 13 looks at financial issues relating to college, including cost and financial aid.

Not set in stone

The ingredients we've discussed throughout this chapter are often, unfortunately, subject to change. For example, College A may have a fabulous Director of Disability Services. The accommodations and services offered by the Office of Disability Services may be first-rate under this administrator. At some point in time the Director resigns from her position and moves on to College B to take a new position. The administrator that replaces her is less than stellar, and the quality of accommodations and services at College A declines. This can mean that from one year to another a college may or may not be a school that has all the key ingredients to support a student with a disability and enable her to have a successful educational experience. It is important to look at what a college offers currently, not at its past reputation or offerings.

---

* Because colleges change and evolve, whether academically, programmatically, or personnel-wise, from one year to another a college may or may not have all the key ingredients.

Although there is no magic list of colleges that are appropriate for students with disabilities, we hope you now have a sense of how to find schools that have the key ingredients you will need for success.

Chapter 7

Application Advice

The college application process can be overwhelming and fraught with deadlines and uncertainty. In addition to the decisions, questions, and tasks faced by all high school seniors, students with disabilities have even more to think about. A student with a disability must consider whether or not he will focus his college essay on his learning, physical, psychological, or other challenge and explain how he has persevered in the face of it all. He must find out if there is a separate application for the disability support program in which he is interested in participating and whether an interview is required for him to be considered. As seen in the previous chapter on selecting a college, he has already had to consider the kinds of support available to him and think about his physical needs and campus accessibility.

You've already done a lot of work, so, as you begin thinking about your applications, we urge you to take a deep breath and try to stay calm. Even though applying to college may seem hopelessly complicated, we're going to help you take the stress level down a notch and guide both students and parents, step by step, through completing your application.

The timeline

Remember the term "chunking" from the previous chapter? We want you to take the seemingly overwhelming application process and break it into smaller, more manageable parts. Decide on a goal for when you want to submit applications, keeping in mind the fact that our experience has made it clear that the earlier in senior year students submit their applications, the better. We suggest that by Thanksgiving of twelfth grade, students should have their applications complete and ready to submit. So as not to confuse you, we need to point out that the Thanksgiving deadline is our creation rather than that of any particular college. In the section that follows, we'll look at formal application deadlines set by colleges.

We've had success using Thanksgiving as the deadline because this practice relieves excess stress on the student and his family. Students are less likely to make mistakes on applications if they are not rushing to get them in on time. Teachers who write recommendations and guidance counselors who submit academic transcripts and recommendations are less overwhelmed earlier in the application process. Colleges are less inundated with applications early on and therefore less likely to misplace or lose submitted applications. If a student is considering applying Early Decision (ED), or Early Action (EA), for which most colleges have a November 15 or December 1 deadline, he will be ready to meet that early date. Our Thanksgiving date offers students a better chance of being admitted to the school(s) of their choice since there are generally fewer applicants at this early point in the process. The same applicant accepted in November, for example, could be rejected in January. This may make the critical difference for an applicant whose disability has impacted his high school academic performance, resulting in grades or standardized testing scores that are not as high as he had hoped.

For students with learning disabilities who are applying to the separate fee-based support programs offered by a select number of colleges, there is quite a demand for the few available spots. Directors of these college support programs encourage students to submit their applications by the fall of their senior year to give them a better chance of being admitted, since qualified students are usually accepted on a first-come-first-served basis.

Once you have set your deadline for having your applications ready to go, work backwards from that date to create a timeline for the tasks that need to be completed before you can actually submit your applications. Much of junior year in high school should be spent prepping for and taking standardized exams, improving grades, taking a rigorous curriculum, creating a list of colleges to apply to, and visiting college campuses. For a student with a disability, junior year should also be spent getting documentation in order. As detailed in Chapter 4, this includes making sure the documentation of your disability is up to date and complete, and that, for students with learning and attention difficulties, it includes all the specific psychoeducational testing that will be needed to qualify for accommodations at the college level.

The summer before senior year is the ideal time for writing a college essay and a resume. Most, though not all, four-year colleges require a student essay or personal statement, and some require more than one. If a student is using the Common Application, which we will discuss in a moment, he can use the same essay for each application. Double-check your essay, not just for grammar, spelling, and the usual concerns, but to make sure that you don't send the version declaring that you have always wanted to attend College X in the admissions packet you send to College Y!

You should use the fall of your senior year to obtain teacher recommendations, keep grades up, and continue taking a rigorous curriculum. Fall of senior year is also a good time to visit or revisit campuses and to take standardized exams one last time. Most colleges require one or two teacher recommendations and the popular teachers—generally those who can be counted upon not only to write and provide a well-written, positive recommendation but, as important, to get it in on time—usually book up early. You should also be having regular conversations with your guidance counselor to make sure you have submitted all the necessary documents and that your applications are submitted on time and are complete.

---

* Start early and chunk. The earlier an application is submitted, the better. Acceptance rates for LD programs and the university at large are affected by when the application is submitted. Break down the process into smaller tasks and take it one step at a time, to keep things from becoming overwhelming.

Application options galore

In years past there was only one kind of college application—the paper kind you received in the mail and returned the same way. Not any more. In hopes of making things easier for both colleges and applicants, schools have begun to use several different types of applications in recent years. There is still the hardcopy paper version that can be obtained from the college through the mail. But there is also the online application, the Common Application, and the Universal College Application.

The Common Application can be accessed online[1] and is accepted by over 400 colleges. The Common Application requires that applicants submit at least one essay and one teacher evaluation. Private liberal arts colleges make up the majority of Common Application schools and most of them have such requirements already, but many public institutions do not. If a student fills out the Common Application once, they will likely be able to submit it to more than one college—hence making the life of the applicant easier. However, many universities also require a supplemental application that asks a student to respond to a brief essay question that is unique to that particular school. The list of colleges that require the supplemental application can be found on the Common Application website.

There are over 80 schools that accept the Universal College Application, a clearing-house application, similar to the Common Application.[2] The goal of the Universal College Application is to attract a great variety of colleges and a diverse pool of applicants. The organization that produces the application requires only that member colleges be accredited and that they abide by the *Statement of Principles of Good Practice* of the National Association for College Admission Counseling, which focuses on ethical principles.[3]

The final application dilemma is deciding whether to apply online or to print the application, fill it out, and send it via mail the old-fashioned way. In our experience, colleges prefer that students submit their applications online. There is often a statement on their website to this effect. However, through conversations with admissions representatives, we've found that if a student decides to mail in the application rather than submit it online, it does not reflect negatively on his application.

In working with students with disabilities, we haven't found one type of application or one particular way of submitting applications that works best across the board for everyone. But we have developed some important strategies that may be helpful for students with a particular disability. For a student whose disability impacts their organizational skills, filling out applications is a tremendous challenge. Having a folder for each college to which the student is applying is helpful for all students, but crucial to those with organizational deficits. A student who is a strong visual learner will find it advantageous to have hard copies of all applications and to lay them out on the largest table or desk he can find. Students diagnosed with dysgraphia are better served by applying online rather than handwriting the application. The opposite is true for a student who is impulsive; there is a real danger of this student pressing "submit" before he fully completes his online version of the application.

Let's look at Joey, who is a student diagnosed with attention deficit hyperactivity disorder (ADHD). Beginning in the spring of his junior year in high school, the dining room at his family's house had become the dumping ground for all his college application material. Every piece of mail he'd received from prospective colleges, brochure materials he had picked up from college fairs, and hard copies of his standardized testing scores were all stored on the dining-room table. Having poor executive function skills, Joey was prone to losing important items. He knew that the dining-room table was his safe place to keep important college information and, fortunately, his family decided that having him manage his applications outweighed the importance of having the dining-room table available for actual dining. The summer before senior year, when it was time to write his college essay, the dining-room table was where he sat down with his laptop. Come fall of senior year, when he began to fill out college applications, he brought his laptop to the dining-room table once more. Although this very casual method of dealing with important papers is nothing we would recommend, at least Joey found a way to keep all his documents together and to avoid losing anything he needed for his applications.

But that wasn't enough to keep Joey out of trouble completely. Without careful forethought, a common state of affairs for students with ADHD, he went to the webpage of his first choice school, accessed the online application, completed it, and with a click of a button submitted it. Moments later he realized that he had attached the wrong version of his college essay and submitted it to the college. He immediately panicked. After lengthy conversation with his parents and guidance counselor, his counselor contacted the college explaining the situation. The college agreed to allow Joey to resubmit his essay. With his parents' assistance, Joey resubmitted his essay online, this time the correct one. In addition, he mailed a hard copy of the correct essay to the college's Admissions Office, along with an explanatory letter indicating his previous mistake. He was lucky the college had allowed him to resubmit, but his mistake may not reflect positively on him in the eyes of the school.

* Tricks of the trade—There are many different types of applications. Focus on making decisions regarding what type of application works best for you—hard copy, online, the college's own, the Common Application, or the Universal College Application. Students should be aware of their specific disabilities and personal style, and employ strategies that will assist them in completing their applications.

* Use paper management strategies. Even students who are using online application forms should have a file folder for each school to which they are applying and for other relevant documents, such as standardized test scores, disability documentation, records of which teachers will be sending recommendations, and college responses. Too many of the students we see are more like Joey, and they end up losing papers and sometimes missing important deadlines.

Varying application deadlines

In recent years colleges have developed a number of deadlines other than "Regular Decision" including Early Decision (ED), Early Action (EA), Early Action Single Choice (EASC), and Rolling Admissions. What do these terms mean? Not all colleges have all types of deadlines, but many have more than one. You must be sure what you are getting into before you sign on the dotted line, since one type of decision deadline actually creates a binding agreement requiring you to attend that college if they accept you.

Rolling Admissions is a system that has been around for quite a while. The college has no specific deadline to which the student must adhere. The college begins accepting applications in late summer or early fall and continues to do so until they have filled all the spots for their freshman class. As the admissions staff receives applications, they review them and send the student an admissions decision within a few weeks.

A student who has a solid idea of which colleges will be a good fit for him may consider applying Early Action (EA), which sets an early deadline but will also result in an early admissions decision. This is a type of non-binding application. When a student applies EA, he is showing the admissions staff that he has a very serious interest in the school. It has been our experience that EA gives students a slightly better chance of being admitted to schools because there are fewer applications, therefore less competition, at this early point in the process. Colleges are trying to predict their yield—the percentage of students they accept who actually enroll—so if they accept a certain number of students before the bulk of high school seniors apply, they are that much closer to guaranteeing a full class. Schools that don't accurately predict their yield will have fewer students than they want or may have more students than they can fit in their dorms.

Submission of an application Early Decision (ED) is a binding agreement between the student and the college. The student actually signs a contract with the college agreeing to enroll if he is accepted. The only possible exception to this rule, which may permit a student to be released from this binding agreement in some cases, is if the college cannot give the student the financial aid needed to afford the tuition payment for that college. Since this exception to the binding nature of ED applications varies by school and is not well publicized, students who require a specific level or kind of financial aid may want to avoid applying ED. A student who applies ED to a particular college can apply to other colleges under their EA or [AQ]Regular Decision programs, but he can't apply ED to other colleges. A recent list of over 100 colleges showed that their acceptance rates for students who applied ED ranged from 16 percent to 100 percent.[4] ED is taken very seriously and there have been serious repercussions for students who try to back out of this binding agreement. There are documented cases of students who have had offers rescinded from other colleges when they find out that the student did not honor their ED agreement to a particular college. Like EA, ED benefits a student because it demonstrates to the college that it is the student's first choice. This student's application is looked upon much more favorably because the admissions staff is trying to build a class and trying to predict a yield. The downside is that colleges may offer a less generous aid package to an ED applicant whose agreement does not provide an escape clause for inadequate financial aid. Knowing that an ED student is already committed to going there once accepted, a college may not be motivated to offer a particularly generous aid package.

Early Action Single Choice (EASC) is a much less common practice and is usually seen at the more competitive colleges. Colleges that have EASC do not allow applicants to apply to more than one school EA.

Finally, there is Regular Decision. This straightforward deadline is the original deadline of days gone by before colleges got creative and developed the admissions policies we have just discussed. In addition to a deadline for applications, many schools advise all of their Regular Decision applicants regarding acceptance or rejection on the same date, usually mid-April.

For a student with a learning disability, the choices for application deadlines may be somewhat limited because of practical considerations. Andrew is a high school senior who wanted to apply ED to his first choice school. He also planned to apply to this university's LD program and would be submitting an additional application specifically for this support. As he moved forward in the application process, he learned that because he was applying to the LD program, the college would not allow him also to apply ED. He decided that he would need to proceed by applying to the college's LD program without applying ED. He and his family felt that his chance for succeeding at the college would be significantly diminished if he applied ED and was accepted but did not have the support of the LD program. Andrew applied Regular Decision and also applied to the LD program. He ended up being wait-listed by the university. Before hearing back from the university definitely as to whether he would be eventually accepted or denied admission, he decided to accept admission at another college and submit his enrollment deposit. The college where he ultimately enrolled did admit him to their LD program.

---

* Multiple deadline choices—Understand the distinctions between the terms Early Decision, Early Action, Early Action Single Choice, Rolling Admissions, and Regular Decision. Only apply ED if you will absolutely, without a doubt, attend that college if accepted, since ED is a binding agreement.

To disclose or not to disclose?

Over the years, we've heard the same question over and over again at the dozens of workshops where we have presented on the topic of college applications: Should a student disclose his disability in a college application? Like Hamlet, for students with disabilities, that really is the question.

We have discussed this issue with admissions representatives from colleges throughout the country, and the wisdom gleaned from these conversations by and large points to the fact that it is okay—and usually more than okay—to disclose a disability on a college application. The rule of thumb that has emerged is that if disclosing the disability adds something positive to the application or explains a gap in the student's academic profile, then he should go ahead and disclose. Admissions representatives want to get to know a student through his application. If disclosing a disability that impacts a student's high school experience, and particularly his academic performance, helps the admissions counselor get to know the student better and predict his potential for success at the college level, then sharing this information is suggested. This goes for other pertinent pieces of information as well: For example, the death of a family member or a parental divorce that has severely impacted a student. Admissions representatives are looking for reasons to admit students more than they are looking for reasons to reject a student's application. When an admissions counselor sits around a table with the other members of his department and presents a student for admission to the committee at large, his role is to advocate for admission by carefully weighing any additional significant factors.

Let's take a look at John, who was not diagnosed with a visual disability until halfway through his junior year of high school. Once he was diagnosed and began receiving accommodations in school, his grades improved significantly. His grades for freshman and sophomore years, as well as for the first half of junior year, were much lower than his grades for the rest of his high school career. Rather than leaving admissions counselors to believe he was just lazy in his freshman and sophomore year, he took this opportunity to explain his visual disability and how and when it was discovered during a long overdue eye examination. This is an example of when disclosing a disability is clearly appropriate.

In a similar situation, Jennifer, who is a junior in high school, has been diagnosed with a neurological condition called dystonia.

Dystonia causes Jennifer to have tremors in her hands and to suffer from severe pain. This directly impacts her ability to write and her level of concentration. Over her high school career her condition has continued to worsen and now rises to the level of a disability. As we discuss in Chapter 3, an illness is not necessarily a disability unless it substantially limits major life activities, which for Jennifer would be writing and learning. In her freshman and sophomore years of high school Jennifer had a 504 plan to provide her with accommodations. By her junior year, as a result of her worsening condition, Jennifer needed special education services and her school district classified her as "other health impaired" under the Individuals with Disabilities Education Act (IDEA). She was given an Individual Education Program (IEP) to address her educational needs. Her grades throughout her first two years in high school were consistently in the 90s. During the summer going into her junior year she began taking a new medication in hopes of arresting the progression of the dystonia and managing her pain.

Unfortunately, this medication has medically documented side effects which include an impact on cognitive ability. Jennifer's grades have gone from 90s to 80s. In such a case, disclosing a disability on a college application is appropriate and encouraged. Jennifer can disclose through her college essay, or by writing a letter explaining to the admissions counselors, what factors are contributing to the downward trend in her grades. It is also appropriate to include detailed documentation from doctors explaining her medical condition and how the medication is impacting her ability to learn. Although Jennifer chose not to focus her college essay on her significant health challenges, she did indeed write a letter to college admissions representatives at the schools where she applied, explaining her disability and the factors that had contributed to the drop in her grades. When Jennifer interviewed at two of the colleges to which she applied, she was told by her interviewers that they were impressed with her disclosure and the maturity and initiative with which she approached it. She was ultimately accepted to six out of the seven schools to which she submitted applications. She enrolled at a competitive college and is faring well with accommodations. Some semesters have been more challenging for her than others, but most of the time she is holding her head above water. The one characteristic in her favor is that she is not afraid to ask for help from the Office of Disability Services when she needs it, or directly from her professors when she needs clarification. The symptoms of her dystonia have essentially stayed the same; it hasn't become more severe, but hasn't improved. Her college is located an hour's plane ride from home, which has been helpful because of the frequency with which she has had to fly home for doctors' appointments.

Some college representatives will not take a disclosed disability into account one way or another. These Admissions Officers essentially disregard the disclosure, out of fear of legal action. Colleges know that it is illegal under the Americans with Disabilities Act (ADA) and Section 504 to deny admission to an applicant based on a disability. If a college denies a student admission based on the fact that he doesn't meet the admissions standards—academic grades and standardized test scores—the institution does not want to risk being sued, so they take disability out of the equation completely.

Students should be aware that although the ADA and Section 504 prohibit a college or other post-secondary program from denying admission based on a disability, they are not prohibited from giving extra consideration to a student with a disability, just as they may accept a gifted musician or athlete who would not ordinarily be accepted based just upon his grades and test scores. They don't have quotas as to the number of students with disabilities they must admit, but they do have flexibility. Additionally, there are a number of colleges that welcome student diversity and believe that accepting students with disabilities enriches the student body of their school.

In certain cases it may not be appropriate to disclose a disability. Again, the best way to determine whether or not to disclose a particular disability is by weighing whether disclosing adds something positive to the application or would assist an admissions counselor in obtaining a fuller picture of the student. For example, writing about your peanut allergy, may not be the best use of space in your application.

The tragedy at Virginia Tech in 2007 has impacted college staff, programming, curriculum, and training in various ways. In the aftermath of that shooting, in which a student with a documented mental illness killed 32 people and wounded many others in the deadliest campus violence in history, university staff members, including admissions representatives, have become more aware of students who may pose a serious risk to the safety of others or themselves. If red flags are raised on the college application, by disclosing an unmanaged mental health condition, most colleges have a system in place to evaluate applications with risk to self or others in mind. Students should be mindful that certain information may hint at a problem, even if the student decides not to disclose the mental health condition. For example, missed semesters or extended absences could indicate that a student has been hospitalized or in some sort of rehabilitation facility. Students whose attendance at high school was interrupted should be able to offer an explanation of this interruption to the admissions representatives.

The International Association of Campus Law Enforcement Administrators' 2008 report entitled "Overview of the Virginia Tech Tragedy and Implications of Campus Safety" recommends that institutions implement a process whereby all applicants are asked whether or not they have been convicted or charged with a crime and that colleges should conduct criminal record checks for their students as appropriate.[5] A 2008 report from the Midwestern Higher Education Compact entitled "The Ripple Effect of Virginia Tech: Assessing the Nationwide Impact on Campus Safety and Security Policy and Practice" found that only a small percentage of colleges made changes to their admissions procedures. Most changes are related to background checks, asking applicants to disclose convictions of crimes involving violent behavior, and asking applicants if they are currently taking medication to treat a psychiatric or psychological condition,[6] even though questions relating to medication or medical conditions are barred by the ADA.

If families are hesitant to disclose a student's psychological difficulties for fear of having that student denied admission because he may be deemed a danger to himself or others, they must recognize the reality that even when schools have some information about a student's psychological state, the college is usually in no position to supervise the student. Full disclosure is often most helpful to the student and the university community. The university counseling center, Office of Disability Services, and residence life staff (if the student is residing on campus) can help support the student. As we note in Chapter 10, parents, the young adult, and the prescribing psychiatrists need to have serious discussions about the need to monitor the student for depression and other psychiatric conditions that can worsen under stress or in the event of medication avoidance and can have life-threatening consequences.

As we have seen, the practice of flagging SAT or ACT exams taken with accommodations was deemed to be discriminatory as the result of a lawsuit brought in 1999. Flags (actually, asterisks with explanatory footnotes) have been removed from all score reports since October of 2003. Even though flagging is no longer allowed, many admissions officers attest to the fact that they can usually tell if the application they are reviewing is that of a student who receives special education services. The student's academic transcript may show that he is enrolled in resource room, or the transcript lacks any evidence that he has taken a foreign language in high school. Even though a student may decide not to disclose a disability formally on his application, the presence of a disability may be assumed by an admissions counselor for other reasons. Given this reality, it is better for a student to disclose his disability and explain it than for an admissions counselor to piece together a situation that may not be completely accurate. We are told over and over again by admissions representatives that it is a plus if a student writes and explains to them in his own words the challenges of his disability. This illustrates maturity and motivation on the applicant's part.

---

* Disclosure decisions—It is okay to disclose a disability on a college application if it adds something positive to the application or explains a gap in the student's academic profile. Colleges know that it is illegal under the ADA to deny admission to an applicant based on a disability. Interestingly, it is important to know that although colleges can't deny admission to an applicant based on a disability, they can accept the student because of a disability. If disclosing a disability does not add something positive to the application or would not assist an admissions counselor in obtaining a fuller picture of the student, then it may not be appropriate to disclose.

Fee-based support programs

A select number of colleges offer a separate program of support to students with particular disabilities. Most of these programs are geared towards students with learning disabilities and ADHD. To qualify for participation in these separate support programs, the student's learning disabilities usually must be language based, which includes disorders of reading or writing. These separate programs of support are offered at an extra cost in addition to tuition and generally average about $1500 per semester and up. There are a few colleges that offer a fee-based program to students with high-functioning autism or Asperger's syndrome. Separate programs of support may be able to offer students one-on-one time with a learning specialist to assist with course content and organizational, studying, and note-taking skills. Although this is the highest level of support offered in college, it is important to note that it does not come close to the level of support offered by a high school resource room or a private school specifically for students with disabilities.

Many of the colleges that offer a fee-based program require applicants to fill out an additional application, separate from the general admissions application. Calling the Office of Disability Services or looking at a college's website for the LD program's webpage may help to answer the question of whether an additional application is required. Sometimes you are even able to download the application from the website. Fee-based support programs are often competitive; 25 spots for 75 applications is not unusual. It is important to send in this application early—again using Thanksgiving as the deadline—to ensure a better chance of being accepted. These applications usually ask the student to respond in writing to three to four short questions regarding his disability. The application may also require a recommendation from a special education teacher. Recent psychoeducational testing is required and will need to meet the standards discussed in Chapter 4 on documentation.

In addition to a separate application and disability documentation, an interview may be required to be considered for the program; this varies by college. Some colleges screen applications first and then only invite viable candidates for an interview. Support program personnel are looking for students to be aware of what their disability is and how it impacts their learning. Students should be able to articulate how they learn best and what accommodations are essential for them. Students who are good candidates for such a program are self-motivated and interested in improving their self-advocacy skills. They should be more than agreeable to being part of this program and willing to commit to it freely, rather than be pushed to apply by their parents or counselors.

---

* Key aspects of LD programs—Although fee-based support programs are the highest level of support at college, they do not come close to the level of support offered by a high school resource room or a private school specifically for students with

disabilities. Fee-based support programs are often competitive and usually require applicants to fill out an additional application. An interview may be required to be considered for these programs.

The resume

Throughout the college application process, a resume may also be referred to as an activity sheet. We recommend students create a succinct record of the activities they've been involved in during high school and the honors they've received. If you submit a paper version of a college's application, then include a copy of your resume, along with your application, in the envelope you mail out. If you are submitting an online application, we suggest giving your guidance counselor a copy of your resume and asking him to mail it along with your transcript and his recommendation.

The resume is a great tool to bring to an admissions interview and share with your interviewer. It shows you are motivated and excited about the prospect of attending college. Colleges like to see that students are engaged outside the classroom. They want to see that you have leadership skills. So, rather than join every club your high school has to offer, focus on sustained involvement and a commitment to a particular club or two. By the time you are a junior or a senior, you could hold a leadership position within this club, sport, or part-time job. Colleges want evidence of what makes you tick and to understand your passion. Why do they want to see this? Because they want to accept students who can make their college a better place. Admissions Officers are reading your resume and your entire application, evaluating your leadership potential, unique gifts and talents, and envisioning how you may apply these to their campus in order to enrich the educational community of their institution.

For students with disabilities who may struggle in the classroom, the resume is the perfect place to highlight their accomplishments outside the academic realm. Sam was diagnosed with a learning disability at the age of nine. His strengths were mainly in verbal expression, whereas he struggled with reading and writing. Although he liked school, it had always been tough for him academically. He achieved average grades even though he put much more effort into his work than most of his peers. He didn't shine in the classroom, but outside the classroom he had quite an accomplished reputation among doctors traveling to Africa. Sam had been to Africa more times than he could remember. Since the age of four, he and his family had been making regular trips there to work with a nonprofit organization his father had created. Sam spent most school vacations and summers in Africa interacting with children who were sick and assisting the doctors that came to lend their expertise. Sam would help provide any supplies the doctors needed for their patients or daily living necessities they needed for themselves. As time passed and Sam entered his teenage years, not only would he assist during his trips but he would help out even when he wasn't in Africa. In the United States he was actively working for the nonprofit and he raised money for the organization by assisting his father in writing grants. He was also solely in charge of arranging all the travel plans for the visiting doctors who came from all over the world to volunteer for the nonprofit organization. Sam was known as the one to contact at all hours of the day or night if your flight was canceled at the last minute and you needed assistance getting from point A to point B. In looking at his resume, Admissions Officers couldn't help but notice Sam's commitment and his work in Africa. They were so impressed that this topic came up regularly throughout his college interviews. Clearly, his commitment to this activity said something very positive about Sam and his leadership ability, not to mention his first-hand knowledge of the world and peoples different from himself. Many colleges found Sam to be a very attractive candidate for admission.

---

* Highlight your interests, talents, and accomplishments. A resume or activity sheet is a wonderful tool to share with colleges, especially for a student who struggles academically. Not only does it indicate an applicant's motivation and pride but it assists students in showcasing multiple aspects of who they are and their potential for success in college.

Additional parts of the application process

As part of the application packet, standardized testing scores will need to be submitted to those colleges that require them. Applying to at least some colleges that do not require these scores is usually a good idea for a student whose disability has impacted his performance on standardized tests. As we discuss at length in Chapter 5, there are hundreds of colleges that don't require either the SAT or ACT tests for admission. Some colleges that don't require these standardized tests will have some other requirement that will factor into their admissions decision. For example, some will require one or two graded papers of a substantial length. Others may require an on-campus interview with a member of the admissions committee who will want to become familiar with the applicant and discuss his high school curriculum.

As we will see, Admissions Officers look favorably upon students who have shown great interest in their school throughout the application process. Applicants can earn extra points through admissions practices that reward a prospective student for visiting campus and making contact with a particular college. Each additional contact—a call to the Admissions Office with a question, a second campus visit to stay overnight in the dorm, a letter to admissions to let them know about some new and substantial achievement—will add to the points total. Again, for a student whose disability has impacted his high school performance in a less than stellar way, making a consistent effort to illustrate how interested he is in a particular college can be to his advantage.

Some college applications may ask the student to check a box indicating if he has a disability. It is illegal to require students to check the box and disclose a disability, but if a student chooses to do so, they may. The reasons an institution may ask this question vary, but it is likely for planning and logistical purposes. If the college requires that admitted students take subject placement tests, then staff may be able to predict how many students with disabilities may take the test and possibly need accommodations. Colleges that offer a fee-based support program may make an admissions decision in cooperation with staff from the LD program. A checked box allows the admissions staff to share the application with the LD staff.

Applicants must provide their contact information to the college. There is proper etiquette for sharing this information. The proliferation of web-based communications such as Facebook has made the risks of cyber mischief very real. Not only will many colleges deduct application points for inappropriate student email addresses or cell phone voicemail greetings, but they have rescinded admissions acceptances to students who have been caught engaging in inappropriate or illegal behavior, in word or deed, on their cyberspace page. We have received emails from students whose email addresses include "huggable," "hotstuff," and "studly;" we can only imagine the impact these highly undignified choices must have on a college Admissions Officer.

---

* Wrapping up loose ends—If a college does not require an applicant to submit ACT/SAT scores, then you must find out what may be required in lieu of standardized testing scores. Students can earn points by showing initiative and visiting campus and making contact with the college through phone or email. Points refer to how admissions representatives evaluate an application in terms of favorability and admissibility. Applications may ask a student to check a box if he has a disability. Legally, you are not required to check this box, but it may be to your advantage if you are applying to a fee-based program of support. Students need to be hyperaware of the risks of cyberspace. They should be sure their Facebook page, voicemail greetings, and email addresses are professional and appropriate.

How a college's Admissions Committee assesses an application

College admissions representatives place the most weight in the decision process on a student's academic transcript. They want to see evidence of a student taking a rigorous curriculum throughout his high school career. They want to know that a student is challenging himself. Advanced Placement (AP), honors classes, and the International Baccalaureate (IB) curriculum are pluses. Grade point average and SAT or ACT scores are critical factors, along with an upward trend in grades. Colleges want to see a certain number of years of core subject areas such as English, social studies, math, science, and foreign language.

A student who is exempt from a foreign language in high school because of a disability needs to make an admissions counselor aware of this fact. Otherwise, a student's chance of admission may be diminished if a college requires applicants to have a certain number of years of foreign language in high school in order to be considered for admissions. In such a case, it is looked upon most favorably by a college if the student writes a letter disclosing the language exemption. We then advise the student to give a release of information to his guidance counselor allowing the counselor to include the exemption in his recommendation letter, thereby supporting the student's written statement.

The type of diploma a student receives is also important. Some states have only one kind of diploma; others have diplomas that reflect high scores on state-wide exams or other evidence of proficiency. Colleges want to see that a public high school student is on track to receive the highest academic diploma offered by his state. A local high school diploma, usually indicating that the student has met district criteria, but not necessarily completed all state-wide exams, is generally acceptable, especially since many private schools with excellent reputations offer this kind of diploma so as not to be constricted by state curriculum.

It is critical to note that a student who does not receive a regular high school diploma will not be accepted at many colleges. Some community colleges across the country do not require a high school diploma to matriculate, but they are the exception. Some public and private colleges offer non-degree courses, or certificates of completion, to individuals without a regular high school diploma.

A 2007 report from the National Association for College Admission Counseling (NACAC) looked at what the responding colleges considered important admissions factors. Eighty percent mentioned AP/honors grades; 65 percent the difficulty of high school coursework; 60 percent admissions test SAT/ACT; 50 percent all grades; 25 percent college essay; 23 percent class rank; 22 percent interest in college; 20 percent teacher recommendations; 11 percent interview; and 8 percent extracurricular activities. Although much has been written and discussed in recent years about how colleges have begun to place less emphasis on standardized testing as a reliable means of predicting college success, this report concluded reliance upon these tests has actually grown in the past decade.[7]

---

* The impact of high school academics on college—The courses that high school students choose to take during their secondary education greatly impact how favorably colleges view them. Students should take courses that challenge them academically, as long as their disability permits. A student who is exempt from a foreign language, and who is applying to a college that requires a certain number of years of a foreign language be taken in high school, should disclose this exemption in his application so that he is not inadvertently viewed less favorably by an admissions committee.

So you've made it to the waiting list

One of the most unsettling parts of the admissions process is being "wait-listed" for a school you really want to attend. It's good to know they haven't rejected you, but it raises many questions about what to do—and not to do. First of all, keep a positive attitude. Schools don't place students on their waiting list just to torture them. They'll only extend waiting-list status to students they'd like to accept but who they are not sure they will have room for. Although there may be some flexibility in the number of students a college can accommodate in its classes, there is rarely any room for additional students in dorms. The college needs to see how many of the students it has accepted actually enroll, to see if its yield is what it expected based on past experience.

So, what can you do if you are placed on a waiting list? Definitely send back the postcard that came with your wait-list letter, advising that you do want to be retained on the waiting list. Then, contact the Admissions Office by regular mail, letting them know that you were disappointed not to be admitted and indicating that their college was, and remains, your first choice. Make it clear that, if accepted, you plan to enroll in their school. Let them know about awards, achievements, and activities that took place after your application was submitted.

Many high schools have awards ceremonies in the spring that would not make it into an application submitted in November. A follow-up letter a few weeks later, including more updated information and reminding the Admissions Office of your interest, is also a good idea. You want to remain on their radar, but not be an annoyance.[8] Meanwhile, you should keep track of deposit deadlines for the colleges that admit you to make sure that you are assured of a place even if you are ultimately rejected from the school that placed you on the waiting list.

---

* The waiting game—If wait-listed, don't just wait, but rather take the initiative to show your interest and commitment to the college.

Chapter 8

The Campus Visit

"This is it! I can really see myself spending the next four years here!" There is certainly much work on the student's part to get to this point, but such a declaration is often music to a parent's ear. Every parent wants to know their child is in a good place. Each of us can vividly remember the first time we stepped foot on the campus of the college we would eventually attend. It was an "Aha!" moment for sure. We had so many hopes and dreams as we were about to embark on a journey full of unknowns. We knew we would be okay, though, because we fit that college and it fit us. This realization is the goal of a campus visit.

Maybe the plan is to spend two years at a school, if you are planning to work towards an associate's degree. Maybe you only expect to spend one year at community college, get your grades up, and then transfer to a more competitive school. That's okay. The goal is to find the right match for each individual student. But this match business is really quite tricky; it requires a 17-year-old to be aware of her needs, talents, and interests, and then to choose a college based on the fit between her goals (which may be changing from week to week), what the college has to offer, and what it may be lacking. It is great when students know themselves well enough to be involved in this process and not get overwhelmed. It's even better if they have goals and can articulate them. But since this is often not the case, we're going to help guide you through this process. Now that we've shown you the goal of the campus visit and, we hope, have gotten you psyched for it, let's get started on the steps you'll need to get there.

The importance of the visit

Pretend, for a moment, that you are a member of an elite special forces unit. You have been in training for years and now it is time to put your skills to use. You are charged with leading your unit in reconnaissance work to gather information for your mission. And what is your mission? To find the right college match. You must go on-site to investigate how this college will meet your needs; to identify what you like about the college and what you don't like. Better yet, you are going to meet with the locals (the current students) to find out what they think of this school. It's your responsibility to take all the facts you've gathered, along with your gut feeling, and report back to your supervisors (in this case your parents, your guidance counselor, and other adults you trust). Then they will help to debrief you from your mission and you will work together as a team to figure out the most important things to take away from your visit.

Lucky for you, your reconnaissance work does not go unnoticed. You are actually rewarded for your initiative by most colleges. Admissions applications often ask students to check a box to indicate if they have visited the college. You should also make sure that you sign in with the Admissions Office and anywhere else on campus you visit. Unlike military reconnaissance, you want everyone to know you have been there. When a college knows that you've visited, they recognize your interest, and this can weigh in your favor in your application and may even offer you certain perks. One kind of perk is a fast-track application which some colleges send to their priority applicants. Often this fast-track application is free, as opposed to the online or snailmail versions which require application fees ranging from around $50 and up. Fast-track applications may also offer a quicker turnaround time when it comes to an admissions decision.

The campus visit is a key part of your college selection process. Make sure you prepare for it ahead of time. "What?" you're thinking to yourself. "I thought I just had to show up! Now what?" A little preparation goes a long way. Take a look at the college's website. Read about the school's mission and what is currently happening on campus. In addition to learning the basics about the number of students who attend, the locations, and the courses offered, take note of any special academic programs (for example, a five-year combined bachelor's and master's degree in social work, or the opportunity to create your own major). Prepare two or three questions that you may want to ask your campus tour guide or an Admissions Officer.

---

* Your mission is to find the right college match.
* You may get extra "points" on your admissions application if you've visited that college. Colleges want to know that students have enough interest in their school to take the time and trouble to visit.
* Prepare ahead of time for your campus visit. A little preparation goes a long way.

We're off to see the Wizard! The campus tour

If you are planning to visit a college, we strongly suggest calling ahead to schedule a campus tour rather than just showing up and hoping there is room for you. Tour schedules vary by college; some offer tours every day of the week including the weekend, others do not. Most tours are led by student volunteers who have been trained by the Admissions Office. Many colleges also offer an information session before the tour which is usually led by an Admissions Officer.

If the idea of a campus tour seems overwhelming or too far off in the future—for students who are sophomores in high school, for example—then we suggest taking a driving tour through a local college or university. This type of experience "gets your feet wet" and will perhaps excite you enough to schedule a college-led tour for next time. Speaking of getting your feet wet, the next time you are about to go on vacation, do a little research before your trip and find out which colleges may be near your vacation destination. Take an hour or so out of your relaxation time and visit a local college. The more opportunities you have to visit a variety of campuses, the easier it will be to figure out what type of campus and college fits you best. This being said, as you visit numerous campuses, they have a tendency to all blend together in your mind. We have found success by keeping a written log of each college visit. Much of our time is spent visiting colleges across the country so we have created our own college visit form. You can find a copy of this form in the Resources chapter.

So what kinds of things would you want to jot down or remember about your tour? Is it an aesthetically pleasing campus? Do the students look happy and engaged by what the school has to offer? If, for example, you are interested in majoring in communications, does the university have an entire building dedicated to it? Maybe this communications building hosts a state-of-the-art broadcasting studio. Or is your intended area of study just one of many majors housed in a nondescript building on campus?

We have a word or two of caution from our own tours of numerous campuses. Try to avoid basing your impression of the college on your student tour guide. The quality of student tour guides varies greatly, although they all seem to have an uncanny ability to walk backwards in rubber flipflops, even on days when everyone else is wearing hats and gloves. Some are terrific and will inspire you to put their campus at the top of your list. Others will be so annoying or provide so little information that you begin to think that you hate the school you are seeing and would never want to go there. You need to keep in mind that your guide is simply one student on one particular day—possibly early in the morning after a long evening. Don't let your reaction to the job she does have a serious impact on your reaction to the campus. You should also keep in mind that, just like people, campuses look better at some times than at others. We can't help but recall the story of Dave who visited a campus in upstate New York with his father. It was late April, and they were looking forward to seeing an attractive campus, with budding trees and the green grass of early spring. Instead, as it sometimes does in that latitude, it snowed—a lot. They were wet and cold as they slipped around campus. Fortunately, they were able to look beyond the ice, the mud, and the cold, and were able to consider the other factors that would make the school a good fit for Dave. He ended up enrolling and had an enjoyable and successful four years there. And although the winters were certainly cold, he never again encountered a late April snowstorm.

* Call ahead to schedule a campus tour. Don't just show up. There may not be room for you on a tour, or there may not be a tour scheduled on the day you arrive on campus.

* Get your feet wet. Do a drive-through of local colleges and plan to visit a nearby college for a tour while you are away on vacation.

* Campuses begin to blend in your memory after you have visited several schools. Keep a log and write down your impressions of the college while visiting or when you get in the car to go home.

* The campus tour guide and the weather shouldn't be determinative. Don't base everything about the college on these two factors on the particular day you visit.

Two key questions to ask while visiting

The campus tour and information session may be the perfect time to ask a question or two of a college Admissions Officer. There are two topics that most students with disabilities need to know about: what is the college's foreign language requirement—for admission and for graduation—and what is their disclosure policy for a student who may share disability information in her application?

Let's first talk about how many years of foreign language study the college requires for admission. This is an important and appropriate question to ask a college Admissions Officer. It is also important and appropriate to ask whether a student who has been exempt from a foreign language requirement in high school due to a disability should note this on her application. Many students with disabilities, usually language-based learning disabilities or hearing impairments, are exempt from studying a foreign language in high school. Colleges will generally not hold it against a student who does not meet their admission requirements for a foreign language if this is due to a disability. Admissions Offices often suggest a student submit an extra paragraph explaining the basis for her foreign language exemption in high school.

The other question that you need to ask the Admissions Officer is how many semesters of a foreign language does a student need to take in order to graduate from that college? This is where a language waiver becomes a two-edged sword: It does no good to be admitted to a college if you can't meet the graduation requirements. Some colleges will require that every student, or every student in a particular major, take a predetermined number of semesters of foreign language courses even if she was exempt in high school. Remember, accommodations from high school do not automatically carry over to college. If a college determines that a foreign language makes up an essential component of their degree program, then the college does not have to alter this requirement for a student with a disability. To do so would be going beyond providing the equal access required by the ADA or Section 504, and would be modifying the curriculum, which the college is not required to do. Colleges that have determined that a foreign language does not make up an essential component of their degree may have more flexibility. We know of very few schools that allow an exemption, but permitting a student to substitute another course, perhaps on the history or culture of a particular foreign country, is not uncommon. The process of requesting a foreign language substitution varies by college. Some colleges have a committee that reviews a student's disability documentation and makes the determination as to whether the substitution is warranted. Other colleges have students submit the request to the Office of Disability Services and the Director of Disability Services makes the decision on her own. Complicating matters is the fact that in most instances, as is the case with almost all accommodations, a student who is exempt from taking a foreign language in high school will not know if she will be given a foreign language substitution in college until after the point where she has to pay a nonrefundable deposit to a college and declare her intention to enroll.

Let's look at the case of Jimmy, who was in the process of transferring colleges. Jimmy was thrilled to be accepted as a transfer student to his first choice school. The only thing holding him back from finalizing his enrollment was that it was still unclear to him whether he would be required to take a foreign language in order to obtain a bachelor's degree from this college. With the deadline to submit his deposit a few days away, he spoke with the Office of Disability Services about his concern.

The Director apologized that she could not give him a definitive answer as to the possibility of a substitution, because his documentation had to be reviewed by a committee, which made the final determination on this issue. This would only happen once he enrolled at the college. Jimmy didn't know what to do. He really could not take and pass three semesters of a foreign language in high school, let alone manage the fast pace and intensity of the three required college-level courses. The Director of Disability Services was honest with Jimmy and explained that, in her experience, other students with learning disabilities had been denied a foreign language waiver and really struggled because of this. She suggested to Jimmy that her college may not be his best choice. Of course, Jimmy had to decide for himself, but she asked him to consider why he would enroll at a school where there may already be a stumbling block set up for him. Ultimately, Jimmy decided to go to another college where he did not have to take a foreign language in order to graduate.

We believe the foreign language question to be essential for students with a learning disability or hearing impairment. The last thing we want is for a student who has been exempt from a foreign language in high school to matriculate at a college that requires two, three, or even four semesters of a foreign language in order to graduate. One semester, okay, you may be able to struggle through it with accommodations and tutors, but four semesters seems like an unnecessary hurdle. Once you decide to make the foreign language question part of your college match process, then the doors of some colleges may close. It is important to remember that there are more than 3000 colleges out there, so the right match will come along.

Having tackled the foreign language issue, let's move to the question of whether a college wants students to disclose their disability at the time of application. You may think this is a strange question; after all, we recommend contacting the Office of Disability Services. Why would we even ask if a student should mention her disability? Believe it or not, there are some colleges that don't want to know if a student has a disability until after they make their admissions decision. These schools claim that they don't factor in disability and, in fact, would rather ignore any consideration of a student's disability because they are concerned about liability. They don't want to have any accusations of disability discrimination raised if they are denying a student admission based on factors such as poor grades or low standardized testing scores.

Fortunately, much more often, college Admissions Officers tell us that disclosing a disability is a fine thing for an application; it helps them learn more about the student and oftentimes puts her grades in context. You can find more information about disclosing in an application in Chapter 7.

You don't necessarily need to ask about foreign language requirements and disclosure policies in a public forum—either on the tour or in the information session. If you are concerned about anonymity, by all means feel free to ask these questions privately. You can do this in person or via email. You can even call the Admissions Officer and speak with her without revealing your name. This will not be a problem and it is not uncommon. Rest assured, most Admissions Officers are professionals, and it is increasingly common for them to see applications from students with disabilities and for them to admit such students to their college. In addition, if you speak with them in person, it would be rare for the Admissions Officer to remember who you are once it comes time to read your application, since they meet hundreds of prospective students each year.

---

* Coming in and going out, what is the college's foreign language requirement? Do not leave the campus without getting an answer from the Admissions Office and the Office of Disability Services about how many semesters of high school foreign language may be required to be considered for admission and how many of semesters of college-level foreign language are required to graduate with a degree.

* Prospective applicants should also check about a college's disclosure policy. Do they want students to share disability information in their application?

A golden opportunity

When visiting a college, most students and families miss out on a prime opportunity: The chance to meet with someone from the Office of

Disability Services. This is the place you'll be coming every semester to arrange your accommodations, so you'll want to make sure the office will be able to serve you well.

You should begin by checking out the person sitting behind the desk. How long has the Director been there? Does she seem to like her job? Do you like the people in charge? How many staff members are employed in the office? If you make an appointment ahead of time, which we strongly suggest, ask if a staff member can look over your documentation, knowing she can't make you any promises regarding accommodations if you matriculate. Another important reason to make an appointment ahead of time, rather than just stop by, is that midterms and finals times are especially busy and no staff member may be available to speak with you.

While visiting the Office of Disability Services, find out if there is a separate computer room only accessible to students with disabilities. Are various types of assistive technology offered? Is there a separate quiet testing room? If you receive extended testing time or a distraction-reduced testing site, then it becomes more complicated for you to arrange your accommodations in college if there is no designated testing room or testing center. With no place to take a test through the Office of Disability Services, then each time you are scheduled for an exam you have to rely on the professor to come early or stay late and to find you a quiet and separate location for testing. This has the potential to become a headache for you. You may also want to ask whether tutoring in course content is offered through the Office of Disability Services or at a tutoring center elsewhere on campus. Are academic coaches employed to work weekly with students on organizational and time-management skills? For a student with high-functioning autism or a pervasive development disorder, is social skills counseling available? Also, ask yourself if the Office of Disability Services is attractive? Where is it located on campus—in a prime spot in the student union or out of the way and stuck in the basement of a building somewhere? The location of the office may indicate the priority that the university gives to Disability Services and can be a good predictor of the quality and quantity of resources that may be allocated to students with disabilities. Is there a full-time sign language interpreter employed through the Office of Disability Services? With a shortage of qualified sign language interpreters nationally, having one employed full time by the college can make a big difference for a student with a hearing impairment.

Be sure to verify the foreign language question with the Office of Disability Services. Just because you already received a response from the Admissions Office on this one, it doesn't mean it was correct. In our experience, foreign language is an area where there is a notorious lack of correct information among college personnel. You may also find it helpful to ask if the Office of Disability Services offers a reduced course load, four courses instead of five, for a student with a disability, especially the first semester of freshman year. Some colleges do and others don't. Pay attention to the quantity and quality of curb cuts on campus if you use a wheelchair—are they adequate? Would a hilly campus make it challenging to operate a wheelchair, especially in bad weather? Is there a separate Learning Disabilities program? Do admissions staff and Disability Services' personnel ever make admissions decisions together regarding particular students with disabilities, especially if the university has a Learning Disabilities program? While you are visiting, obtain a documentation guideline. Each college should have written guidelines as to what evidence and documents they will require to document specific types of disabilities. These guidelines are generally available on colleges' websites and may be published as a separate document or as part of the official college handbook. Chapter 4 offers more detailed information about what type of documentation is needed for various disabilities.

The Office of Disability Services often works together with Counseling Services, Health Services, and Residential Housing in trying to accommodate students. If you need an accommodation that may overlap with one of these offices, then don't miss the opportunity to stop by and speak with a director from these services to discuss the feasibility of your accommodation request. To request a single-occupancy dorm room rather than the double- or even triple-occupancy rooms often assigned to freshmen, contact the Office of Residential Housing. Many colleges do not offer this accommodation. They can barely accommodate all their students in double or triple rooms and just don't have the space to provide singles. When one is available, it can sometimes be offered to students with Asperger's syndrome, for whom the social issues of living with a roommate may be overwhelming. You can ask the Counseling Center if it has a waiting list and if there is a limit on how many sessions a student can have with a counselor. You should also inquire as to the qualifications of the counselors. Are they graduate students or qualified, seasoned professionals? You can speak with Health Services about the possibility of filling your medication prescription or to obtain off-campus referrals to local pharmacies. When a student and family think ahead, and request accommodations in advance or even just discuss the feasibility of an accommodation, college personnel often appreciate the forethought. Try out the cafeteria food. If you have digestive or food issues, will there be sufficient healthy choices available for you all the time? What about allergy issues? We've been impressed at several colleges to notice jars of jelly and jam in a "peanut butter free" area. That sure beats finding out that someone dipped the peanut butter knife in the strawberry jam you just spread on your toast!

One other important stop for students with learning disabilities should be the Office of Academic Support, or Learning Center, or whatever name that college has given to the center where tutoring and other academic supports are headquartered. This is crucial for students who will be applying to a separate program run by such a center and is a key stop for those students who suspect they may just need some course-specific tutoring. Look around with the same concerns you brought to your visit to the Office of Disability Services. Check out whether there are fees for tutoring and whether the tutoring is done by students or professionals. Are there extra help sessions scheduled before exams? Is there a limit to the number of tutoring sessions per week or per subject? What is the physical condition of the facility? This can reflect the commitment of the college to its support program.

---

* When visiting campus, don't miss out on the chance to meet with someone from the Office of Disability Services. This is the place you'll be coming to every semester to arrange your accommodations, so you'll want to make sure the office will be able to serve you well. Make an appointment ahead of time.

* Ask the Office of Disability Services staff about accommodations and services that pertain to your specific disability. Is there a quiet testing room or center? Are academic coaches employed to work weekly with students on organizational and time-management skills? Is social skills counseling available? Is there a full-time sign language interpreter?

* Verify the foreign language question with the Office of Disability Services. Just because you already received a response from the Admissions Office on this one, it doesn't mean it was correct.

* Counseling Services, Health Services, or Residential Housing. If you need an accommodation that may overlap with the Office of Disability Services (a single-occupancy dorm room, for example), stop by and speak with a director from these other offices to discuss the feasibility of your accommodation request.

Sign me up! Other things to do on the visit

When visiting a college campus, there is a lot more for a prospective student to do than just take the campus tour. These days there are a variety of opportunities available to give students the chance to "try on" a school to see if it is the right match. You can stay overnight in a dorm, sit in on a class, or meet with a professor or student from your intended major. Most colleges offer at least some of these options, but they generally need to be arranged in advance, so call the college before you visit. For some reason, the overnight visit arranged by the college doesn't always work out as planned. We know of two students, at different schools, who arrived for an overnight visit only to find their assigned host had gone out for the evening. Fortunately, neither of these applicants was in town on their own, and both were able to call their parents at nearby hotels and arrange to stay with them. For the record, both students eventually enrolled at the schools where these events occurred.

Interviewing with an Admissions Officer is another option offered by some schools. Again, it is best to schedule this ahead of time. Know that some colleges may offer you an on-the-spot interview while you are visiting. We speak to many students and families who have been offered such an interview and they all have told us that they felt taken off guard and really didn't know what to do.

We met with a father who, in retrospect, realized it was not a good idea for him to have sat in on his daughter's admissions interview. It was the spring of Jessica's junior year and she was visiting a college that would quickly become her first choice. She had already visited two other colleges both of which she liked, but "didn't love," as she explained to us. At the end of the student-led campus tour, the guide offered prospective students the opportunity to interview with an admissions representative. Jessica looked at her dad excitedly; she hadn't planned to interview that day, and hadn't interviewed at any college yet, but since she didn't know when she would make it back (the college was a six-hour drive away) and she loved the school, she wanted to go for it. Jessica and her dad were soon ushered into the office of an awaiting admissions counselor. Although many of the questions she was asked were basic, Jessica found her dad answering for her. In the rare event she responded first, her father found a way to add to or clarify what she had just said. At the end of the interview, when the admissions counselor asked if Jessica had any questions for him, she just shrugged her shoulders and shook her head. Not only did she not have any questions prepared because she hadn't planned on having an interview, but she was thrown off by her dad being there with her. After the interview, Jessica was upset with her dad and herself.

Jessica's experience illustrates the need to be prepared when visiting a college. By the time a student sits for a college interview, how many formal interviews have they had previously? Maybe one, if they have had a paid job or internship with significant responsibility, and, more often, none. So keep in mind that practice makes perfect! We've heard of high schools that offer mock college interviews to students. Although this is rare, there is no reason why you can't participate in a mock interview with a few friends or family members. You can even have a friend record your mock interview, to allow you to go back and watch it, evaluating which parts you nailed and what you still need to work on. In addition, we suggest scheduling your first real college interview with an Admissions Officer from a safety school. This way, if it should go poorly, you're not ruining your chances at your first choice school.

Many schools do not offer on campus interviews. They just don't have the staff given the number of applicants they get. What some schools use instead is the alumni interview. This is done in the student's home town by a graduate of the college who has volunteered to meet with applicants. Generally, the alumni interviewers are asked only to let the Admissions Office know of information that might not be reflected fully in a student's application. It is a chance for a student to shine, not for her to be surprised with difficult questions. We sometimes get inquiries from families where a student wants to attend a school that one of her parents attended. These applicants are referred to as legacies, and although they may get an extra look from the Admissions Office, they are not assured of admission. A student has to meet all the standards of other applicants, and only then might it be of some help. As an Admissions Officer at a very competitive college (where legacies probably get more advantage than at most schools) noted, being a legacy "can cure the sick, but can't raise the dead."

---

* 'Try on" the school to see if it is the right match for you. Stay overnight in a dorm, sit in on a class, and meet with a professor or student from your intended major. Call ahead to arrange these activities in advance.

* An invitation to an on-the-spot interview—Don't be caught off guard if, while you are visiting, you are offered an interview with an Admissions Officer. Whatever you decide, just be prepared, because if it goes poorly, it could hurt your chances of being accepted to the college.

* Practice makes perfect! Participate in a mock interview with family and friends before sitting for an official college interview.

When to visit? And how often?

There is much value in visiting colleges before you apply to them. Some say it's a waste of time and money to apply to a school that you haven't visited. Colleges that look good in a glossy catalog or are suggested by your friends (or your parents or even your guidance counselor) may not be what you are looking for. But don't feel you have to visit every school you plan on applying to before you submit your application. Maybe visit your top-choice schools and a few others that are clearly different from each other before you send in your application. It's okay to save your serious visiting until after you've been accepted by a college and before you make your final decision. With the tables turned, and the school now wanting *you*, chances are you are much more focused and realistic during your visit.

The bulk of your pre-application visits should take place during your junior and senior years. Ideally, you want to visit when the students are in session; if you can avoid visiting during the summer or holiday break, this is best. Some high schools allow you two to three college visit days which are counted as excused absences. Be sure to check with your high school about their policy. This flexibility makes it easier for you to go see colleges while their students are on campus.

As you begin the campus visit process, it's helpful to keep in mind the scores you earned on your practice standardized exam, whether you took the PSAT or PLAN (the preliminary versions of the SAT and ACT exams). Based on your scores, you can get an idea of the colleges that may be target schools for you. Even if you increase your scores when you take the actual exam—SAT or ACT—you want to have a general idea of your target schools so that you are not wasting your time by visiting Harvard when that won't be an option for you. Also, keep in mind that some colleges are SAT and ACT optional as we discuss in Chapter 5. However, there is usually more emphasis on your grades when a school does not require you to submit SAT or ACT scores.

It's probably best not to begin visiting colleges in earnest while a freshman in high school. On the other hand, not visiting any colleges until senior year and then cramming a dozen campus visits into a three-month period is not the best idea either. It's important to strike a balance and avoid burnout. If you visit a few colleges during junior year, once you narrow them down, you may even want to return to your first choice again come senior year. On a second visit you can choose to take advantage of the chance to sit in on a class in your prospective major or stay overnight in a student dorm.

---

* There is much value in visiting colleges before you apply to them, but don't feel you have to visit every school to which you plan on applying.

* Most visits should take place during junior and senior years of high school. Visit when college classes are in session.

* Don't start too early or visit too many colleges because burnout is likely to occur.

Red flags

It is important to keep an eye out for red flags when you are visiting and researching colleges. A red flag may be an indication that this college is not the right match for you. Finding a red flag is not necessarily a reason to take the college off your list, but it is a cautionary sign that means you may need to investigate the issue further. One red flag that we've encountered over the years is when a college has a low retention rate. Retention rate describes the percentage of students who begin as freshmen and then return sophomore year. A college whose retention rate is in the 90th percentile or higher indicates a high level of student satisfaction. A retention rate in the 70th percentile is abysmal, indicating a low level of student satisfaction and raising the question of what is going wrong at that school. The reasons students leave a college can include financial challenges, homesickness, or a change of major to a program of study which the college lacks. Other reasons for leaving a school may include the perception that it does not have a sense of community, that coursework is too challenging, or that academic support is insufficient. But when a college's retention rate is unusually low, you need to ask yourself if this is simply coincidental or whether the college is doing something wrong or lacking something important.

We remember one particular college we visited that made us question the drinking culture of the school. Driving down the street where all the fraternities and sororities were located, the number of empty kegs lining the street was mind-boggling. This was not a Saturday or Sunday but a Wednesday morning. Now, we are seasoned enough to know that, unfortunately, underage and excessive drinking happens on nearly every college campus and we discuss ways to deal with that in Chapter 11. But, what this indicated to us, in comparison to other colleges we've visited, is that there is likely to be an overwhelming culture of drinking at this school. It is very possible that drinking is a crucial part of campus social life.

Other red flags include colleges with counseling centers that have a waiting list, a career services office that doesn't offer many internships, inaccessible professors, and current students who do not have good things to say about their experience at that college. What do students have to say about the Director of the Office of Disability Services? Does she genuinely care about students? Or is she clearly overworked, frenzied, and not particularly accessible? If this is the case, a prospective student should be concerned about the kind of assistance that the Office of Disability Services will be able to provide.

Post-visit follow-up

One aspect of the college selection process that is often neglected is the post-visit follow-up. The first part of this process involves following up with the college staff that you met. Not only is sending a thank-you polite, but it also offers you another chance to remind college personnel of who you are, why you want to attend that college, and what you could add to that college community. Thank-you notes can be emailed, but it always reflects more positively on you if you take the time to send a handwritten note.

Interestingly, not only are you doing a post-visit follow-up, but the college may be doing the same with you. Be prepared to receive a phone call from the colleges you visit. They often call after a student visits to ask how your visit was and if you have any further questions. It is terrific if you can be composed and ready to ask a question or two when and if you do receive such a phone call. But, if you are caught off guard, do not worry. A phone conversation that goes okay, rather than great, is usually not enough for a college to deny you admission. Knowing that a college may be calling you, take the opportunity, right now, to double-check and make sure your voicemail greeting is appropriate. The last thing you want is for an Admissions Officer to hear a greeting on your phone that is immature or which otherwise reflects poorly on you. That could be a more legitimate reason for a college to think twice about admitting you.

The second part of the post-visit follow-up is using the information from your college visit to determine if this is the best college for you. As we mentioned earlier in the chapter, we have found it helpful to write down our impressions of a college as we visit. Whether you use the form we include in our Resources chapter or create your own, don't wait for more than a day or two to record your thoughts. It also helps if you talk to a parent or counselor about what you thought of each school.

Soon enough you will be standing on the campus that is the best match for you, and we hope you have an "Aha!" moment of your own. This realization will come because you've done your homework. You'll have visited the college and investigated what it has to offer you and what it may be lacking. You'll have asked key questions and paid attention to factors that impact students with disabilities, including red flags. You'll have taken advantage of that golden opportunity to meet with a staff member from the Office of Disability Services, and followed up after a visit by both thanking administrators you met on your visit and reviewing the pros and cons of the college with an adult you trust. And, in the process, we hope you will have gotten to know yourself and your goals for college and beyond.

Chapter 9

It's Off to Work We Go...

A college education is no longer only for the wealthy or the very highest levels of gifted students, as was the case just a couple of generations ago. College is an increasingly common choice for students of modest economic means and those with more average academic abilities.[1]

We need to keep something in mind, however, as we talk about the expansion of college opportunities: College is not the best path for everyone, especially some students with disabilities. Even students who eventually enroll in college may want to take time off after high school to consider whether college is the right path for them—or at least the right path, right now. We have encountered a number of students with disabilities who have decided to forgo or delay a college education for a variety of reasons. Some of these students had disabilities that would have made college an extraordinary challenge. Others had interests or abilities they could best explore by getting a different kind of training or immediately entering the workplace. Still others were tired of the struggles of high school and wanted to take a break before deciding what kind of additional education, if any, they might pursue.

Of course, even students who decide to attend college or obtain vocational training will eventually enter the workplace. It can be pretty scary to think about it, but once you finish school—whether high school, college, or graduate or professional school—you need to spend the next 40 or 50 years at work. Sure, not everyone is employed at every point in their lives. People stay home with their kids, take time off, and may even be unemployed for some period of time when they would like to be working. But unless you are independently wealthy or have extraordinary good fortune (lottery winnings come to mind), you will spend much of your adult life on the job.

Individuals with disabilities are not exempt from the need to earn a living. There are programs that we will discuss later in this chapter that can assist those who have difficulty finding work, and there is financial support available for those who are disabled to the extent that they cannot earn enough to support themselves. This is a real issue for many individuals with very significant disabilities. But for most of our readers, the next step after school—whether that is high school, college, or beyond—is the workplace.

---

* Although a college education is more available to students of all levels than ever before, it is important to realize that college is not the right next step for all high school students. Even students who move on to college or post-college education will eventually need to enter the workplace; school doesn't last forever.

Working after high school

We met Greg when he was a tenth grader, when his parents brought him to speak with us to explore post-high school options. "He doesn't want to go to college," his mother told us when she called to set up the appointment. "School has always been a struggle for him, and he says he just wants to put it behind him and get on with his life. But we worry about him. His dad and I both went to college and so does his older sister. How will he manage if he doesn't get more education?"

Greg was a friendly young man who had been classified under the Individuals with Disabilities Education Act (IDEA) since third grade because of severe dyslexia. He had received remedial reading services from his public school and managed to get through his mainstream classes, with extra time for reading assignments and exams. Even with the support of an excellent reading program, he found academics to be a challenge. He got mostly Cs in his classes, except for his tech courses, where he consistently got As. "I just don't like school," he told us. "Oh, the social stuff is fun and gym is okay, but the regular classes don't really interest me. I just want to build stuff." As we continued our conversation, we learned that Greg was building a small boat and that he loved to sail. His face lit up when he described the satisfaction he got from working on his boat and sailing on weekends with a local sailing club.

We had several meetings with Greg and his parents and spoke about options for continuing Greg's education after high school. We pointed out the disparity in income between individuals with high school diplomas and those who attend even a community college. For example, a US Census Bureau estimate put lifetime earnings for high school graduates at $1.2 million, those of graduates of two-year community colleges at $1.6 million, and those of graduates with a four-year college degree at $2.1 million.[2] We suggested several colleges that offered a sailing program and could also provide support for Greg's dyslexia. He was adamant. He simply did not want to go to any kind of college or continue his education after high school. Greg and his parents worked with his guidance counselor to enroll him in a part-time high school program that taught carpentry and building trades, jointly run by several area school districts. Greg attended the program his junior and senior years of high school. He liked being out of the school building part of the day and was able to expand his skills. We learned from Greg's parents that after graduation he had taken a job in a local boatyard.

The story didn't end there. We recently received a call from Greg's mother. "You're not going to believe it," she told us, "but he's going to community college. He loved working in the boatyard but he realized after a year or so that he didn't have the skills to run a business of his own. So he's working part time and taking business courses. It will take him a while, but it looks like he may end up with a degree after all!" We weren't surprised. Sometimes, particularly for students who have struggled with a disability, the idea of continuing beyond high school just seems overwhelming. Students and their parents need to recognize that a decision not to move on to college now doesn't mean that they will never want to continue their education.

---

* College isn't a "now or never" decision. Some students—with and without disabilities—take some time working before deciding that they want to continue their education.

Community colleges and vocational training

We've been using the term "college" throughout this book and want to pause for a moment to point out that going to college no longer means just enrolling in a four-year degree program and emerging eight semesters later with a bachelor's degree. There are numerous ways for students—with and without disabilities—to obtain a college degree or job training by using a community college or technical institute as a starting point. We look at some alternatives to four-year colleges, including community college and vocational programs, in Chapter 6. Students and parents should also keep in mind that much of what we discuss in this chapter about forgoing or delaying college also applies to the decision to forgo or delay attending a vocational or technical program.

---

* Don't forget to consider vocational or technical training as a way of continuing your education without enrolling in college.

Other reasons not to move on to college

Sometimes, the decision not to move on to college after high school is strictly a financial one. It is not unusual for students with and without disabilities to need to work for a time to accumulate funds to make college possible. Sometimes family or personal circumstances require that a young person help out at home to care for a family member, or their own child (more about avoiding teen pregnancy in Chapter 11!). Students may have disabilities that impair cognition. Or they may have serious difficulties interacting with others, such as with some forms of autism. For these students, getting through high school with an IEP diploma (which, as you may recall from Chapter 2, only certifies that a student has completed the goals set out in his IEP) is an enormous achievement and moving on to further education may be out of the question.

* There are many reasons that some students delay or end their education after high school. These can include financial limitations, family responsibilities, and the impact of serious disabilities.

Vocational Rehabilitation System

For most students with disabilities who decide not to move on to college (at least not right away), there is an agency in each state that can offer a path to training and employment. Those of you who paid careful attention to Chapter 1 may recall the Rehabilitation Act of 1973. That same federal law that established the 504 plan you may have had in high school also created the national Vocational Rehabilitation System that is designed to assist individuals with disabilities attain "meaningful and gainful employment and independent living."[3] The program works by providing funds to states to establish and administer statewide Vocational Rehabilitation Programs. This is a service designed for adults; the only time it deals with students who are still in high school is during their transition planning, when those students who are likely to qualify for vocational rehabilitation services as an adult may start the vocational rehabilitation intake process and work with a counselor to formulate goals, starting at age 16. As you may recall, the Vocational Rehabilitation Program is one of the agencies that can be brought into the IDEA transition process to help with post-high school planning.

Let's start by looking at just who is entitled to services under this program. We'll try not to get bogged down in too many details, but you should be aware that the Vocational Rehabilitation Program makes distinctions among different levels of disabilities and provides more extensive services for those individuals with the most disabling conditions. These levels of disability start with people who have "a physical or mental impairment which...results in a substantial impediment to employment."[4] This category includes individuals who need assistance with training or job placement but who can be expected eventually to enter the workplace and hold a job.

A more extensive level of services would be provided to an "individual with a significant disability"[5] which would generally be someone with "a severe physical or mental impairment which seriously limits one or more functional capacities (such as mobility, communication, self-care, self-direction, interpersonal skills, work tolerance, or work skills) in terms of an employment outcome." These individuals would be "expected to require multiple vocational rehabilitation services over an extended period of time" and their disability would fall within a long list of major debilitating conditions.[6]

We should take a moment here to note that the Vocational Rehabilitation Programs are specifically not available to individuals whose disabilities are related to drug use. In Chapter 1 we noted that the ADA can protect someone who is presently an alcoholic but not someone who is actively using illegal drugs; the Vocational Rehabilitation Programs have the same restrictions.[7]

We've seen that the extent of services available to a student with disabilities under the Vocational Rehabilitation Act is going to depend upon the nature of his disability. For most students graduating high school who are not moving on to a post-secondary education program, their state Vocational Rehabilitation Program will start with an assessment process, to determine whether the student meets one of the definitions of disability to qualify him for services. Once that determination is made, he will be assigned a counselor, who will determine his interests and experience and usually arrange for him to undergo an evaluation to determine his skill levels and readiness for work. This assessment will often be done by an agency located in the student's community, and can involve pen and paper testing, as well as trial work settings, to help determine what kind of work situation would be most suitable for this individual. Finally, the student will be placed in a work situation—sometimes paid and sometimes as an unpaid trainee or intern to start—where the employer is aware of his disability and has indicated a willingness to accommodate his needs (yes, we know that all employers are required by law to do this, but these employers have actively agreed to work with individuals sent to them by the Vocational Rehabilitation Program). For some individuals, this initial placement will be sufficient to "jump start" their entry into the workforce. For those whose disabilities are more extensive, this initial process may be followed by more extensive support services to facilitate employment in the community or in a sheltered environment.

Students and families should be aware that the services offered by the Vocational Rehabilitation Programs can continue throughout an individual's lifetime. Although we are looking at the role they can play for individuals with disabilities who are graduating high school and need help finding a job, their services can include a variety of supports for individuals who are going on to college, and for older students and adults at all stages of their work life. Donald, for example, was a high school senior with a form of autism, who planned to attend a community college while living at home with his family. In his suburban community there was no direct bus or train transport available to the college, and his parents both worked full time and could not drive him to school. Donald needed to learn to drive, but drivers' education classes and parental lessons were proving to be insufficient to overcome his anxiety about the process. He had begun to work with a Vocational Rehabilitation counselor as part of his IDEA transition, and the counselor arranged for him to take individual driving lessons the summer after high school graduation, working daily with an experienced driving instructor until he was ready to take and pass his road test.

The mandate behind this and other services provided by Vocational Rehabilitation Programs is that individuals with disabilities be given what they need to prepare them for productive work and independent lives, to the extent that they are able. So, students who are moving right into the workplace may need training or placement, while a student who wants to continue his education by going to college or a training program may need and get a laptop computer to take class notes or get help purchasing necessary text books. One young man we know described the services he received from his Vocational Rehabilitation Program as "having a guidance counselor for life" for someone with a disability. We'll mention some of their services at other points in this book, but we hope you keep them in mind when an individual with a disability needs assistance in preparing for or finding employment. We have included information about how to find your state's Vocational Rehabilitation Program in our Resources chapter.

Families should be aware of other agencies operating in their state and local community that may be helpful to students who will be entering the workforce right after high school. Some of these groups focus on students with a single, specific disability, such as visual disabilities. Others work with students with cognitive or learning impairments more severe than those we address in this book, and can provide sheltered workshops or supportive living situations for individuals who are unable to work in the competitive marketplace or live on their own. Sheltered workshops are sometimes controversial employment settings for individuals with substantial disabilities who are employed at low wages to do simple tasks such as assembling or packing.[8] Still others provide training and support services to individuals with disabilities from disadvantaged backgrounds. The best source for local community resources is the high school transition team, school social worker, or, for those students who have one, their case manager. We've included information on where to locate some of these agencies and programs in our Resources chapter.

Another group of agencies focus on both the level of disability and the financial situation of an individual. These include the federal programs known as SSI and Medicaid. We'll discuss these in Chapters 10 and 13

---

* State Vocational Rehabilitation Programs offer services for students with disabilities. The goal of these services is to make individuals with disabilities independent and productive members of the workforce. Services are offered only to adults, but planning for services can begin during high school, once a student is 16.

* The level of services offered depends on the extent of an individual's disabilities. Individuals with more extensive disabilities will receive more services than those whose disabilities have less of an impact on their ability to work.

* These services are not just available for students who are seeking employment right after high school. Services can include technology (such as laptop computers), books, and other individualized services for college students with disabilities.

Military service

One option for students who choose not to continue their education immediately beyond high school is to enlist in the military. Having a disability does not automatically disqualify someone from joining the military, but much depends upon the type of disability and the extent to which it has been active in recent years. As we mentioned in Chapter 1, the ADA does not apply to the military services; each branch technically has its own standards and requirements for the physical and mental abilities of applicants, although they all refer back to Army standards which implement Department of Defense guidelines for determining what conditions will disqualify an individual from military service.[9] All of these standards arise from a provision in the Selective Service Act that permits the military branches to declare someone unacceptable for service.[10] Potential recruits need to be able to pass a test of physical readiness and psychological screenings for every branch of the military, and additional requirements exist for specific job categories. It makes sense that a pilot or a Navy SEAL will need to meet different physical standards than a clerk in a supply depot. Certain items in an individual's medical history will automatically disqualify him from enlistment, including a history of behavior or personality disorders and suicide attempts, or a physical condition that limits mobility or stamina. The unifying principle behind the list of disqualifying medical, psychiatric, or behavioral disorders is that they will interfere with an individual's ability to function as part of group, to operate anywhere in the world, to deal with stress, and to be able to make effective decisions under pressure.

Even though the list of disqualifying conditions is long and may seem an insurmountable barrier to military service for anyone with a disability, each branch of the military will grant waivers for certain conditions that have not been active or required medication for many years. Two of the most frequently encountered conditions of this type are asthma and attention deficit hyperactivity disorder (ADHD). In general, if an individual has not had symptoms of asthma nor needed asthma medication since age 13 he will be able to enlist in most branches of the military. If a high school graduate with diagnosed ADHD has not needed medication for his condition for three years or more, he would not be automatically disqualified to enlist in every military service.[11]

Students who are interested in enrolling in ROTC (Reserve Officers' Training Corps) while in college need to be aware that the training they receive will culminate in their commissioning as an officer in a branch of the military service. Students who do not meet the military guidelines will generally not be permitted to enroll in ROTC. One important word of caution if you are considering enlisting in the military: Do not rely solely upon information provided by a recruiter. The only accurate advice is that put in writing by the branch of the service in which you are interested. The rules can be confusing and recruiters are under some pressure to meet quotas.

As the number of military personnel who return from the battlefield with significant physical and emotional disabilities grows, there is a new population of young people who will eventually be ready to enter the workplace as individuals with disabilities. The complex issues that these wounded warriors must deal with as they adjust to the significant changes in their lives are beyond the scope of this book, but we have included in our Resources chapter information on how to find some of the programs and agencies that are in place to assist with their post-service transition to civilian life and employment.

---

* The US military does not have to comply with the ADA. Each branch of the military can make its own rules about who is qualified to serve.

* Most, but not all, disabilities will disqualify an individual for military service. Mild disabilities that have not been active for many years may not always be a bar to military enlistment. It is important to check written rules for each branch of service.

Disclosure

You've read a great deal in Chapter 7 about whether or not to disclose a disability on a college application, but the decision to disclose a disability to a potential employer involves a number of different considerations. Colleges are fundamentally in existence to educate and support students. They tend to be supportive of the needs of applicants with disabilities, especially when they have mechanisms in place to provide the kind of accommodations and support such students will need. Businesses are in existence to make a profit. Sure, most businesses want to do the right thing for their employees and their communities, and to comply with the law, but their mission differs from that of a college, and we need to look at the issues they are concerned with as we consider whether individuals with disabilities should disclose their disabilities to employers—and, if so, how and when this should happen.

Let's begin this discussion by recognizing that the ADA does not permit employers to ask about disabilities. Even questions that indirectly reveal the existence of a disability, when that is the intention of the question, are not permitted. So, although an employer can state that they require regular attendance and that they offer limited time off, they can't then ask a potential employee if he will need regular time off for doctor visits. Employers are permitted, however, to ask questions that relate to fundamental aspects of the job. So, for example, the manager of a commercial printing company who is hiring someone for general office work, which can also include some proofreading duties, can require that a prospective employee be able to read without difficulty.

Another important issue to keep in mind is that an employer is not required to provide accommodations for a disability they do not know about. If an employee does not tell the employer about a disability or request accommodations, the employer does not have to provide them. The employer must maintain a generally accessible workplace, but the specific accommodations that may be required by a particular employee need to be made known by the employee to the employer.

We will also need to distinguish between obvious and hidden disabilities as we discuss the issue of disclosure. Certainly, an individual who uses a wheelchair does not have the liberty of deciding whether or not to disclose his disability to an employer. It is obvious to all. But, as we will see, even someone with an obvious disability needs to consider whether to disclose his condition when he first submits his resume or application for the job. We see no reason why he should. If he is applying for a job for which he is otherwise qualified, his resume or application should reflect his qualifications, not his disability. The job applicant may want to discuss the fact that he does not intend initially to disclose his disability with those people he is listing as his references. He doesn't want to decide not to disclose at this point and then have one of his references make mention of how well he gets around in his wheelchair.

We don't suggest, however, that the applicant with the obvious disability arrive for his initial interview without disclosing his circumstances to his potential employer. At that point, the employer has determined that he is interested in this applicant and that his qualifications are sufficient for the job. When the applicant gets a call to come in for an interview, we'd suggest this is the time to mention, "By the way, you may want to know I use a wheelchair." Any employer who responds with "Well, let's not go ahead, then" is clearly violating the ADA—take a look in our Resources chapter for how to find legal help. On the other hand, not mentioning anything until you show up for the interview may make the employer feel you somehow didn't trust their fairness and will deny them the opportunity to think in advance about how they can modify the non-fundamental aspects of the job to make it work for someone in a wheelchair.

We have similar advice for those whose disabilities are not initially obvious to the potential employer. Whether we are talking about a learning disability or a seizure disorder, employers generally want to know about disabilities they don't see, and, more importantly, they cannot be required to accommodate disabilities that are unknown to them. We discussed this very issue during a visit to a college-based post-secondary program in Cambridge, Massachusetts. The program, for individuals with learning disabilities, has been around for many years, serving those who seek job training and social growth but who would be unable to do college-level work. These students study for two to four years and emerge with a certificate, not a college diploma. The program conducted a study of its alumni on a variety of subjects, including whether the students disclosed their disabilities to their employers, when they disclosed them, and what impact their disclosure had on their success in the workplace and their satisfaction with their job.

The results of the study were dramatic. Most of the students disclosed their disability "on the job application, at the interview, or when they first met their employers." Of those who disclosed their disability before they actually began the job, 79 percent received promotions and/or raises at that job. Of those who did not disclose their disability before they began to work, only 25 percent received raises or promotions. Not surprisingly, employers gave higher ratings to those employees who disclosed early on, compared to those whose disability was disclosed over time, after their employment began.[12]

One area that is far less clear when it comes to the issue of disclosure is when a job applicant has been diagnosed with a mental or emotional illness. We can all see how a serious learning disability will impact job performance and how sharing the existence of such a disability with the employer early on will enable the employer to understand better what issues the employee is bringing to the workplace. Some employers actively seek out individuals with significant learning disabilities to do tasks that others might find repetitive. But mental or emotional illness presents more complex issues. Not only does the employer have to be concerned about the ability of the potential employee to do his job, but employers will also have concerns, rightly or not, that individuals with mental or emotional disabilities may be disruptive or, worse, violent, in the workplace.

Still, the basic principles apply. The potential employee needs to have an actual disability (note that certain behaviors, such as irritability, chronic lateness, or poor judgment are not considered to be disabilities themselves, although they may be linked to mental impairments).[13] The individual needs to be otherwise qualified for the job. He needs to understand that the employer is obligated to offer reasonable accommodations to him, and he needs to be aware that the employer is not obligated to offer accommodations for a disability that is not made known to him.

A unique situation arises where an individual with a mental or emotional illness has been denied a professional license that is generally required for a particular job. The employer, who cannot legitimately inquire as to whether or not the individual has a disability, can properly ask if he has a license and may require proof of licensure as a requirement of the job. Even if the reason the individual is not licensed is because of a mental or emotional illness, the employer can decline to hire him, as long as the license really is a requirement for the job.

---

* Employers cannot ask an employee whether he has a disability. However, unless an employer has been made aware of an employee's disability, the employer has no obligation to provide accommodations for that employee.

* Employers do not have to hire individuals with disabilities unless they are otherwise qualified for the job. Applicants

who may be unable to do every part of a job, even with accommodations, may still be considered qualified.

* Disclosing a disability to an employer at or before the start of employment may lead to greater employer satisfaction with the employee. The employer will have had a chance to consider accommodations and will better understand any of the employee's limitations.

Practical considerations

Most businesses are covered by the ADA and, in some cases, by Section 504 of the Rehabilitation Act as well. Since we've seen that these two laws have very similar definitions and requirements, we'll stick to the ADA when discussing what businesses are obligated—and not obligated—to do, and how that impacts individuals with disabilities. It is also important to remember that individual states often have laws in place that extend significant rights to individuals with disabilities dealing with businesses of any size, even those that would not be covered by the ADA. We've included information on how to find out about your state's laws in our Resources chapter.

It is important to remember that no law requires a business to hire someone unless that individual is otherwise qualified for that position. So, Roger, who uses crutches because of an orthopedic disability, need not be hired for a position in a factory where he will be required to climb ladders or carry heavy objects with two hands. The ability to climb and carry is a fundamental part of the job and Roger will not be able to do that job safely or effectively, even if he is provided with significant accommodations. On the other hand, if Roger applies for an office position with the same factory, where the workday activities are primarily done at a computer, the employer must give him the same consideration as any other applicant. Since physical agility and mobility are not fundamental to the job, the employer may not use the disability as a disqualifying factor in considering Roger for that position. If that job would also occasionally require that Roger personally deliver documents throughout the employer's premises, and if prior individuals in that job used a nearby staircase instead of a slow and poorly located elevator to get from one floor of the building to another, the employer still could not disqualify Roger for that position based upon his orthopedic disability. The ADA requires that the employer provide an individual with a disability with reasonable accommodations necessary to do the job, and having Roger use the elevator or, even better, having someone else do the delivery portion of the job, would be a reasonable accommodation.

Employers may have to undertake a reasonable additional expense in order to accommodate an employee with a disability, and what is reasonable will depend upon the amount of the expense, the size of the employer, and whether there are other ways of accommodating the employee's needs. There is evidence that a large majority of employees with disabilities do not require any accommodations.[14] A study reported by the US Department of Labor found that there was no cost to employers for 15 percent of accommodations; that 51 percent of accommodations cost employers $500 or less; that another 12 percent cost between $501 and $1000; and that only 22 percent cost the employer more than $1000.[15] But an employer does not need to provide the exact accommodation the employee requests. The employer can provide other accommodations designed to achieve the same purpose even if the employee would prefer another approach.

In the same way that a college will require documentation of a disability before providing accommodations to a student, an employer has the right to request documentation of a disability that is not physically obvious. Documentation can be required to include information about what kind of accommodations the employee will need to perform his job.

---

* Employers need to look at what is fundamental to any particular job and be willing to modify secondary aspects of a job to accommodate an employee with a disability.

* Employers have the right to require documentation of a "hidden" disability as a condition to providing accommodations.

Whether you will be entering the workforce right after high school, following a period of training by your state Vocational Rehabilitation Program, or after a successful stint as a college and graduate student, we hope this look at the workplace has helped you to understand better what lies ahead.

Chapter 10

Medical Management Without Mom

Medical independence may be the hardest step for young people with disabilities—and their parents—to take on the road to adulthood. There is no more fundamental role for parents than making sure the health needs of their child are met and no more significant step towards becoming an adult than for a student to manage her own medical needs. Many students with disabilities take medication. Some deal with complex medical or psychological issues that have been treated throughout childhood and adolescence by specialists with whom the student and her parents have formed a close bond. For most of these students, Mom and Dad have played a major role in arranging doctors' appointments, filling prescriptions, and monitoring their child's health. Even for students who live at home while they attend college, or while working, learning to handle their own health and medication needs is an important part of their transition to adult life.

Jack is a college freshman with more than his share of medical and learning issues. He was diagnosed with Crohn's disease, a form of inflammatory bowel syndrome, at the age of five. He has Tourette's syndrome, which can cause tics and impulsivity, and he has difficulty regulating his mood and his attention. On top of all that he has learning disabilities which make math and spatial issues difficult for him, although he reads and writes quite well. He has numerous physicians and takes a number of medications. Jack and his parents have struggled to help him maintain his health—and his independence—while he is away from home for the first time, attending a college with strong supports for his learning difficulties located in an adjacent state. Let's look how Jack and his parents have worked to enable Jack to handle his physical and behavioral issues while attending college.

A tough pill to swallow

Jack's mom began working with him in high school to get him to take responsibility for taking his medications each morning. It wasn't an easy process. Jack didn't like needing pills in the first place. It was hard enough to remember to take them when they were right in front of him as he gulped down some juice on his way out of the door on school mornings. Getting involved in setting them up was just more than he wanted to bother with. Jack absolutely refused to use any sort of pill tray, the kind with room for each day's medication to be set up in advance, sometimes divided into morning and evening pills. "They are for old people, not kids," he would state in an annoyed tone. "I just don't want to use it."

Eventually, even Jack recognized that the quantity of pill bottles his mom had to deal with was a burden on school mornings, and he decided by his senior year of high school that a pill tray was more of a convenience than a stigma. His parents worked with him for much of his senior year to have him take responsibility for his medications. His mother insisted that Jack sit with her while she distributed his pills for the week into the pill tray, and if he balked, she reminded him that she would not be with him in college to do this.

She and Jack informally discussed each pill and why he was taking it: "These brown pills are for your Crohn's. Remember, Dr. Mark prescribed it a few years ago. You can add a pill each day if you need it, but just let me know so you can tell Dr. Mark when you see him." They continued this process for a number of weeks until it was clear that Jack fully understood not just what pills he was supposed to take, but also what each pill was intended to do and what side effects, if any, each pill might have. As his senior year in high school proceeded, Jack became comfortable filling his pill tray once a week. It was a gradual process, and there were a number of days when the tray was empty on a busy school morning, but by the time he graduated, Jack took on this responsibility fully.

Jack found it particularly helpful when one of his doctors, a psychiatrist who was helping him deal with his mood and behavior, made a list of all the medications Jack had tried for these issues. The doctor wrote each medication on a large whiteboard in his office and grouped them together. He then went through each medication with Jack and Jack's parents, discussing what worked and what didn't, and noting any side effects. Finally, he showed Jack how he seemed to be helped most by a particular class of medications and explained to Jack that he wanted Jack to try a new medication that was related to those that had worked before but could be more effective with fewer side effects. By sharing his decision process with Jack, this psychiatrist made the reasons behind his choice of medication clear. Jack understood why he was trying this medication and felt as if he was part of his own medical team. It was an extremely empowering experience for Jack, and he clearly felt as if he was in partnership with his doctor in trying this new medication.

One realization that grew out of Jack's sense of empowerment was that he really could only manage to take medication once a day, in the morning. Somehow, if he needed to take a pill in the afternoon or evening, it just never made it to his "to do" list. By sharing this with his doctors, they have tried whenever possible to avoid medications that needed to be taken any time other than in the morning. Of course, morning for a college student may well mean lunchtime for anyone else, but it was still at the beginning of Jack's day.

The next step for Jack in this process was for him to become aware of the need to have sufficient supplies of each medication on hand to fill his pill tray. This involved understanding what medications were prescribed with several renewals and which ones were "controlled substances" that needed a new prescription every month. There were issues of prescription drug coverage and payment to consider. Jack and his parents decided that Jack would keep tabs on whether he was running low on medication, but that his parents would continue to arrange for prescriptions to be filled. They agreed that each time Jack came home for a vacation he would bring all of his pills with him so his mom could double-check to see if he had an adequate supply. It wasn't full independence, but both Jack and his parents felt it was all he could manage along with all the other transitions that freshman year required.

Some of Jack's medications were pills he had taken for years, and the dosage rarely changed. But other medications, particularly the ones that helped with his mood and attention issues, were frequently in need of adjustment. With help from his parents, who contacted the college health center for guidance, Jack learned about a pharmacy in his college town that would deliver to the campus health center. The pharmacy would accept Jack's prescription plan and would bill his parent's credit card for any co-payment. This gave Jack the option of having a prescription written that could be filled at school. For medications that did not require frequent adjustments, Jack's mom arranged for prescriptions to be filled at the family's home pharmacy and she sent Jack any pills that could not wait until his visits home.

We can see from the experiences of Jack and his family that there are many steps that need to be taken before a student or working young adult can become an independent manager of her own medication. Of course, for students who take a single pill each day, the process of medication independence may be simpler than it is for someone who needs multiple medications prescribed by several different physicians. But the basic steps remain the same.

---

* Start early. The first day away from home is too late to undertake self-management of medication. This process should begin in high school, with less parent supervision and involvement as high school graduation approaches.

* Understanding is crucial. No one can accept responsibility for a medication they are simply told they need to take. Understanding why a medication has been prescribed, what it is expected to do, and what side effects it may cause are necessary parts of taking ownership of the responsibility of taking medication. This understanding needs to come from the student's physician and needs to be reinforced by her parents as part of the move towards independence.

* It does not have to be "all or nothing." Medication management can be a complex subject, involving insurance, doctors of varying degrees of accessibility, and a young person whose medical needs may complicate her ability to manage this entire subject on her own. Jack's family found a compromise in having his parents arrange for prescriptions to be filled, with Jack being responsible for letting them know when he was running low. Other families need to find their own comfort level in dividing responsibility. What is important is that the student be

increasingly involved in managing her own medication needs, with the ultimate goal of being an independent adult who takes full responsibility, to the extent she is physically and cognitively able, for all aspects of her own medical needs.

It doesn't do any good in the bottle

Of course, having the medication on hand is only one step towards taking it regularly as prescribed. Many students get caught up in the excitement and sudden independence of being away from home—or even of starting college or work while living at home—by stopping their medication. Some do it intentionally, others with less thought. Some stop completely, and others just become very casual about remembering their pills, missing more doses than they take. The impact of this medication change may not be readily apparent to the student or her parents, which can lead to a sense in some students that the medications weren't so important after all. What they fail to realize is that some medications continue to provide some effect for days or weeks after they are stopped. The impact of not taking these medications may not be immediate, but it is eventually very real.

Within several weeks of the start of Jack's freshman year, Jack's parents noticed a change in his behavior during their telephone calls. Jack was irritable and complained of stomach pain. He was evasive when asked if he was taking his medication and eventually admitted that he only took it "sometimes." It soon became clear to Jack's parents that he was not taking it at all.

Jack explains it this way: "It wasn't that I made up my mind to stop taking my pills. It just sort of happened. One day I was late to class and couldn't find my pill tray. Then it happened a couple of days in a row. Somehow, without the pills to kind of keep me on track, it seemed less important to me to actually take them. I thought I was doing okay, until I realized that I was feeling lousy, with stomach pains, and that I wasn't in a good mood very much. I guess I need to take my pills to be focused enough to take my pills."

Jack had a break from school over Columbus Day—a four-day weekend at home. His mom handed him his pill tray each morning—

not saying anything, just making it very easy for Jack to have his pills with some orange juice in the morning. By the end of the weekend Jack was feeling better, and he and his parents had a talk about what had happened. He has had lapses since then, but has been much better about taking his pills.

Remembering to take your pills is sometimes only part of the problem. Jack and his parents still remember his frantic telephone call one day not long after he had gotten back on track, announcing dramatically that "Someone stole my pills!" After some questions from Jack's dad, the pill tray was located in Jack's dorm room, behind a pile of papers and under some laundry of dubious cleanliness. Jack learned to take a deep breath and look around before he panicked when he could not find his pills. He tried to keep them in one place on his desk to make them easier to find.

Jack's experiences with medication are not unusual. We have encountered numerous students who managed well in high school but who could not manage their medication needs when they moved from home, often with predictably disastrous results. Rory took medication to manage his attention deficit hyperactivity disorder (ADHD). The distractions of living in a college dorm made it hard for him to remember to take his medication and he found that he could not keep up with his classroom work. Rory withdrew from his college program to regroup at home, and the following year enrolled in a local college, where he could pursue his interest in art and still have the support of his parents to help manage his medication. Today, several years after graduation with a degree in art, Rory is enjoying his work in art direction for an advertising agency. He says, "I needed more time than I had realized to be able to function independently. Maybe I just took longer to mature than some other guys, but going to school while living at home made the most sense for me. It took a few tries for me to accept responsibility for taking my own attention medications, but by the time I graduated from college I had taken this job on as my own. I guess I needed my parents' help for longer than I expected."

Another problem with some medications, especially those for attention difficulties, is that the demands of a day at college or in the workplace are often not the same as those in high school. Days may be longer or start at different times than the more structured days of high school. Evening classes or work schedules may mean that shorter-acting medications are no longer good choices for some students. Students, parents, and their physicians need to be mindful of this change in lifestyle when considering what medications may be most helpful to these young adults.

Medications for psychiatric disorders can pose particular difficulties for students, families, and the schools and workplaces of the young people with these conditions. Issues of what to disclose about a mental or emotional illness are dealt with in depth in Chapter 7, but we should acknowledge here that some families decide not to disclose fully a student's emotional difficulties for fear of having that student denied admission because she may be deemed a danger to herself or others. Many of these students can do quite well when regularly taking appropriate medications. But several factors, including the side effects of these medications and the underlying conditions themselves, can make medication compliance more difficult than for other students with disabilities. Even when schools have some information about a student's emotional state, they are usually in no position to supervise the student. Parents, the young adult, and the prescribing psychiatrists need to have serious discussions about the need to monitor these young adults for depression and other psychiatric conditions that can worsen under stress or in the event of medication avoidance and can have life-threatening consequences. The safety of the student and school community must take precedence over any educational decision.

---

* Disorganization is the enemy. We will focus on organization as a key to success in college and the workplace in Chapter 11. But there are few places where being organized is more important than in medication management. You can't take a pill that you can't find. Keeping medication in the same place all the time and taking it roughly the same time each day reduces the chances of missing doses.

* Medication complications don't have to interfere with success. Although he could not manage to handle his own medication needs as a college freshman, Rory found an alternative way to attend college and is a successful adult in every meaning of the term. Rory could have tried living on campus a year or two into his studies and may have found that he was ready to handle his own medical needs at that point in time. The key is

that students who need some extra time to fully manage their medical needs should be forgiving of their own setbacks and look for alternative paths to their educational goals.

Complicating conditions

Our friend Jack had to deal with issues beyond managing his medication. His Crohn's disease was pretty well controlled, but would occasionally flare up without warning, causing bouts of stomach pain and diarrhea. He had encountered some difficulties in high school when he needed to leave a class suddenly, and he had learned to explain to his high school teachers at the beginning of the semester that he might need to leave class abruptly. Jack found that it helped to speak to the teacher soon after a sudden departure to explain why he left class and to remind her about his medical condition. He knew that he would need to do that with his professors in college as well, although, as he noticed after a few weeks, "College is really different from high school. If you need to get up to use the bathroom, you just need to get up and go. They treat you more like an adult, and figure that if you are leaving the room, you have a reason for it."

Kate, who also has Crohn's disease, but with more frequent and debilitating flare-ups, decided to forgo specifically requesting accommodations from her college professors at the state university she attended. When she moved on to graduate school, where the classes were smaller than at the large state university, she made a different choice. "I decided to email my professors at the beginning of the semester and explain my situation. Classes were smaller and it was obvious if I wasn't there or had to leave in the middle of a lecture. My professors were very understanding and worked with me on days I couldn't make it to class or had to leave in the middle of a class because I wasn't feeling well. I would *highly* recommend doing this...it makes bad days less stressful!"

Kate considered the availability of a private bathroom early on in the process of considering colleges, and before she accepted admission to the state university she was in contact with the Office of Disability Services to make sure this would be available. "They were very helpful with this," she noted.

Jack and his family were also concerned about bathroom access in the dorm. Jack made sure to mention his Crohn's disease on his roommate information form, along with his preference for loud music and the fact that he liked to sleep late. He communicated with the college Office of Disability Services and advised them of his Crohn's and his need for easy bathroom access. The college initially placed Jack in a small dorm, with two bathrooms for the six people on his corridor. About a month into the year, however, campus logistics made in necessary for Jack and his roommate to move to a larger dorm, where far more students shared a bathroom and where the bathroom would be located some distance from Jack's room. Jack didn't even have a chance to be concerned about this news; the Director of Residence Life told him about the move and in the next instant handed him a key: "This is your personal key to the staff bathroom right near your room. Please don't share it with anyone, but we wanted to make sure you had access to a bathroom right near your room at any time you need it."

Jacob, who has a severe hearing impairment and has had a cochlear implant since elementary school, had disclosed his condition at the time he applied to his small private college. He needed specific academic accommodations but was disappointed to realize that he also needed—and his school insisted upon—a dorm room equipped with strobe lights that would flash and alert him to a fire or other emergency. "It was tough," his mother explained. "Jacob wanted to live where everyone else lived, but there were a very limited number of rooms with strobes and he was frustrated that this limited his choice of dorms."

We know of other colleges that have put students with Crohn's or related ailments in small suites, or made other provisions for bathroom access. What is important for students like Kate, Jacob, or Jack is to inform the appropriate individuals in the Office of Residence Life and the Office of Disability Services as to the medical issue and what will be needed to accommodate the affected student.

Sometimes, however, even when students inform the right offices on campus about a specific medical need, things don't go smoothly. Elise has celiac disease, an immune reaction to gluten, a protein found in wheat, rye, and barley. The only way to avoid the damage to the digestive system that can be caused by celiac disease is to eliminate any gluten from the diet. That means no bread products, but also no products with hidden gluten, which can be found in many processed foods and things not commonly regarded as bread products, such as gravy. Before Elise started college as a residential student at a small campus not far from her suburban home, she and her parents met with the Office of Disability Services and the Food Services Department, which operated the school meal program. The Food Services Department seemed to understand the situation and gave Elise and her parents a list of alternative, gluten-free products they promised would be available to Elise at all times.

What wasn't considered in this carefully thought-out plan was that it would need to be implemented by the actual cafeteria workers, some of whom did not seem to understand the serious consequences that could result to Elise from eating gluten or who did not speak enough English for her to explain her needs. Elise found it difficult to get the food she needed and began to subsist on baked potatoes—gluten free, but hardly nutritionally sound. Telephone calls from Elise's parents, cordial at first and ultimately ending with shouting and claims of violations of the Americans with Disabilities Act, preceded Elise's withdrawal from the dorms and the meal plan by Thanksgiving. She continued her college education at the same school as a commuter, living at home and bringing her own lunches to campus when needed.

Although a good argument could be made that Elise's college failed to provide her with reasonable accommodations under the Americans with Disabilities Act, Elise and her family decided not to pursue legal action, either by filing a complaint with the US Department of Justice (which would generally refer the complaint to the Office of Civil Rights at the US Department of Education) or by filing a suit in a state or federal court; they wanted Elise to continue her education at that college and felt that there was no purpose in "rocking the boat" with the school.

Kate didn't include specific food needs when she made her request for bathroom accommodations to her campus Office of Disability Services. It was a mistake, she says, since the dining hall and food courts on campus were "a nightmare." She explained that "a lot of the food is greasy and processed and is not easy on the stomach. It's a good idea to stock your dorm room with 'safe foods' that are easy to make. For me, it was things like crackers, peanut butter, soup—basically anything you know you will do okay with."

This solution worked for Kate. Another student at another school might have found different alternatives, perhaps living facilities with a kitchen where she could prepare her own meals.

* Disclosure of physical needs is a necessary step in getting accommodations. Chapter 7 discusses issues of when, what, and how to disclose disabilities to colleges, and Chapter 9 discusses disclosing to an employer. But one area where disclosure is always appropriate—and necessary—is when dealing with a condition that requires physical or logistical accommodations. As we can see from the difficulties faced by Elise, disclosure is not always sufficient to get what a student may need, but unless you are clear about your needs, even the most accommodating college or employer can't meet them.

What's up, Doc?

Let's look at still another medical issue that students with disabilities need to navigate after high school. Age 18 is a crucial turning point for young people with medical issues. Under FERPA and HIPAA, two laws which we discussed in detail in Chapter 1, the right to medical and educational information about an individual transfers at that age from parents to the young person. That means that under federal law, a physician must speak to the student/patient, not her parents. The young adult is the only one with the right to her educational records and her medical records.

Jack and his family encountered these laws in several ways. Jack still saw his childhood pediatrician in his senior year of high school, during which he turned 18. He was surprised, and pleased, when the receptionist looked at his chart one day and said, "Oh, you are 18 now. You need to sign this form, not Mom." Jack's mom was a bit concerned, however, since she realized that she might not have the right to get information such as test results from the doctor's office. She mentioned this to Jack, and, despite his pleasure at his adult status, he realized that he still wanted his parents to be able to assist him medically. He signed a form to place in his medical chart which stated that the doctor had Jack's consent to communicate with his parents about medical information. Not every physician follows the rules of HIPAA to the letter. A number of doctors, especially ones that Jack has been seeing for many years, haven't changed their practice of speaking to both Jack and his parents about his medical condition. Still, all young adults should be aware of these issues, and families should recognize that there are steps they can take to make sure that parents can still have access to medical information where that is desired. Of course, the other side of this issue is that young people should be aware that they have the right to the privacy of their medical information, and that their physicians cannot disclose information to their patients' parents unless or until their patient gives consent. Every family will work this out their own way, but the important thing is that they become aware of the subject in the first place.

Another aspect of working with physicians is moving from parent-managed medical treatment to the student's handling of her own medical needs. As with medication, this subject is often complicated by insurance and payment issues. It is a rare college student who has her own medical insurance or funds to pay a doctor. Most students are still covered by their parents' policies and may not fully understand such terminology as "participating physician," "co-pay," and "out-of-network." Part of the transition to adulthood for a young person is understanding health insurance and making sure that she has coverage. That means parents need to initiate a series of conversations, beginning before the student's eighteenth birthday, explaining the kind of insurance that covers the student, its source (Mom's job, Dad's job, Medicaid or otherwise), and the scope of its coverage. Individuals with severe disabilities may be entitled to Supplemental Security Income (SSI) and Medicaid medical coverage, but the requirements for this are sufficiently strict that it will not generally be available to most individuals who are able to attend school or work. Individuals who qualify as legally blind have different standards for SSI and should contact the Social Security Administration for specific guidelines. We discuss availability of SSI and Medicaid in Chapter 13, and information on SSI and Medicaid is included in our Resources chapter.

Still another aspect of managing one's own medical care is to know what to do in an emergency. Students should carry their own medical insurance and prescription medicine coverage card. Parents may want to make copies in case they are called upon to assist in an emergency or in case the student's card is lost. The student should understand that this card needs to be in her wallet and should be available if she is admitted to a hospital in the event of illness or an accident.

Communicating with a physician can be difficult even for experienced adults. Young people with medical issues may have questions about symptoms, medication, or unanticipated challenges. We have seen that some doctors won't speak to parents once a student turns 18. Even when doctors are willing to speak to parents, this form of communication is much like the party game of telephone, where information can become mangled as it passes through each stage. There are also numerous medical issues that students just don't want to filter through their parents: Sex, recreational drug use, tattoos, drinking. In short, part of the transition to adulthood is learning how to communicate with your doctor or doctors.

As with other aspects of self-care for students with disabilities, this process needs to begin during adolescence, when parents should encourage students to contact their doctors directly. Some doctors are comfortable with email and readily provide their patients with their email addresses and sometimes even cell phone numbers. One noted adolescent medicine specialist gives his patients his cell phone number with this cautionary note: "Feel free to call me any time for an emergency. But if you call me for something like a form for school at 3 a.m., you can be sure that I will get back to you at some equally bad time to tell you I have sent it out!" It is not uncommon for more traditional physicians, especially those in large practices, to have one or more layers of office staff who will convey information to and even from the doctor. This may work fine for some medical conditions and for some individuals, but students and their parents should give serious consideration to the accessibility of a physician when deciding who they want to use for a particular condition.

The issue of selecting a doctor is one of the more complex decisions a young person will need to face when becoming medically independent, and depending upon the relationship between the student and her parents, this may be better accomplished as a joint process after college graduation. As with all of the steps towards medical adulthood, this is best done gradually, and use of the college health services for minor issues such as colds and bruises may be a good way for most students to gain experience speaking to health professionals they have not worked with previously.

* Choosing a physician involves a number of complex decisions. Insurance coverage, accessibility, and privacy issues can make this a complicated area for students or young working people to handle on their own. This may be one area where continued parental involvement, gradually diminishing as time progresses, makes sense for both the student and her parents.

Technology

Jacob's parents were concerned about how he would manage living on campus with his cochlear implant. Throughout elementary and secondary school "he wanted to forget he was deaf," explained his mother. "He wanted nothing to do with it other than putting it on. It has lots of settings and controls, and as far as I could tell he never read the manual or watched the video explaining how it operated. Jacob wouldn't attend any sort of support group and wanted nothing to do with other kids with cochlear implants whose parents I met when he went to a special nursery school."

Somehow Jacob became comfortable with his implant and its settings. "He casually mentioned to me about using the beam setting when he was in someplace noisy," noted his mom. "I guess he became comfortable using it by trial and error." She points out that one factor that may have helped Jacob become comfortable with his implanted device was the nine years he spent at summer camp. "It was a small, nurturing camp, and the camp nurse used to call me whenever there was a problem with the device. We'd troubleshoot together on the phone to fix it. The camp nurse had extra batteries and a back-up device, so I guess that helped Jacob understand that it was possible to manage without me being the specific person to help him." Today, Jacob's mom still orders batteries for him, but he tells her when he is running low. "It's not much different than ordering his contact lenses when he tells me he needs them," she says.

Of course, Jacob requires substantial accommodations in the classroom, but we can see how responsibility for managing the technology that he requires has shifted gradually from his parents to Jacob. He still prefers to ignore his deafness and to avoid seeking out others with the same issues, but he is managing his transition to independence and succeeding in his classes and social life.

Different kinds of disabilities raise different technological or logistic concerns. Diabetics need to deal with insulin pumps and testing devices. Students who have difficulty reading, because of a learning difference or low vision, may need to have access to a computer loaded with special programs, such as voice-to-text or text-to-speech software. Most colleges offer technology assistance with customary computer problems, but may not be able to troubleshoot some of the more unusual programs designed for students with disabilities, which students may have loaded on to their own laptops. These issues may differ from those of our friend Jack and his need to take his medication regularly, but the basic principles for mastering these responsibilities remains the same. Students or young working people need to understand the technology on which they rely. They need to become comfortable using it while there is still parental or teacher back-up in high school—or earlier—to help out when needed. They need to know whom to contact if there is a problem, and there needs to be someone available locally to help them in case of an emergency, especially if the technology they use is medically necessary.

---

* Technology provides important opportunities but requires understanding to be used effectively. Students with medical devices need to become accustomed to using the devices and to troubleshooting when they do not work properly, but back-up is important, especially if the device is medically necessary.

* As with medication, the process of mastering the use of technology or medical devices needs to begin gradually before the end of high school. Parents and student need to work as a team to make sure the purpose and process of the device or technology is well understood and that the student can manage the basic maintenance and use of such technology without constant parental supervision.

We have certainly not covered every possible disability or medical issue as we explore the path to handling your own medical concerns, but it is clear that most situations have some basic principles in common. Parents who begin early on to shift responsibility to their child, students who take responsibility for understanding their disability and their medical needs, and physicians who take the time to educate their patients, all contribute to a successful transition to medical independence.

Chapter 11

Keys to Competence

It's not easy to be an adult. Think about it. You need a place to live. You need to get up and dressed on your own. That means shopping, doing laundry, going to the dry cleaners. You need to figure out the weather for the day, decide if you need to wear a warm coat, take an umbrella, or otherwise be prepared to deal with Mother Nature. You need to have a job or source of income and get to work on time, bringing with you all the equipment you will need for the day. You need to eat and pay your bills. That means more shopping as well as financial knowledge and money management skills. And you will want to establish friendships and, perhaps, long-term relationships. That requires some of the most complex skills of all.

As we've looked at decisions about college and the workplace and how to manage your disability as you move beyond high school, we haven't yet focused on one important group of skills that are crucial for success as an independent and successful adult. We call this competence. It includes many of the day-to-day and long-term skills and judgments that young people need in order to succeed. Without these skills, a young person may remain dependent upon others, or limit his success, or place his health or happiness in jeopardy. Most of the areas of competence we'll discuss will be applicable to all students, not just those with disabilities, but we'll make mention of when having a disability has a special impact on one of these important sets of skills.

Sleep

Let's start with something basic. Getting regular and sufficient sleep is something doctors like to call "sleep hygiene."[1] We recognize that young people have busy lives and that in some social situations an evening will just be beginning as older adults are getting ready for bed. We also know that sleeping until early afternoon is not uncommon for college students—sometimes even on days when they have early classes. But the fact remains that studies show that insufficient sleep, even getting as much as four to six hours of sleep a night for a couple of weeks, has a marked impact on cognitive functions—just the functions that college students need the most, particularly at exam times. What's even more critical is that these sleep-deprived individuals don't generally realize that they are affected by lack of sleep. They just think and reason poorly without necessarily connecting their diminished performance to sleep deprivation.[2]

In addition to general poor functioning, certain mental illnesses, particularly bipolar disorder, are impacted by failure to get regular and sufficient sleep. As a psychiatrist specializing in bipolar disorder notes, "The relationship between sleep and bipolar disorder is twofold: BD causes sleep disturbances, and sleep disturbances can destabilize BD."[3] Individuals who take medication to help with mental illnesses or for attention issues may find that the medications impact sleep, either by making it difficult to fall asleep or by making them sleepy during the day. Asking "How will this affect my sleep or my level of alertness?" is important each time you are prescribed a new medication or substantially change the dosage of a medication you have been taking.

One step towards adulthood is recognizing the importance of adequate sleep and taking steps to make sure you get sufficient and regular sleep. That may sometimes mean turning in before the party has ended, because you have an early class. It may mean not registering for early classes and sleeping until mid-morning most days, because you like to stay up late. For a young adult in the workplace, it may mean seeking or avoiding a particular work schedule because of the way it will impact your sleep schedule. It may mean a frank conversation with your roommate about noise and light at night. There is no one perfect amount of sleep or one best way to make sure that you get it regularly. What is key to this area of competence is giving it priority, even when it would be more fun to ignore it.

---

* Understanding the importance of sufficient sleep is an important step towards adulthood.

* Even minor sleep deprivation, over a period of time, can affect thinking and learning. This can happen even when you don't feel tired.

Traveling

Some young people want to be able to travel around the world. Others would be happy being able to get around their home town. Different temperaments, and levels of disability can all affect a young person's travel goals. But whatever they may be, mastering them is an important step to independence and adulthood.

In many areas outside of large cities, driving is a crucial skill for getting from one place to another. For some individuals with visual impairments, seizure disorders, or cognitive or anxiety disorders, driving may not be an option. For individuals with most other disabilities, learning to drive may take some time, and may require technology or vehicle modifications, but can eventually be accomplished. We've seen in Chapter 9 on work issues that State Vocational Rehabilitation Programs will sometimes assist individuals with disabilities to learn to drive when this is necessary for them to work or attend school. Families need to start the learning process early, and stick with it, realizing that just because a young person can pass the state road test doesn't mean he is ready to drive. We know of a number of families that required their children to take a second road test after they passed the state version. Mom's road test was far more rigorous and took place over the course of several weeks. Only when Mom was satisfied that her teenager was ready did he get access to a car. We've included information on how to find driving instruction and safety issues for young drivers in our Resources chapter.

Other kinds of travel competence are also important for independence. Starting in early elementary school, students need to be guided in the use of all forms of public transportation. Whether it is an airport security line, an interstate train, or a local subway system, early and consistent familiarity is the best way to develop the competence with travel that all young people, including those with disabilities, will need for independence. Individuals with impaired mobility, whether they use a wheelchair or walk with difficulty, need to be aware of physical obstacles that can be a barrier to their travel. Even though the Americans with Disabilities Act (ADA) requires that public places be made accessible,[4] the truth is that the law and the reality are not always in sync. It may make sense to have someone assist you with reconnaissance before traveling an unfamiliar route.

Sometimes it's the things you haven't considered that will cause problems. Justin has learning disabilities that include difficulty with spatial awareness. He attended a secondary school for students with learning disabilities located in a nearby city and was transported back and forth to his home in one of those little yellow school buses that has become a much vilified symbol for some students with disabilities.[5] Like many city schools, Justin's high school did not have a formal cafeteria, and students were permitted to go to nearby food shops to pick up lunch and bring it back to eat at their desks. All was well until the day when Justin got tired of the local fare and decided to walk a couple of blocks further than usual to see if he could find a more interesting lunch. He bought a sandwich at a shop he hadn't seen before, but quickly realized that he couldn't find his way back to school. He went one street this way and another street that way and ended up even more confused than before. He finally called his mom at her office and wailed, "I'm lost!" The story ended with someone from the school locating Justin and walking him back the few short blocks to the school building. Justin put the school telephone number into his cell phone and his teachers made a point of walking him out to lunch for the next few weeks, until he was comfortable with the entire neighborhood. Justin is in college now, and still has difficulties with spatial orientation, but he has learned to pay closer attention when he is in unfamiliar places and to identify landmarks that can help him find his way.

---

* Being able to travel independently can open up the world to any young person, particularly one with disabilities. Different individuals will have different travel needs, but starting early, with parental guidance, is the best route to travel independence.

* Driving may be a difficult skill for some young people to master. Parents need to be sure their child is truly ready to drive before handing over the car keys.

Organization: Time

Another important area of competence is the need to organize your time and your responsibilities. The existence of innumerable personal organizers in paper formats and in phone and email applications makes it clear that this is not an uncommon problem. But for some individuals, organization of time and tasks is particularly difficult.

Martin struggled with learning and attention difficulties, but both he and his parents felt that the biggest obstacle to his success after high school was going to be his lack of something that psychologists call executive function skills. Executive function is a complex symphony of brain activities responsible for the "project management" parts of school and life. Generally, successful completion of any complex project requires the ability to break the project into a series of discrete steps, developing a plan for completing each step, and then executing the plan. Students whose executive function is not fully developed typically have trouble creating or executing a step-wise plan. Martin's difficulty with executive function made it difficult for him to organize time and space, to move from step to step or task to task without forgetting what he had already done or what should come next, and generally to plan and stage his daily activities. Throughout high school Martin had trouble with things like getting out of the house on time, remembering his belongings, meeting assignment deadlines, and planning for social activities. He lost so many cell phones that his parents collected old phones from friends and relatives who used the same cell phone carrier and arranged to transfer his cell phone number to a new phone each time one disappeared. His alarm clock would be ringing and he'd still be in bed 20 minutes later, so his mom would bang on the kitchen ceiling with a broom, to rouse Martin in his bedroom just above. He grew a beard in his senior year of high school because it was just too complicated to try to find time to shave. But, worst of all, Martin would lose schoolwork, forget assignments, and when he did homework he would not hand it in on time. Although he graduated high school with a regular diploma, his grades suffered significantly from the credit he has lost due to late or missing assignments.

Martin and his parents decided that he wasn't ready to move on to college immediately and that he needed time to remain at home and improve his skills. When we last spoke to Martin's mom, she told us that he had tried and lost one job, in a fast-paced restaurant. She added that after losing his restaurant job he had agreed to put in place some helpful tools that were enabling him to handle his schedule better. He was less likely to forget important obligations, had taken a job at a local department store, and was considering attending a local community college part time.

When we spoke to Martin to discuss what tools were helping him, he told us that there were three primary things that were improving management of his schedule. The first was a large whiteboard in the kitchen of his home, with a bunch of different colored markers and an eraser. When Martin needed to be somewhere at a particular time, he'd figure out the day before when he'd need to leave the house and would write down his departure time and a list of the things he'd need to bring on the whiteboard. He made a point of checking the whiteboard every morning and then updating it in the evening. So, on a day when he needed to take a train into a nearby city to see a doctor, he'd check the train schedule from his suburban home the night before, and write down, "Leave at 10:10 for 10:30 train. See Dr. at 11:30. Bring check." Because the whiteboard was in a public area of the house, Martin's parents and brothers could see it too and, when needed, would give him a reminder. "Look," Martin said, "I still sometimes screw up, and I know that I should be more organized, but at least this way I get out of the house in time for important stuff."

Another tool that was proving helpful to Martin was a large calendar in his room, where he wrote down deadlines and dates. He transferred these each day from a smaller calendar he kept in his backpack (which he took everywhere) and the fact that appointments and other time-sensitive matters were staring down at him whenever he was in his room helped him keep them in mind.

Finally, Martin got a watch with an alarm. He set it to go off (in a silent vibrate mode) in time for him to leave the house and at times he had to take his attention medication. Like his other tools for managing his time and schedule, it wasn't foolproof, but all of the devices together clearly helped him improve his ability to get through his day. It is still not clear how Martin will manage in the future, but his steps to overcome his difficulties give us cause for optimism.

Martin's difficulties with executive function are pretty severe and you may not need so many tools to manage your schedule. You may want to stick with the newest technology, or you may prefer old-fashioned tools such as lists and calendars. Sometimes trial and error is the only way to know what works for you. We've listed some good starting points for time-management issues in our Resources chapter.

---

* Young people who struggle with time management can use a variety of tools to help themselves manage appointments, assignments, and medication. These can include simple devices, such as whiteboards and calendars, or more high-tech items such as electronic organizers, multi-function cell phones, or computer programs. Trial and error may be the best way to decide what works for you.

Organization: Where's my stuff?

Another aspect of poor executive function is keeping track of belongings. This can also be an issue for young people with attention difficulties. Maybe you tend to lose items, like Martin and his cell phone. Or maybe you live in a messy room or house that seems to make important papers and objects disappear into some mysterious black hole. Maybe you have a poor memory and simply can't remember where you put things. Whatever the cause, keeping track of belongings is a problem that most people face to some degree. Competent adults are able to keep this problem to a minimum by using some helpful techniques.

Being successful at keeping track of things will also help you keep track of time and stay on schedule. If you can't locate the items you need, you will have to spend time looking for them. That can upset your carefully planned departure. Tyler was a student who came to us with his parents for advice on what college might be a good match for him. We discussed his hearing impairment and talked about the accommodations he would need and where he would fit in academically. As our meeting was winding down, Tyler's mother commented, "You know, I am worried that most of the schools we are talking about are campus-based." She turned to her son. "Tyler, you are so disorganized I just don't know how you are going to manage living in a dorm room. I'm really worried that you won't be able to keep track of your stuff." Tyler just shrugged his shoulders, but we ended up extending our conversation and spoke about some of the techniques we have seen students—and others—use successfully to keep track of the many objects that are part of their lives.

One of these techniques is to create a daily "launching pad," a chair or shelf or other place that exists only to hold those things—clothing, books, papers, and electronics—that you will need to take with you when you next leave your room or home. We know space can be tight in a dorm, so you may need to be creative and perhaps use something you hang from the back of a door or on a wall. But the concept remains the same. Every item you will need for the next day is placed on the launching pad when you complete it or remove it. So, your shoes will be placed there when you take them off. Your class assignments for the next day's classes will be placed there (in a "work to hand in" folder) once they are completed. So will your phone, keys, and other stuff that generally goes in your pockets. It's not a perfect system, but it definitely helps.

A similar process can be extremely helpful for those young people who have trouble deciding what to wear each morning. We know that some students grab the closest pair of jeans and a t-shirt (clean or not) off of their floor. Others (and you know who you are!) may look casually dressed, but can try on and discard several items before they get the properly casual look they are seeking. This can take time on a busy morning and is best done the night before. So, if you care what you wear, make a practice of setting out your clothes before you climb into bed each evening.

Another basic method for keeping track of things is the lump check. This was described to us by a professor who admits that he has organizational difficulties. "Every morning, before I leave my house," he explained, "I pat my pockets, checking to see that I have all my lumps—my wallet, my cell phone, my keys, my glasses. And I do it every time I move from one place to another: my office, my car, a lecture hall. If I'm missing one of my lumps, then I know I need to check the place I'm in, since I had it when I got here." This may not work well for those who carry a purse or backpack, but if you rely on your pockets to carry your stuff, it can be extremely helpful.

For students who struggle with organization, managing papers and assignments can seem overwhelming. High-tech and low-tech solutions can be used separately or together to help with these processes. We suggest to students that even in a messy room there can be one or two places where important papers and school items are kept organized. A large open file box, with a folder for each class, can keep handouts, assignments, and other important papers for each class in one place for the entire semester. Make sure you have one folder marked "work to hand in" that you place on the launching pad before you go to sleep. The equivalent of this system can be used with a computer; dedicated folders on your computer desktop for each class can keep course materials in one place. If a professor wants papers or tests submitted in electronic format, this system will keep a copy of everything sent and received in one place, along with a record of when and where it was sent. Of course, every computer user knows the importance of backing up files, but sometimes this gets put off in the rush to get a document completed. If you don't back up your electronic data each and every time you complete a work session, you will eventually run into trouble. And since multi-gig back-up devices are relatively inexpensive and can be carried on a key chain, we urge you to use more than one portable back-up device, perhaps one you carry with you and one you keep in a desk drawer, alternating between the two so that even if you lose your portable back-up device, you will have fairly recent back-up from your other data storage device. You can also email something to yourself so that it will be preserved on the email server, which creates a time-stamped record of what the file is and where it is from. It also allows you to access the file from other computers, no matter what may happen to your computer or where you may be. We include some resources for organization and paper management in our Resources chapter, but realize that the solutions to organizational problems will differ for each individual. What is important is the realization that part of becoming an adult is coming up with systems that enable you to manage your schedule and belongings in a way that makes it possible for you to meet your daily and long-term responsibilities.

* An important step towards adult competence is learning to keep track of belongings. This will also help manage time and schedules, since time won't be wasted looking for missing items.

* Techniques such as a launching pad, dedicated folders for each class, and a regular lump check may help young people have the daily items they need to succeed. No matter what system works for you, don't forget to back up all electronic information!

Other competencies

Before we move on to some of the more complicated areas that most young people will encounter on the road to adulthood—drinking, drugs, social interactions, and sex—we want to make sure to remind you to take a look at our chapters that deal with medical management (Chapter 10) and money matters (Chapter 13). We haven't included the material in these chapters in this discussion of key competencies, not because they aren't important, but because they are so vital that they each merit their own chapter.

Alcohol

For some young people, alcohol use is not really a concern. They may or may not drink, but it is not a big deal for them and they don't give the subject a lot of thought. For others, drinking is the focus of their social life and the idea of going out on a weekend or attending a college party without some serious drinking is almost unthinkable. Whichever group best describes you (or your student), it is fair to say that drinking is a major issue on many college campuses. It is also an issue that can be particularly complicated for individuals with a variety of disabilities.

Let's start with the simple part. Alcohol and cars don't mix. That means any amount of drinking and it means more than not driving. It also means not getting into a car, even for a short drive home, with anyone who may have been drinking. Whether or not you abstain from alcohol, it won't do you any good if you are in a car with a driver who is impaired.

If you are taking medication of any kind, whether for a disability or a temporary health condition, alcohol can impact the effectiveness of the medication or can interact with the medication to create an unanticipated level of impairment. Some disabilities, including inflammatory bowel disease, depression, and certain forms of mental illness, can themselves be affected by alcohol. We'll discuss the issue of self-medicating in the following section, but whether we are talking about pills or liquor, students with disabilities such as depression, bipolar disorder, and other psychiatric difficulties may sometimes seek relief from their emotional state by drinking or taking illicit drugs.

There are also the legal aspects of drinking to consider. Although the legal drinking age is set by states, there is a federal law linked to highway funding that makes it costly for states to permit anyone under age 21 to drink in most circumstances (with certain exceptions that permit alcohol consumption for religious reasons or with parents).[6] This creates a two-tier system in most colleges: Younger students are legally prohibited from drinking, but older students, those over 21, can legally consume alcohol. Some schools deal with this by banning alcohol on campus, and some go even further and prohibit their students of any age from drinking on or off campus, at the risk of school disciplinary action. Many other schools require organizers of events or parties where alcohol will be served to register with a specific campus office and to check the identification of all students attending. Those who are of legal drinking age get wristbands which are then checked by those who are actually serving the alcoholic beverages. No wristband, no drink.

So what decisions do students and their families need to consider when dealing with the issue of alcohol on campus? First, students with disabilities need to understand the impact of alcohol on their medication and on their disability. We talk about some aspects of this in the previous chapter, and this is really just another component of understanding both your medication and your medical or emotional condition. Next, students and their families need to investigate the campus atmosphere and determine if the school social world revolves around alcohol or if drinking is limited to a few students and a few situations. Your campus visit might be a good time to explore this. You may want to decide if an alcohol-free campus, or perhaps a dorm in a substance-free building, might be desirable. If that is the case, make this a priority when deciding where to apply.

What about students who are alcoholics? Although being an alcoholic is a disability that can be covered under the Americans with Disabilities Act, the ADA also requires that the disability interfere with [AQ]a major life function. This may prove an insurmountable burden for a student who meets the qualifications for acceptance at a college; it may then be difficult or impossible to make the argument that you are unable to function as a student. A similar situation arose for George Bailey (his real name), an employee who lost his job with the Georgia Pacific Corporation when he was incarcerated, even though his employer had been willing to provide work release for other employees who had been jailed. Bailey sued, claiming that he was the victim of discrimination under the ADA. The appellate court agreed that Bailey was disabled because he was an alcoholic, but denied him any recovery because they determined that his condition did not interfere with his ability to function as a worker.[7] Students or young working adults who are alcoholics, who suspect they may be alcoholics, or who are dealing with alcoholic friends or relatives may want to seek help from support groups such as Alcoholics Anonymous[8] or Al-Anon.[9]

Both parents and young people need to also be aware of the risks involved in serving alcohol to minors. Some municipalities have "social host" laws which create criminal responsibility whenever a homeowner serves underage drinkers. These laws vary and some can create liability even if parents are unaware that their teenager is serving alcohol to friends. Even where criminal responsibility is not involved, those serving alcohol to minors or to someone who is clearly inebriated can be liable for civil damages. Leo and Sherry considered themselves very responsible parents and made the decision to spend New Year's Eve at home to keep an eye on their son Evan's party. Evan and his friends were students at out-of-town colleges and were getting together while they were home for vacation. As the students arrived, Sherry reminded them that they were welcome to sleep over, and that they absolutely could not drive if they were planning to drink. As far as Leo and Sherry were aware, all of Evan's friends were 21 or older. While the college students partied downstairs, Leo and Sherry kept a low profile in the living room, and they eventually headed up to bed not long after midnight. They were astonished when they received a call on the morning of January 1, from a very angry father of a high school student who had dropped by at the party long after Leo and Sherry went to sleep. The college group knew him from high school and didn't really watch him carefully. He had way too much to drink and after he walked home his parents discovered him passed out on the floor of his bedroom. He had no ill effects except for a major headache, but his father was understandably upset that his son was allowed to have access to alcohol. Putting aside all other issues of responsibility (of the high school student, his own parents, and the college group that let him in and then failed to supervise him), Leo and Sherry were mortified and just grateful that there was no worse result than a hangover.

---

* Alcohol can be a major issue on some college campuses and for some students. Determining the nature of campus social life at a particular school is important for those concerned about drinking in college. There are support groups for students who are having difficulties with their own drinking or with friends or family members who may be alcoholics.

* Drinking can interfere with some medications and can cause complications of some health difficulties. This is a particular issue for students with disabilities, who need to be aware of whether it is safe for them to drink at all.

* Drinking and driving is always unsafe. Even students who don't drink need to make sure that they don't get into a car with a driver who has been drinking.

Drugs

It would be easier to discuss this subject if we could draw a clear distinction between drugs used to treat medical conditions, which we could then call medications, and drugs used (or abused) for recreation, which we could refer to as illicit or illegal drugs. The problem is that the same pill can belong to both categories, depending upon who is using it, how they obtained it, and why they are taking it. For example, students with attention issues are often prescribed Ritalin or other drugs that are also used, illegally, by students without attention issues to enhance their focus.

So, we need to come up with a better system of classification. We'll start by looking at a drug that is prescribed by a physician and used by the individual for whom it was prescribed in the way his doctor intended for it to be used. We can all probably agree that this would be a *medication*. Any other drug, whether it was prescribed to the individual who uses it but is used in an unintended way, whether it is used by someone else, or whether it is something that cannot be legally prescribed (heroin, cocaine, and, in most states, marijuana), we'll refer to as a *drug*.

We discuss competence in relation to medication in Chapter 10, which deals with medical management, but one topic we don't get into there is keeping your medication secure from others. Depending upon the kinds of medication a student will keep in his dorm room, he may want to consider some sort of locked area—even as simple as the locked drawer of a desk, to keep his medication out of the wrong hands. This will clearly be more of an issue for someone who takes medications that are also commonly abused, such as some prescribed for attention difficulties, pain, and psychiatric disorders.

Another form of competence for students and young working individuals with disabilities is to understand that using drugs (and here we mean the illicit or recreational kind) can have a significant impact on their medical condition and interact with their prescribed medications. This is part of what we discuss in Chapter 10 about understanding your medications, how they work, and what side effects they may have. Don't mix them with drugs. It's difficult enough managing a disability; let's try not to complicate matters.

One reason that drugs and medications are used, whether illegally or as prescribed by a physician, is that they can diminish uncomfortable symptoms or feelings. Anxiety, stress, and social inhibitions (even helpful ones that prevent foolish decisions) can sometimes be reduced by taking prescribed medication or by drinking or using illicit drugs. Some individuals use these substances without medical prescriptions or a doctor's advice in an effort to self-medicate, to try to make themselves feel better or be more comfortable in a particular situation. We aren't preaching. We can appreciate the enjoyment of a glass of wine at the end of a rough day or at a party. Our goal is to make both young people and parents aware of the issues involved when individuals self-medicate—

whether it is done with alcohol, prescription drugs used in unintended ways, or illicit drugs—and to suggest that it should be a topic of discussion by the time a student is in high school, or even earlier.

It's sometimes difficult for parents who used drugs when they were in college to be comfortable counseling their own college-aged offspring to avoid illegal drugs. We suggest you be direct and honest. You don't have to go into details about every party you attended where drugs were offered. You do have to admit that using drugs wasn't the best decision you made and that it may have impacted your schoolwork. You probably have true stories to share about someone you know who moved on to harder drugs, or who died from a drug overdose. You may not be able to be there every time your child is faced with a decision about using drugs, but if you keep the conversation going, starting long before he goes off to college, he will at least have your words of admonition in his head as he makes a decision.

---

* Because it is common for young people with disabilities to use prescription medications, it is important to understand that when prescribed drugs are used by someone other than the intended patient, or by the patient in unintended ways, their use is inappropriate and illegal.

* Physical or emotional pain, stress, or anxiety can be reasons individuals self-medicate with drugs or alcohol. Families should discuss this subject together so that young people gain an understanding of this issue.

* Parents who used drugs when they were younger may be uncomfortable counseling their child. Get over it! You do not need to go into detail, but you should be honest when you are asked if you ever used drugs, and explain why you don't think it is a good choice for your child to make.

Friendships

Parents often ask us what they can do to help their child—from youngster to young adult—make friends. Most young people with disabilities have no difficulty making and keeping friends. They have the same social issues as do others of the same age without disabilities and need no help from parents or anyone else in handling relationships. For some young people, however, the nature of their disability makes establishing and maintaining relationships with classmates, colleagues—indeed, with anyone—a real struggle.

Autism spectrum disorders (including Asperger's syndrome), attention difficulties, and some learning disabilities, especially those in nonverbal areas, can impact the ability to recognize or focus on social cues or to understand some of the verbal banter that so often occurs when friends are together. Young people who just can't get their act together to keep social appointments or who may be lax in personal hygiene, perhaps because they don't always find the time to shower or change clothes, can also find it hard to make friends.

This is one of those areas where the earlier families begin to work on an issue, the more they can do to help with it in the long run. Although parents of a 20-year-old have very limited opportunities to help him make friends, parents of a young adolescent may help him increase his social awareness by enrolling him in a therapeutic group designed to build social skills. We include some suggestions for locating this kind of group in our Resources chapter. Parents can also help by encouraging young people of any age to pursue their interests with others. Collecting, athletics, or the arts are all areas where an individual who may struggle with social situations can meet others. Conversation about shared interests can be a good way to start a friendship.

Another helpful resource may be under your own roof. Siblings (or cousins, or offspring of close family friends) can help create social opportunities for a young person who struggles with social competence. They can also serve as a sounding board and provide advice on everything from etiquette at college events to what to say to a girl (or guy) in ways that parents are just not able.

This is a tough area to navigate, but although parents need to keep their role limited once a young person is about to move on from high school, they can still help by fostering opportunities for their child to meet his peers and preserving positive social interactions within the family.

* For those individuals whose disabilities make it difficult for them to make or keep friends, siblings can be a good source of guidance and support.

* Although parents will have a limited role in helping young adults make friends, it can be helpful to encourage encounters with other young people who share similar interests.

Sexuality

Sex is undoubtedly the most sensitive of topics, one that every young adult thinks about much of the time and, according to the young men with whom we have spoken, possibly all of the time. Religious views, family background, and the type and extent of an individual's disability will all be factors in determining when a young person decides he is ready to become sexually active. We have one additional consideration to add. In fact, we view it as an ironclad rule: you are not ready for sexual activity unless and until you use a condom each and every time you have sex. Let's be clear. We don't mean having a condom in your purse or wallet. We mean knowing how a condom works, having a decent quality condom with you before you consider sexual activity, and using the condom properly every single time you have sex. That includes being able to do this in unexpected situations, with an inexperienced or fumbling partner, and when you are hot and bothered and not thinking clearly. If you can't do this, then you lack the judgment and maturity to be sexually active. Period. Some high schools have extensive sex education programs that include learning about all forms of birth control. Other schools have a more perfunctory health curriculum. Families should make a point of discussing their values and how those values are to be applied in real-life situations. Parents should become knowledgable about what is taught in health courses and make sure that they educate their child about any information that has not been fully covered. And if that means buying a condom and a cucumber to help your teenager practice, that's part of the process. It's not as embarrassing as an unplanned pregnancy, a sexually transmitted disease, or being exposed to HIV.

Using a condom does not mean that a sexually active young woman may not also decide to use a form of birth control such as the pill, as additional protection against unintended pregnancy. But only abstinence or a condom will protect against sexually transmitted diseases.

While we're on this subject, let's finish the lecture with a particular point for our male readers. If your partner is unable or unwilling to consent to a sexual encounter, it's time to stop. You may have heard of some colleges that instruct their students to seek and be given consent for each step forward in an encounter that can end in sexual intercourse. That has always seemed a bit unrealistic to us. But a partner who has had too much to drink to make a sound decision, or one who has a change of heart at *any* point along the way, cannot be considered a willing partner and you need to stop in your tracks, no matter how difficult that may be, and end the encounter.

So far we've discussed sexual situations that are relevant to all students. But there are special concerns that some students with disabilities need to consider. Students with serious allergies can be at risk if their partners have eaten the allergen before kissing them. A well-publicized case in Canada, where a teenage girl with a serious peanut allergy died after her boyfriend had eaten peanut butter several hours earlier, is an extreme example of this concern. Still, students with allergies should make sure their friends and partners not only know about their allergies but also what to do in case of emergencies and where they keep their EpiPen.

Another concern that some young people with disabilities may face is discomfort with some of the very personal aspects of certain disabilities. This can have an impact not only on dating and social relationships, but on living with other students in a dorm. Even minor medical or physical issues—the need to take medication for acne, for example, or the growth hormone shots that need to be stored in the refrigerator—which don't necessarily rise to the level of a disability, are difficult to keep private or personal in the close quarters of shared dorm rooms and communal bathrooms, sometimes on floors that house both men and women.

Other issues can be more complicated. A student who has undergone ostomy surgery as a result of inflammatory bowel disease will generally have an absorbent pad or a pouch to collect bowel material. A student with this condition may decide to request a private bathroom or single room as an accommodation under the ADA. This may deal with his general privacy concerns, but it won't help make him more comfortable with discussing his ostomy with someone with whom he is beginning a dating relationship. As we suggest in other chapters, students and young working people need to become comfortable with their own disabilities and the social issues these disabilities may affect. There are numerous websites that we list in our Resources chapter that offer support for individuals with specific disabilities and give young people a chance to raise questions with others who have similar concerns. Being comfortable with yourself is key to managing the social world of college with a disability.

---

* Dealing with sexual issues is one of the most adult of competencies. Judgment and maturity are important aspects of dealing with sexual relationships, and families need to begin as early as possible to make sure young people understand the issues involved in becoming sexually active.

* If you ever feel uncomfortable or don't wish to continue with sexual activity—even if you've already started—you have the right to change your mind at any time.

* Young people with certain disabilities may be uncomfortable sharing details about their condition when they begin a dating relationship. It is important for young people to become comfortable with their disability. Support groups and websites where other young people with similar conditions can share their experiences and concerns may be helpful.

The developing brain

One thing that parents and students should remember when considering everything from poor organizational skills to risky behaviors is that the brain of a teenager is still developing. Recent research in brain development indicates that the prefrontal cortex and the cerebellum, both of which play a part in executive function, go through major developmental changes through adolescence and beyond.[10] Some young people, with and without diagnosed mental illnesses or other disorders that may cause impulsive behavior, can exhibit poor judgment that might put their lives at risk. Others simply don't yet have their act together as students, workers, or social individuals. It's important for young people and their parents to understand that recent high school graduates are still works in progress, and that sometimes just the passage of time and the additional brain development that comes with it will be enough to greatly improve a young person's judgment and maturity.

---

* The brain of a young adult is still changing. Some difficulties with judgment and maturity may resolve with the passage of time. Young people should work on their skills, but should have reason for optimism that these will develop as key areas of their brain mature.

"Wait a minute!" we can hear parents complain. "You tell us that things may get better over time, but you haven't dealt with my kid's issue with partying, or showering, or gambling, or laziness, or whatever it is that drives parents crazy and keeps young people from maximizing their success." The truth is that there are lots of things that make someone a competent adult, and the list of ways in which young people can sabotage their own success is a long one. But as parents and young people look through this chapter, we hope that you see that each area of competence has a few things in common: Awareness of the skills needed, guidance from parents from an early age about what is expected, and the opportunity for young people to communicate with others who face similar issues to gain ease and confidence about their disability.

Chapter 12

Pulling it All Together

It's a fine Saturday morning in the spring of your senior year of high school. The sun is shining, the birds are singing, and you're relaxing. You don't have a care in the world now that you've received your college acceptances, decided which school you'll attend, and sent in your enrollment deposit. You smile, realizing that you could get used to taking it easy like this. Without the college application process hanging over your head, there's nothing to worry about until college begins in the fall. If you're the parent of the student in this scenario, maybe you're sleeping in on this beautiful weekend morning. The question of where your child will go to college next year has been decided, and you've gotten a restful night's sleep for the first time in as long as you can remember. You're happy not to have to think about college until your child starts to pack.

Not to burst your bubble, but you're not done yet. You seem to have forgotten about a few things that need to be taken care of before classes begin. Students have some more work to do, and Mom and Dad may not want to relax just yet.

The summer before freshman year is a key time to request the accommodations you'll need to manage successfully in college. Often, this process is straightforward, but sometimes there are curves and bumps in the road that you never expected. Some of these obstacles may be due to the particular policies of the college you will be attending. Other snags may be created by the Disability Services administrator at that school or may simply be the nature of the beast that is the accommodation process. It's imperative to give yourself enough time before school begins to get your accommodations in place. You'll also want to bone up on your self-advocacy skills. If you have mastered these skills, or are on your way to mastering them, you will have a great advantage in setting up your accommodations with your professors and the Office of Disability Services. As we'll discuss later on in this chapter, these skills can make or break your success in college. Buckle up; here we go!

The accommodation request process

As you may remember from our earlier discussions of how the disability accommodation process works, each college is required by the Americans with Disabilities Act (ADA) to have at least one person in charge of coordinating accommodations for students with disabilities. This person is usually the Director of Disability Services, but we've visited colleges where the person in charge of accommodations wears many different hats and may carry the title of Dean of Student Affairs, Vice-President of Student Services, or University Compliance Officer. It is not always crystal clear who the go-to person is, but it's the responsibility of the student to do the necessary research to find out. The student handbook and website will generally list the name of this administrator and how to contact her.

Once you have sent in your enrollment deposit to the college you have decided to attend, contact the administrator in charge of accommodations and explain that you'd like to set up a meeting. This is your first step towards formally disclosing your disability to the college. This official disclosure needs to happen before your freshman year classes begin in the fall and, ideally, should happen during the summer before you arrive on campus. It doesn't matter that you may have already mentioned to an admissions officer that you have a disability, or even that you wrote your college essay on your experiences living with your disability, because once you enroll at the college it is your responsibility to present yourself officially as a person with a disability and request accommodations at that time.

In advance of the meeting, the Office of Disability Services will likely want you to send them a copy of your disability documentation, which you may remember we discussed in some detail in Chapter 4. You may be wondering what will take place at the meeting. Do you need to prepare? We suggest that you read your disability documentation, if you have not already done so, and have a conversation with your parents about it. You want to understand your disability and be able to articulate how you learn best. Know what accommodations you'll need in order to be successful in college and why you need them.

At your meeting, the Disability Services Director may ask how your disability impacts your ability to learn. You want to be able to respond in a knowledgable manner. Your responses will help the administrator determine how the college can best level the playing field and give you access to education. You will most likely also need to fill out a few forms. These forms may request that your contact information, as well as your schedule of classes for the current semester, be shared with the Office of Disability Services. The meeting may also include a discussion of general information about the Office of Disability Services and its policies on such issues as letters to professors, note-taking, and proctoring exams. We'll discuss these in more detail later in this chapter. The administrator should also explain to you that you'll need to return to the Office of Disability Services each semester to request accommodations for your new classes.

Due to confidentiality laws such as FERPA, which we discussed in Chapter 1, parents are often not invited to participate in the student's intake meeting with the Office of Disability Services. Parents can be most helpful by understanding that this is an important step towards the student becoming an independent adult. They can help their child prepare for her meeting by making sure that she knows what her disability is and what her strengths and challenges may be. This is yet another reason for students to have mastered the ability to speak up for themselves and be confident in who they are. Their self-advocacy skills will definitely come into play here.

---

* The person in charge of accommodations may wear many different hats and have various titles at different colleges. It is not always crystal clear who the go-to person is, but students will need to do the research to find out.

* After sending in your enrollment deposit, set up a meeting to request accommodations. This is your first step towards formally disclosing your disability to the university. Do this before your freshman year classes begin, ideally during the

summer. Mentioning your disability in your application or to the Admissions Office is not a formal disclosure for these purposes.

* Read your disability documentation and have a conversation with your parents about it. As a student, you need to understand your disability and be able to articulate how you learn best. Know what accommodations you'll need to be successful in college and why you need them.

* Parents are often not invited to participate in the student's intake meeting with the Office of Disability Services.

Students enrolling in a Learning Disabilities program

If you applied to and were accepted into a Learning Disabilities (LD) program, which we discussed in Chapter 7, the accommodation request process may work a bit differently for you than for students with disabilities who will not be participating in such a separate program. Your accommodations will likely be set up directly by the LD program, rather than the Office of Disability Services. This is a more streamlined approach than if you were to go to numerous different offices to secure your accommodations each semester.

Many LD programs require participating students to attend a summer orientation program before freshman year. This will often be a two-week structured experience where students live on campus and get a headstart on classes. You will likely get to move into your dorm room early so that you can get set up and become acclimated before the majority of students return to campus. It may also be during this summer experience that you and the LD program administrator discuss your accommodations and put them in place for the semester.

* If you'll be participating in an LD program, your accommodations will likely be set up directly by this program and its personnel, for a more streamlined approach.

* Many LD programs have a required summer program for participating students. This allows you to set up accommodations and get settled on campus early.

The most important step to success

The single most important skill that will enable students to have a smooth transition to college and a successful academic experience is being a good self-advocate. We can spot a kid who lacks this skill from a mile away. What is a good self-advocate, you ask? Let's look at two different students to help answer that question.

Ethan entered our office, with his mom, at the start of his freshman year of college. Head low, eyes down, he extended his hand and mumbled a hello. Through most of the meeting it was his mom who talked for him. Even when we asked him a direct question, he had a hard time giving more than a one- or two-word response. There are disabilities which may cause these traits—a lack of social skills due to Asperger's, or lack of emotional affect due to depression—but Ethan had a learning disability, not one of these other conditions. We are willing to bet Ethan's lack of advocacy skills came from his lack of self-confidence, his inability to see himself apart from his disability, and embarrassment about having a disability.

We had the opportunity to learn about Jane, a graduate of a very competitive college, from our colleagues in the Office of Disability Services. Jane made her first appearance at the Office of Disability Services early in the semester of her freshman year but was not pleased with how her meeting with the Assistant Director had gone. She followed up by making a call to the Director of Disability Services and, as a result, was invited to a second meeting to re-evaluate her accommodations. Jane had a chance to explain her concerns and ended up receiving the accommodations she requested. We admire Jane's ability to speak up and advocate for her needs. She went on to have a very successful college career and graduated with honors. Jane interned in Washington DC and is now working on Capitol Hill.

From these two stories we can gather that a good self-advocate is someone who is motivated, confident, and not afraid to ask for help or clarification. Jane clearly had all of these attributes and skills. Ethan, on the other had, seemed to have none of them. In our work with students with disabilities who are about to make the transition from high school to college, we can usually predict the likelihood of their success in college within the first five minutes of meeting them. What do we mean by success? From our perspective, a successful student is one who will be happy, will achieve academically (or at least hold her head above water), and who will graduate with a degree. Being a good self-advocate is the difference and the key to success for a student with a disability.

If you are like Ethan, or have a child like Ethan, it's important to realize that self-advocacy skills can be learned, even late in the game. We highlight some of these skills in our discussion of the transition process in Chapter 2, but they are so important that we'll take a moment to remind you about them here. We strongly suggest that as early as possible, and when developmentally appropriate, students with services under the Individuals with Disabilities Education Act (IDEA) should attend a triennial or annual review meeting. Those who receive services under Section 504 (remember these two key laws from Chapter 1?) should attend the meetings of their 504 team. Yes, it can be intimidating for an adult, let alone a teenager, to be sitting around a big table with numerous professionals who are all talking about you, but this is an important step. Maybe by the second or third meeting a student attends, she'll feel comfortable participating and adding in her two cents. After all, this is about her and her future! Has she read her IEP, 504 plan, and psychoeducational testing report? Does she understand what her specific disability is and how it impacts her learning or her daily activities? Does she feel comfortable speaking with her teachers about the accommodations she needs to succeed in school? Does she understand the difference between the IDEA and the ADA? Working closely, especially during the middle school and high school years, with the resource room teacher, school psychologist, guidance counselor, outside therapist, learning specialist, or educational consultant is another way for a student to improve her self-advocacy skills.

At one high school where we offered a presentation, the parents of students with disabilities told us that they had hosted an evening workshop the past January that went over quite well with parents and students alike. They invited recent graduates with disabilities, who were home for the holidays, to speak with high school students and parents about their transition to college. The evening focused on what the alumni wished they had known before heading off to college. The need for self-advocacy skills was a common theme throughout the night. The wisdom shared by the recent graduates was priceless, particularly because it came directly from the college students to their former peers.

Another important part of making students effective advocates is making them comfortable with their disabilities from a very early age. We've spoken about this before, but cannot emphasize it too strongly. Students need to be comfortable with their bodies, whether or not they differ from their peers. They need to appreciate the strengths of their minds and emotions, even if there are some areas that are difficult for them to master or control. The more a disability can be talked about in everyday conversation, as a part of daily life, the more positive it will be for a child as she grows. This approach to dealing with a disability aims to normalize what can be a difficult situation and to give a child as much control as possible over her life. Disabilities are not something to feel embarrassed about. The more a disability can be demystified, the better. Students need to define themselves not by their disability but rather as people who happen to have a disability, along with numerous talents, interests, and strengths. Embracing such a philosophy and way of being in the world builds students' confidence, which is a natural foundation for learning to be a good self-advocate. Parents need to understand this and create an environment where this attitude and the skills it fosters can thrive.

---

* The key to pulling it all together is being a good self-advocate.

* A self-advocate is motivated, confident, and not afraid to ask for help or clarification.

* An effective method to hammer home the importance of self-advocacy skills. Consider inviting recent graduates with

disabilities to speak with high school students and parents about their transition to college.

* Parents need to start the process of building confidence in their children. Students need to define themselves by their strengths and interests. They need to be comfortable with their disability but not let it define who they are.

Nuances of the accommodation process

Once you officially register with the college as a student with a disability, some schools will create your accommodation letters and mail them directly to your professors. What's an accommodation letter? It's a notice to the professor that a particular student has been approved by the college to receive one or more specific accommodations. Most colleges rely on the student to hand-deliver these letters to their professors. If this is the case, then you, as the student, must figure out the best way to get your accommodation letters to each of your professors. Unfortunately, students have been known to toss the letter casually on their professor's desk as they are exiting class. This is not the best way to impart an accommodation letter—in fact, it's a really poor idea.

We recommend finding out when your professor has office hours and then scheduling a time to meet with her. You can ask the professor directly when her office hours are, look on your class syllabus where this information is usually located, or call or email your professor. Meeting during office hours offers a quiet place to have a confidential conversation. Some professors may ask what they can do to assist you in learning the class material. Be prepared to explain how you learn best with an example, such as explaining that you learn best when you can see material set out in front of you, rather than presented orally. You can mention that a PowerPoint presentation or handout will be more effective than a straight lecture. Just as we suggested practicing for an admissions interview, we suggest enlisting a friend or family member for a role-playing exercise where she is the professor and you, obviously, are the student giving her your accommodation letter and explaining what you need to learn successfully.

The accommodation letter to the professor will not mention your specific disability because the college cannot disclose this confidential information. Some professors may ask anyway, usually not out of curiosity but to gain insight on how you learn best. So that you are not caught off guard with the question, decide before you meet with your professors if you would like to share this information. If you decide not to, you can always describe the general nature of the disability and its impact on your ability to learn, without sharing the specific diagnosis. We've included links to examples of college accommodation letters to a professor in the Resources chapter.

Many colleges offer the accommodation of note-taking for students whose disability impacts their ability to take class notes effectively. For example, a student with attention deficit hyperactivity disorder who is easily distracted may attend every class, and be motivated, but still struggle to concentrate. Despite her best efforts, she may miss some of the essential things the professor says. If note-taking is available, it may be offered a few different ways. The professor may give the student with the disability a hard copy of her own notes which she used to teach the class, or the professor may post her notes on a college-sponsored computerized data-sharing system. Another option is for the student to receive her class notes from the Office of Disability Services which has coordinated another student, in the same class, to take notes to be shared. This allows the student with the disability to remain anonymous. The student note-taker is chosen by the professor or volunteers when the professor announces to the class that a note-taker is needed. The quality of note-takers varies by college—some are trained by the Office of Disability Services on how to take good notes; others are not. Some note-takers are paid; others are unpaid volunteers. One more note-taking option is for the student with a disability to disclose her need for assistance and to choose a note-taker from her class. We find this way of receiving copies of class notes works best because the student receiving the accommodation can observe all of her classmates first and then choose the one she thinks will be the best note-taker based on that student's intellect and engagement in the class. She can also communicate directly with the note-taker telling her if she won't be in class and vice versa. This option acknowledges that there is no secretiveness necessary. Why should the person with the disability feel that she must remain anonymous? There is no reason for anyone to feel embarrassed that they have a disability and are entitled to assistance.

Another nuance of the accommodation process is understanding the exam proctoring policy at your college. This is the policy that covers how exams are administered and supervised. Not knowing the policy, or ignoring it, may result in a poor grade, even for a student who has mastered the material. We know of colleges where students have been denied their accommodations because they didn't set up proctoring in advance and, instead, have gone to the Office of Disability Services requesting accommodations for an exam to be given that same day. Arranging accommodations such as extended time and a distraction-reduced location for testing at the eleventh hour is unreasonable and a college is not required to provide them. A student in this situation is usually out of luck and must take her exam without accommodations. Proctoring policies vary based on whether proctoring is the responsibility of the Office of Disability Services, the Academic Resource Center, or the professor. Colleges usually have a proctoring form that must be filled out and signed by the student, professor, and the coordinating office on campus. Forms generally must be returned to the coordinating office at least two weeks in advance of midterms, finals, tests, and quizzes. Because proctoring policies vary from campus to campus, we recommend you find out what the policies are at your college as early as possible.

Students should also be aware that a college does not have to provide the exact accommodation that a student requests if there is another accommodation that may be more cost-effective for the college and may accomplish the same end result. The college has at least to consider the student's accommodation preference but does not have to grant it. We worked with Frank, who has a cochlear implant. He requested C-Print captioning services, a computer-aided speech-to-text service for people who are deaf or hard of hearing that produces text through abbreviated keyboard typing or voice.[1] In general, C-Print can provide a meaning-for-meaning translation of the spoken English content. Instead, the college provided Frank with note-takers and Communications Access Real Time (CART),[2] a system that provides access to spoken information for people with hearing loss by producing a text document that corresponds very closely to the words used by the speaker, similar to what a court reporter would produce. This turned out to be an effective alternative for Frank.

* If your college expects you to deliver accommodation letters to your professors, meet with your professor during office hours. Be prepared to explain how you learn best and to provide examples of the techniques that will be the most helpful for you.

* The accommodation letter to your professors will not state what your disability is, because this is confidential. Decide ahead of time how you want to discuss your disability with your professors.

* Find out about note-taking options. Consider choosing your own note-taker.

* Learn the proctoring policy. Not complying with this policy may result in a denial of your testing accommodations.

* A college does not have to provide the exact accommodation a student requests as long as they consider the student's first choice, and the college's accommodation is just as effective. Try to keep an open mind about trying something new.

Pitfalls to avoid

Some students are great about making first contact with the Office of Disability Services, but then never show their face in the office again. We urge you to be a regular. Make sure the administrators know who you are. Establish a friendly rapport with them and with the staff. If you ever need their support on an issue, you want them to know that you're a hard worker who takes her responsibilities seriously.

After you receive your accommodation letters from the Office of Disability Services, don't forget to give them to your professors. This is a common pitfall for students with disabilities. Regardless of the reason, whether you have difficulties with executive function or lack self-advocacy skills, you won't receive accommodations if the letter is not delivered.

Don't fail to follow up with your professors about your accommodations on a regular basis throughout the semester. Just because you give them an accommodation letter in the beginning of the term, don't assume they'll remember what your accommodations are and that you'll need them every time you take a test. You remember what they say about folks who assume, right? Think of it this way: You have a total of approximately five professors each semester, while they may have a few hundred students at a time. It's up to you to check in with your professors on a regular basis, either by phone, email, or in person, to make sure, well in advance of a test, that your accommodations will be in place.

Before you begin college, it is important to know that accommodations are not retroactive. A student who decides to go it on her own and not request accommodations may change her mind halfway through the semester when she realizes that she is doing very poorly academically. At that point she can request and receive the accommodations to which she would be entitled, but they will only apply going forward. A student can request accommodations at any time in the semester, but they will not be applicable to any work already completed before the accommodations were in place.

To prepare the students we work with about possible pitfalls they may encounter on the road to obtaining their accommodations, we like to play a game we call "Will these students receive accommodations?" Feel free to play along as you read the three imaginary scenarios below.

Huckleberry is a freshman at Old Twain College. In second grade he was diagnosed with a learning disability. Huckleberry submitted the proper documentation and registered with the Office of Disability Services once he was admitted to Old Twain. The day before classes began he returned to the office and picked up the accommodation letters for his professors. His accommodation letters stated that he was entitled to 1.5 times the standard administration time for tests. That night he emailed his professors his letter and spoke with them to confirm they received this letter; they indicated that they had. Before Huckleberry knew it, he had his first midterm exam scheduled—The History of River Travel. As Huckleberry sat taking the test, and the clock ticked down, he was glad he'd followed through to secure his accommodation of extended testing time. Suddenly his history professor announced that time was up and all students must stop working and hand in their exams. Huckleberry became upset and mentioned to his professor that he had extended testing time. He received a confused look in response. His professor stated that he had another teaching commitment; he had to go and could not allow extra testing time. Will Huckleberry receive his accommodation?

Although Huckleberry gave his professor the accommodation letter early in the semester, he never followed up with him during the time leading up to his midterm exam. The issue here is a practical one; the professor may have a technical obligation to provide accommodations offered by the college, but if he is unable or unwilling to do so, Huckleberry will have to involve the Office of Disability Services to mediate this situation.

William is a senior at Twelfth Night University. When he was in high school he was diagnosed with attention deficit hyperactivity disorder (ADHD). Every semester since he began as a freshman at Twelfth Night U. he has registered with the Office of Disability Services. Each semester he has received an accommodation letter from the Office of Disability Services and has given this letter to his professors. He registered with the office this semester, and they prepared his accommodation letters (which state that he has the accommodation for an alternative location for testing). As he sits for his first exam of the semester, he tells the professor that he is eligible to take the test in an alternate location and informs the professor that he can verify with the Office of Disability Services that he is registered as a student with a disability. Will William receive his accommodations?

Although William registered with the Office of Disability Services this semester, he never returned to the office to pick up his accommodation letters. He never delivered the letters to his professors. William is not entitled to an accommodation on this exam. The professor may decide to contact the Office of Disability Services to verify that William is entitled to take the exam in an alternative location and then make an exception for him, but he is not required to do so.

Persephone is a freshman at Goddess College, an all-female school in the town of Mount Olympus. She was diagnosed with depression in middle school. Persephone has learned effective ways of managing her depression, including taking medication and attending regular meetings with a counselor. The only negative to the medication is that it causes her to be groggy most mornings. Persephone feels that even though she had a 504 plan in high school, she doesn't want to identify herself as a person with a disability in college and decides not to register with the Office of Disability Services. She wants to try college on her own, without any accommodations. Persephone's first semester starts out bumpy. Since she is a freshman, she gets stuck with mostly early morning classes. She really likes all her professors, but she is having a hard time keeping up with her work. She finds it hard paying attention so early in the day and is sometimes unable to grasp the points the professor is making. All the other students in class seem to be taking notes furiously as the professor lectures, but she can't seem to keep up. As the semester progresses, Persephone sees her grades fall. By the time finals approach, she is failing three out of her five classes. Persephone decides the only thing she can do is to go to the Office of Disability Services and ask for accommodations. She plans on making up all her classwork once she has her accommodations. Will Persephone receive the accommodations she seeks?

As long as Persephone has the proper disability documentation, as required by her college, she can receive accommodations from this point going forward. In terms of making up her classwork from the past, accommodations are not retroactive so she will not likely be allowed to do so. This will be up to individual professors, and they can, but are not bound to, make an exception for her.

---

* Be a regular at the Office of Disability Services. Make sure the administrators know who you are and establish a friendly rapport with them.

* Don't forget to deliver your accommodation letters. You are not entitled to receive accommodations if the letter is not received by your professors.

* Be sure to follow up with your professors about your accommodations, on a regular basis throughout the semester and prior to all exams for which you may require accommodations.

* Accommodations are not retroactive. A student can request accommodations at any time in the semester. But accommodations will not be applicable to any work already completed before the accommodations were in place.

What to do if you are not receiving your accommodations?

Once in a while we do hear of students who, even though they've done everything right, do not receive accommodations from their professors. In this case we suggest contacting the Office of Disability Services. Administrators from this office have been known to speak with professors to find out why accommodations are not being given. They have even arranged meetings to act as mediator between student and professor. Sometimes it is a simple misunderstanding; other times a professor is new to teaching at the college level and doesn't have the experience to know what the accommodation letter is or that her responsibility is to provide approved accommodations. Unfortunately, there are situations when the professor simply fails or refuses to provide the student with the accommodations to which she is entitled.

If speaking with someone from the Office of Disability Services about the situation does not help, then the student has several options, but none of them will resolve the problem immediately. She has a right to file a grievance; most colleges have an official grievance process. She can also work up the chain of command and contact the Director of Disability Services' supervisor and then the ADA Compliance Officer or the Section 504 Administrator at the college. If the situation still remains unresolved, the student can contact the Department of Justice and file a formal complaint with the federal government. A college that faces a federal inquiry or even a lawsuit will almost always do what is needed to get its professor to cooperate. More detailed information about filing complaints for Section 504 or ADA violations are contained in the section of our Resources chapter dealing with legal issues.

* After registering with the Office of Disability Services and delivering your accommodation letters, if you are not receiving accommodations from a particular professor, you should contact the Office of Disability Services. Personnel from this office may be able to act as a mediator between student and professor.

* If the situation remains unresolved, you can file a grievance, work your way up the chain of command, and file a formal legal complaint.

Setting up your safety net

The final link to help you pull it all together is putting your support in place. The transition to college is challenging for any student, with or without a disability. You have the best chance of success if you create a safety net of support and call on assistance from the professionals around you. If you stop and think about it, there are lots of individuals in your college life who can help you on an occasional or regular basis. All you have to do is ask. Depending upon the nature of your disability, you may need regular medication from a pharmacy, or regular visits to the university health services. There are people in both places who can help you with medication or health issues. You may need to make contact with local medical specialists or academic tutors, or to set up weekly appointments with a therapist on or off campus. These people are also available to help. You may have a learning specialist who may or may not be associated with your college and with whom you meet regularly. You may meet in person or remotely via text, email, or phone. She may be the go-to person for academic issues. If you are living in campus housing, confide in your Resident Assistant, or RA, so that she knows what your disability is, what your accommodations are, and what additional housing challenges you may have, given your disability. The best thing about a safety net is that it is there in case you need it, but you don't have to use it unless the need arises.

One reminder when dealing with your safety net people: they all have the ability to help you, so it is important to build a positive relationship with them. Showing your appreciation, whether by a simple "thank you" or a quick email note, or even just by being polite, can go a long way to making these important people eager to help you the next time you need it.

---

* Call on assistance from the professionals around you—pharmacists, university health services, local medical specialists, academic tutors, therapist, learning specialist, and your Resident Assistant (RA) are all there to help you.

* The best thing about a safety net is that it is there in case you need it, but you don't have to use it unless the need arises.

After reading this chapter, we hope you feel that you are in the driver's seat and that you know every bump and curve that may come your way. Now, when the spring of your senior year rolls around and your enrollment deposit is submitted, you know what else needs to be taken care of before classes begin. Once your accommodations are in place, you really can put your feet up, kick back, and relax—at least for a few minutes!

Chapter 13

Money Matters

Would you pay $50,000 for a coffee mug, or maybe a sweatshirt or a tote bag? What about $200,000—or more? We didn't think so. But when you proudly place that college sticker on the rear window of your car, announcing to the world that your child (or you, the student) has been accepted to college, that's what it can cost. And since almost no one can handle that kind of expense out of their regular budget, an entire industry has sprung up to help families afford college expenses. We can't hope to give you all the information you will need on this complex topic in a single chapter, so we will try to walk you through the basic issues and terminology, and refer you to some of the extensive resources—books, websites, and government agencies—that can provide you with the very detailed information you will need to navigate the world of financing a college education.

You'll notice that we have not mentioned disabilities when we talk about college expenses. That's because, as is the case with other topics we have discussed, many of the issues relating to paying for college are the same for students with disabilities and those without. We will mention a few areas where students with disabilities may need to do things a bit differently, where they may incur additional expenses, or where there may be special funding available to them, but for the most part the road to funding a college education is similar for all students.

What will it cost?

Let's begin by looking at what kind of expenses will be involved in attending college. First, there are application fees, which generally cost $50 and up for each school. Some schools will waive these fees for students who cannot afford them or those students the college is inviting to apply (we talk about priority applicants in Chapter 8); check with the individual Admissions Office for each college. Then there is the cost of tuition, which will vary enormously from city and state universities to the most expensive private colleges. Fees are generally billed separately, and can include things such as mandatory student activity fees, required student health fees, and separate student health insurance. For students with learning disabilities who are also enrolling in a specialized support program, there may be an additional fee for such a program, which can run to several thousand dollars a year.

Living expenses will vary, depending upon whether the student lives on campus, at home, or in a private house or apartment near the college. Even if a student decides to live at home for personal, medical, or financial reasons, the costs of getting to and from campus by public transportation or car need to be considered. If a student is attending a school some distance from his home, travel back and forth to campus can involve train, plane, or bus rides. Many campus-based colleges require that all freshman students live on campus and participate in a meal plan, which can often result in paying for meals that a student might not otherwise eat. (We have never known a college student who gets up for breakfast on weekends!)

Students with disabilities who require special living conditions—for example a room equipped with flashing lights to warn of a fire, for a student with a hearing impairment—will generally be provided with such accommodations without charge as part of the obligation of the college to comply with the Americans with Disabilities Act (ADA). This is a good time to mention that whenever a college is required to provide an accommodation under the ADA, this must be done at no cost to the student. The college is permitted to consider the cost of an accommodation (such as voice-to-text software from one manufacturer versus another) when deciding how to meet the needs of a particular student, but they cannot decline to provide a needed accommodation unless the cost is so great that it would be a hardship for the college to provide it at all. Given the multimillion dollar budgets of even small colleges, this is a highly unlikely scenario.

Books are a major expense for all students and can run to hundreds of dollars per semester. Similar expenses would include laboratory equipment, art supplies, and a personal computer. When specialized software is required for a student with a disability, it will not generally be supplied by the college as software for the student's personal computer. Usually, the college provides the student with access to a computer equipped with such software, and that computer may be located in the library, the Office of Disability Services, or an assistive technology lab. If a student wants that software on his own computer, he will generally have to purchase it. In addition, remember that the college does not have to supply exactly what the student prefers, as long as the hardware or software it selects serves essentially the same purpose. Students with very specific preferences may have to purchase their own technology or equipment.

As we noted at the start of this section, many of the expenses we mention are applicable to students with and without disabilities. But students with disabilities may have expenses for certain items that will not generally be provided by their school as part of the accommodation process. These can include upkeep and repair of hearing aids, wheelchairs, or scooters. Personal assistants, tutors, and the care of guide dogs or other personal assistance animals would also not generally be covered by the college. There may also be substantial deductibles under the personal, family, or school-provided medical insurance policy for medications, medical equipment, and medical treatment that can be an additional cost.

Finally, every student will want some additional money available for recreation and incidental expenses. Where the line between want and need is drawn will be different for each student and family, and parents and students will want to reach a clear understanding of how much will be available for such expenses.

There are a number of websites that will help you calculate your costs of a college education and we list several in our Resources chapter.

---

* There are numerous items besides tuition that are part of the cost of a college education. These can include living expenses,

books, activity fees, and costs of travel to and from home and campus.

* Students with disabilities may have additional costs beyond those of other students. Special learning support programs can have fees that run into thousands of dollars per year. Other expenses can include personal copies of software, as well as medical and medication costs not covered by insurance.

How to control costs

Before even looking at sources of financial aid, students and their parents may want to consider ways to lower the costs of college. One key decision is whether a community college or a city or state university makes sense for some, or all, of a student's undergraduate career. Dan was a strong student who knew, even before he applied to college, that he wanted to attend medical school. His parents were supportive of his goals, but they were not wealthy and they had to plan for educating not just Dan but his younger brother as well. They knew that sources of financial support for medical education were limited and they were concerned that when his education was completed Dan would be burdened by loans that could reach $200,000 or more. Dan decided to apply to both private colleges and to several branches of his state university, hoping that the private schools would offer him sufficient financial aid to enable him to enroll with minimal loans. He was accepted everywhere he applied, but was disappointed at the financial aid packages he was offered by the private colleges; they would require his parents to contribute more than they comfortably could and would put him substantially in debt before he even graduated college.

Dan decided to attend a branch of his state university, which would allow him to graduate without having to take on loans. He did very well in his undergraduate premedical courses. But he was concerned that he was not going to be considered for the best medical school programs because he wasn't coming out of a top national school, and worried that his preparation would not be sufficient to meet the demands of medical school. Fortunately, his fears were unfounded and Dan is now enrolled in an excellent medical school, where all is going well. And, although he is borrowing large sums to help pay his tuition, his loan burden is substantially less than it would have been if he had begun borrowing as an undergraduate.

Bridget was a student with inflammatory bowel disease whom we met at a summer conference. She told us how excited she was to be starting a top university in the fall, where she hoped to pursue her dream of becoming a veterinarian. The university which she would attend as an undergraduate also housed a school of veterinary medicine at which she hoped to eventually enroll. As we spoke, it became clear that Bridget would be entering as a junior, not a freshman. When we asked why, she said that she had decided to begin her studies at a community college near her home, where the tuition cost was minimal. This also gave her a chance to recover from the time she was out of school in her senior year, when she was hospitalized for surgery related to her medical condition. "I saved a lot of money and had a chance to get my health in a better place," she noted. "Now I'm ready to move on to a larger school with a campus." She mentioned that the school had provided her with an excellent financial aid package that helped make her decision an easier one.

In addition to starting at a community college or state university, some students reduce their college costs by working while attending school. This can be done by finding a part-time position, with or without a reduction in course load, or by utilizing work-study opportunities offered by a college as part of a financial aid package. Work-study programs are jobs arranged by the college and designed to coordinate with a student's academic schedule. They can range from assisting a professor with research to washing dishes in the cafeteria. The money earned from a work-study job is part of the calculation when a school offers financial aid. A word of caution about working at outside jobs: students who take a reduced course load may jeopardize their financial aid. Federal loan and aid programs set standards for full- and part-time study and failure to meet these course or credit minimums can disqualify a student from federal loans and subsidies. If a student will need a reduced course load for disability-related reasons, many colleges will try to make special arrangements so that financial aid is not unduly impacted. Students who are considering a reduced course load should check with both their college Financial Aid office and the federal loan programs themselves. Contact information for these programs is included in our Resources chapter.

We mention Vocational Rehabilitation Programs in Chapter 9, and want to remind students and parents of something we cover there in more detail. For students whose disabilities qualify them for such state-run programs, certain costs of college may be covered, usually by direct payment to the college. These could include computers, books, and other equipment that will enable a student with a disability to access an education and thereby become a productive, independent individual.

---

* Attending a branch of your city or state university or starting your college education at a community college can help reduce the overall costs of a college education. Families need to consider whether long-term educational and career goals require that a student enroll for four years or more at an expensive undergraduate college.

FAFSA

The key to receiving financial aid is the FAFSA form—the Free Application for Federal Student Aid. This form is available online and is the universal first step in seeking college financial aid. It establishes the eligibility of a student for grants, loans, and work-study funding from the US Department of Education's Office of Federal Student Aid. It is also used by virtually every college to determine what funds the college itself will make available to the student.

The FAFSA website contains extensive information and instructions for completing the form. The information provided on the form is plugged into a formula called the Federal Methodology, which is established by the US Higher Education Act.[1] The report generated by these calculations is the Student Aid Report, which includes the financial information the student has provided. It also sets forth a crucial number, the Expected Family Contribution (EFC), which is the sum that the student and his family are expected to be able to contribute to the cost of college for the coming year. When the EFC is subtracted from the expected cost of a particular school, the result is the amount of financial aid a student will be expected to need to attend that school. Families should be aware that the US Department of Education and the Internal Revenue Service can compare information and that false information on FAFSA forms can have serious legal ramifications.

There are many details of the FAFSA process that students and their families have to consider. One is whether the student is considered as dependent upon his parents and required to include information about his family's financial situation, or if he only has to submit his own financial details. The FAFSA website includes a calculator to determine student dependency status, but the short answer is that unless a student is over 24, married, a veteran, or has dependents, he is generally required to submit financial information about his parents, no matter who will be helping to pay for college expenses. Another consideration is timing. FAFSA forms need to be submitted as soon as possible after January 1 of each year, but they require information from the family's federal tax return, which is generally not completed until shortly before the April 15 filing deadline. In fact, much of the documentation that goes into the preparation of the tax return isn't even available in January. It's a squeeze we've seen families go through, but we haven't yet come up with an effective solution. What needs to be kept in mind is that it generally takes about three weeks for Student Aid Reports to be generated, and families will want to make sure that the schools to which their son or daughter is applying have time to review this report and put together a financial aid offer in advance of the date when they notify the student of an acceptance.

We discuss Early Decision (ED) and other early acceptance arrangements in Chapter 7, but want to remind students who are applying for ED that this can present a dilemma with respect to financial aid. Students whose college decision will depend upon the financial aid package they receive will probably want to avoid ED applications. Some schools indicate that they may release a student from a binding agreement to attend if the student is not awarded the amount of financial aid he needs, but schools are reluctant to publicize this fact. This is a very tricky area, and students should check with all arms of the college that are involved with admissions and financial aid before embarking on the ED process.

Students with disabilities will be chagrined to see that the FAFSA is a very narrow form with no room for narratives or explanations. Students who will have special expenses related to their disability will need to bring these directly to the attention of the colleges to which they are applying. The colleges can then adjust the cost of attendance to include these expenses, and proceed to deduct the Expected Family Contribution from that larger number. We caution families to check the FAFSA website carefully for the most up-to-date information. The details, deadlines, and other aspects of this process change from year to year, and only the information set out on the website itself can be considered definitive.

---

* The FAFSA form is the starting point for receiving financial aid of all kinds. Families should be careful to check the details of each year's form and the deadlines for submitting information directly on the FAFSA website.

Types of funding: The financial aid package

Once a college has reviewed the information they receive from FAFSA, as well as any additional information that the student may have submitted regarding disability-related expenses, they put together what is referred to as a financial aid package. That package uses a number of different funding sources to enable a student to meet the costs of college without placing an unrealistic burden upon his family or incurring debt that is so great that he will not be able to repay it.

A typical financial aid package may contain a grant or scholarship, which does not need to be repaid and may be based on merit or financial need. It can also include a federal loan that incurs no interest during the time the student is enrolled in school, another federal loan that does incur interest while the student is enrolled, and a work-study job that will cover another portion of the student's costs. Depending on the kind of disability with which they are dealing, it may be difficult for some students to manage a work-study job. The demands of a job for someone who is struggling with a physical or learning difficulty may be overwhelming. This is one of the important kinds of information that a student should bring directly to the attention of the college, since there is no place to discuss this issue on the FAFSA form.

Returning veterans, with and without disabilities, are eligible for a number of sources of financing college, provided by legislation generally referred to as the GI Bill. We list sources of information for veterans seeking college funding in our Resources chapter.

The issue of loans is a particular concern for students with disabilities. Depending upon the nature or extent of a student's disability, his ability to earn a living may be affected. Just as our friend Dan knew he would be able to pay back his loans for medical school, because he could be expected to earn a good income after finishing his program, a student with a substantial learning disability or health limitation might have fewer high-paying jobs available to him upon graduation. Other college graduates with disabilities may want to work with students who struggle with disabilities of their own; although this work will bring them great satisfaction, it may not make it easy for them to pay back large loans.

Some colleges with large endowment funds have a commitment to meeting the entire cost of attendance for every student they accept. Others will offer what they can, in a combination of loans, grants, and work-study jobs, even if they are aware that they haven't covered the gap between the cost of attendance and the expected family contribution. You may have heard that some colleges offer "need blind" admissions. Families need to understand that for many colleges, the term "need blind" doesn't mean that the college commits to meeting the student's full financial need. It may only mean that the school will admit students whether or not they will require financial aid to attend. Recent research indicates that only a very small number of schools—18 percent of private colleges and 32 percent of public ones—actually make a commitment to meet the entire financial need of each student they accept.[2] Some schools will accomplish this with only very small student loans and others without any loan obligations at all. This can be a real benefit for the students that these schools accept. What about other schools? Although most colleges will not be comfortable admitting it, we believe that students who will not require any financial aid from the college (even if they take out loans, these don't cost the college anything) may be more attractive candidates to the Admissions Offices in some schools. However, we haven't seen evidence of this, and the ADA prohibits schools from placing students who require accommodations—even expensive ones—at any disadvantage.

* A typical financial aid package from a college may contain grants, different kinds of loans, and a work-study job. Students who have disabilities that will make a work-study job impractical should bring this fact to the attention of the individual colleges to which they are applying.

* "Need blind" admission doesn't always translate into full financial support. Families need to investigate carefully the financial aid policies of each college they are considering and look behind the labels colleges affix to their financial aid practices.

Personal financial management

Let's turn our attention in a very different direction and look at another kind of money matter that students with disabilities and their families need to consider. Arielle has bipolar disorder. She was diagnosed at age 16 after a number of episodes of depression and impulsive behavior. She is taking medication that goes a long way to stabilizing her moods, but she still has episodes of impulsivity and poor judgment. One manifestation of her disorder is trouble controlling her spending. She finds it difficult to weigh the considerations most people think about before they purchase something: Can I afford it? Do I need it? How will I pay for it? Is it fairly priced? She just knows that she wants it and is unable to process anything else. As you might imagine, there have been a number of problems with this behavior, and her parents have resorted to putting her on a strictly limited cash-only budget. They do not let Arielle access any credit or debit cards and give her cash (and require a receipt) when she needs to buy something. This system has been awkward but functional throughout high school. But now Arielle wants to attend a college just a couple of hours away from her home, where she would be living on campus.

Although their issues are very different, Avi and his family also must deal with concerns about how to handle money when he begins a post-high school program on the campus of a New England college. Although this one-year certificate program is very structured, students still have the chance to leave campus and to participate in campus activities. Avi will need money for daily expenses and recreation, but he has struggled with mathematical concepts for his entire academic career and is just not comfortable with calculations involving money. He has trouble deciding if he has spent too much and with figuring out how much money he has left. His parents are concerned about giving him a credit or debit card or having him manage his own banking.

Both Arielle and Avi have older siblings, and each of their parents knew from prior experience that they needed to start early to create financial understanding and independence. They had given their children a weekly stipend from early in elementary school and made them responsible for certain expenses to be paid from their allowance. They created opportunities for their children to earn money by undertaking extra jobs around the house. Each family slowly expanded the list of items for which their child would be responsible and made talk about money part of everyday conversations. But Arielle's impulsiveness and Avi's discomfort with money concepts were just too intractable for their parents' efforts.

Fortunately for both of these students, their respective campuses have a version of "campus cash," a system that uses different names at different schools, but generally links a student's identification card to an account that can be used to pay for laundry machines, extra food in the campus cafeteria, and books and supplies in the school bookstore. Students get a monthly statement and can arrange for their parents to get one as well. If a student uses up all the money that has been deposited into his account, he cannot get additional credit.

Although the campus cash system was helpful, it did not cover all situations that these students might encounter. Avi and his parents decided that the best way to handle his financial needs was to open an account with a bank right near his campus. They went in together and met with a banker, who advised them that a savings account, unlike a checking account, had a limited number of transactions each month. They decided to open a checking account for Avi, which would be a joint account with his mom. Despite the urging of the banker that they arrange a debit or credit card, they decided that they would begin with a simple ATM card that allowed Avi to take out money but not incur other charges. Avi and his parents agreed upon a weekly sum for his personal expenses. His mom checked the account regularly to see how much he was taking out and, if it was more than they had agreed, she contacted Avi and they went over his budget and expenditures. After a couple of months, both Avi and his parents became a bit more comfortable with this arrangement, and while Avi was home for a long weekend, his parents set him up with some personal banking software that let him track his account and categorize his expenses. Things didn't always go smoothly and Avi made some missteps with his spending (which his parents now refer to as "the rock concert incident"), but he very slowly began to understand the rudiments of his own financial life and to take responsibility for his own expenditures.

Arielle's parents took a different approach. They were concerned that her impulsive spending would make any sort of credit or debit card, or any bank account which she could access, more than she could handle along with the adjustment to college. They sat down with Arielle and came up with an amount that they all agreed should be sufficient for her weekly recreational expenses and they mailed her cash, by secure delivery, once a week. They told her that, if she could prove herself capable of saving some of this money, they would revisit the system they devised. It was an interesting year. When her parents first came up for Parents' Weekend in late October, Arielle was completely out of money and got very upset when her parents stuck to their guns and only gave her the agreed weekly allowance. By the time she came home for Thanksgiving, she had spent all her money, but was more accepting of the allowance system. "I guess I realized that some of my classmates didn't have nearly as much as I had to spend and I felt kind of foolish making such a fuss about money. I also started to realize that my parents weren't being mean, just concerned about my problem with buying stuff," she explained to us.

When we checked in with Arielle in the spring of her freshman year, she had been consistently on her medication for most of the school year and her moods and impulses were relatively stable. Her parents had arranged for her to have access to a debit card connected to a checking account.

The banker they met with explained that a law which became effective in early 2010 limited the ability of banks to allow debit charges beyond the limits of the linked account. He also told them that individuals who were not yet 21 could no longer obtain a credit card unless they could show independent assets or income sufficient to pay for their charges. If not, as was the case with Arielle and most other students, they would need a parent to co-sign and the parent would have joint liability for any charges incurred on the credit card.[3]

Arielle and her parents realize that her financial responsibility will be linked to the control of her bipolar disorder, and that it is likely problems will crop up in the future. Still, they are committed to working together to try to find ways to keep Arielle's spending responsible.

---

* Students whose disabilities directly impact their ability to manage their own financial affairs often need special arrangements and careful family guidance. Joint or supervised bank accounts, using only cash, or having credit or debit cards with small limits and no possibility for overcharges or overdrafts are some possible techniques for managing difficult financial situations.

Supplemental Security Income (SSI)

Individuals with substantial disabilities, which impact their ability to earn a living, may be eligible for several government programs. One of the broadest of these is Supplemental Security Income, commonly known as SSI. SSI offers benefits to both children and adults, and many of those who would be eligible as adults will have been eligible to receive benefits as children and will already be enrolled with the Social Security Administration, which administers the SSI program. For children and adults (anyone 18 or over), individuals must meet eligibility standards for both the nature and extent of their disability and their available income and resources. Students who have not graduated high school and are younger than 19 are considered based upon their family income and assets. Individuals over 18 or who have graduated high school are considered adults and their eligibility is based only on their own income or assets, even if they reside with their parents. The key for these adults is whether they have income or assets over the very low limits set by the Social Security Administration and whether they are unable to engage in "substantial gainful activity."

Keep in mind that the financial eligibility limits for SSI are extremely low and change from time to time and from state to state. Families and individuals with more than very small amounts of savings or other assets will fail to meet these standards. Most states provide Medicaid coverage for individuals who qualify for SSI, either as part of the same qualification process or with a separate application. This will ensure basic medical coverage for individuals with very substantial disabilities and little or no funds or income.

Another kind of federal support that may be available to a young person with disabilities is not limited by income or assets. This is Social Security Disability Insurance (SSDI). Just as an adult is entitled to Social Security payments upon retirement, or at any time if he has become disabled, the disabled dependent of someone who has paid into the Social Security system can receive disability payments under certain conditions. The parent needs to be deceased or to have worked long enough to be eligible to receive Social Security retirement or disability benefits. The young adult needs to have been disabled before age 22. The disabled young adult may also qualify for Medicaid after a waiting period by virtue of his receipt of SSDI.

Ronald has Asperger's syndrome, and although he graduated from college, he has been unable to find a job and has lived at home for the two years since he graduated. He has some money he inherited from his grandfather, and his parents are middle class and would in no way qualify for SSI or Medicaid. Ronald's father, Henry, was in his 40s when Ronald was born and is now 65 and has just retired from his job as a library supervisor. He has begun receiving Social Security payments based upon his prior years of employment. Thanks to the suggestion of a helpful counselor with whom Ronald has worked in his efforts to find employment, Henry arranged for Ronald to receive SSDI benefits. Ronald will be able to keep these benefits for some time even if he is able to get and hold a job, and once he loses the benefits he can have them reinstated without having to reapply if he becomes eligible again within several years of his last payment. Time limits and details keep changing for these benefits. Check with the Social Security websites noted in our Resources chapter for the most up-to-date information. We want to stress that the programs we have mentioned are limited to specific populations and, for SSI, to those in truly impoverished circumstances. The benefits they provide are not great. However, they can make a substantial difference to an individual with a serious disability who is unable to work—for a long or short period of time—and you should be aware of their existence. We provide several sources of additional information about these programs in our Resources chapter.

---

* Federal programs such as Supplemental Security Income, Social Security Disability Insurance, and Medicaid may be available to young adults with serious disabilities which prevent them from working. Qualifications for these programs are complicated and subject to change and families should consult with the agencies involved for specific information.

Special needs trusts

Parents of students with disabilities sometimes ask us whether they need to set up a trust for their child with a disability. Our answer depends on a number of different factors, primarily the kind and extent of the disability with which they are dealing. Let's start our explanation by looking at what a special needs trust is and what it can—and cannot—do.

As we've seen earlier in this chapter, young people with disabilities may be entitled to SSI, Medicaid, and other government services if their disability keeps them from earning a living and if they lack the resources, such as savings, investments, and other sources of funds, to support themselves. If parents prepare a will that is designed to take care of the needs of their child with a disability, any direct bequest to that child will generally disqualify him from government benefits. This puts parents in a quandary. They want to make sure their child is taken care of even after they are no longer around to offer supplemental financial support, but they know that their child's lifetime needs will probably be greater than any sums they can leave in their wills. And they also worry about what kind of marginal existence their child will have without all the extras they have provided during their lifetime, such as trips, recreation, additional education, and a comfortable home.

A special needs trust is designed to meet these concerns. Most commonly, it creates a trust under the parents' wills that sets aside money or other assets for the benefit of the disabled child, but specifies that such funds cannot be used to take the place of government benefits. Instead, the funds are used to enrich the child's life and to provide the many things that will enhance his existence beyond what government programs will provide. Less common are trusts set up by parents during the parents' lifetimes, which sometimes can offer more flexibility by allowing changes to the trust terms by the parents.

Clearly, a special needs trust is not necessary or appropriate in every situation. Remember, it has the effect of withholding an outright bequest to an individual where his siblings are probably receiving their bequests outright. These situations can lead to family conflict. It also prevents the disabled individual from having any control over the trust assets or from receiving direct payments; all payments from the trust must be made directly to providers or sellers. Even so, we suggest that families in which young people have cognitive disabilities, mental illness, autism, and serious physical disabilities that will impact their ability to earn a living should at least discuss whether a special needs trust might be helpful.

Sometimes the decision to set up a trust, and the details of the trust, will rest upon the extent of the family's assets and whether there are other individuals in the family who can take on the responsibility of caring for the financial and other needs of the individual with a disability. Thought should be given to naming the trustees who will administer the trust. Roberta and Brian, whose son was diagnosed with a mental illness during his sophomore year of college, eventually decided to set up a supplemental needs trust for him in their wills. They wanted to name his two sisters as trustees, but knew that their daughters didn't see eye to eye about how best to deal with their brother's needs. So they named both daughters, but also a well-respected uncle who could act as a buffer between their daughters and make sure things worked smoothly. Families who have no relative or close friend who would be a suitable trustee may decide to name a nonprofit organization in that role. These organizations often have expertise in the needs of individuals with a particular disability and will keep track of each individual's trust assets, while pooling the funds they handle for investment purposes. Still other families decide to name a professional trustee to manage the trust alone, or along with family members. Trustees are entitled by law to receive compensation for their services, but most family members choose not to take such fees, leaving more assets for the beneficiary.

As you can see, this is a complex area, which involves many personal, financial, and legal issues. Keep in mind, too, that there is never a guarantee with something like a special needs trust. Congress can always swoop down and change the laws covering this field, throwing all carefully laid plans awry. If you think that a special needs trust is something that your family wants to consider, we urge you to work with an attorney who is experienced in this area. We offer some suggestions as to how you can find someone with these qualifications in our Resources chapter.

---

* Young people with disabilities that impair their ability to handle their own financial affairs, or which may substantially limit their ability to earn a living, may benefit from a special needs trust. There are numerous issues that must be considered when parents set up such a trust and this process should only be undertaken with the assistance of an attorney with experience in this field.

We've really run the gamut of financial issues in this chapter, from college expenses and funding, to personal financial management, to government programs. We know we haven't given you all the answers on many of these topics, but the very nature of FAFSA and government-funded programs makes that impossible. Anything that is timely as this book goes to press will be changed by the time you pick it up to read, even a few months later. So please bear with us and check our Resources chapter for how to find the most up-to-date information on these ever-changing, but very important, topics.

Resources

Throughout this book we mention programs, books, laws, and services that can help students with disabilities and their families navigate the path from high school to college, the workplace, and adult independence. Many of these are listed in the endnotes to each chapter, but others are listed here, where we can explain how they can be helpful and give some background information where appropriate. We have listed these resources by chapter (although not every chapter has resources in this section), but many resources will apply to more than one of the subjects we discuss.

One word about websites: Unless a site is difficult to navigate or has a particular section we want to bring to your attention, we have listed only the main website address. Internal pages change and most sites have a search feature that will allow you to seek out the specific information you need.

Chapter 1: The Legal Landscape

For general legal information

www.wrightslaw.com This commercial site is particularly helpful for information on the IDEA, Section 504 and transition issues. Ignore the clutter and use the search feature.

www.ldonline.org Contains helpful articles that give context and details to numerous issues.

www.thomas.loc.gov This legislative resource from the Library of Congress, named after Thomas Jefferson, is a good place to find the text of the laws we discuss.

www.law.cornell.edu The Cornell University Law School website includes search features and links to federal and state laws, as well as the Code of Federal Regulations, which contains procedures for implementing the federal laws we mention in this chapter.

http://scholar.google.com Legal decisions of courts can be found on Google Scholar. Make sure you check the "legal opinions" option if you want the actual text of a court decision.

Government agencies

http://idea.ed.gov/explore/home The US Department of Education's site for information on the IDEA.

www.ed.gov/about/offices/list/ocr/index.html The Office of Civil Rights of the US Department of Education has information on how to file a discrimination complaint under Section 504 or the ADA.

www.ada.gov/cguide.pdf This is a helpful guide to a number of federal laws with links to other agencies.

www.ed.gov/policy/gen/guid/fpco/ferpa/index.html Contains information on FERPA.

www.hhs.gov/ocr/privacy/hipaa/understanding/consumers/index.html A consumer-oriented site on HIPAA rules and regulations. This helps simplify a very complex law.

Finding an attorney

www.copaa.org The Council of Parent Attorneys and Advocates website has a national "find an attorney" feature. Look for individuals who practice general disability law for all ages.

www.hg.org/northam-bar.html Links to state and local bar associations throughout the US. These will generally offer referrals to members who practice disability or education law.

www.napas.org/aboutus/PA_CAP.htm The website of the National Disability Rights Network contains state-by-state lists of Protection and Advocacy Agencies, including information on the federal law which created them.

Chapter 2: Getting Started

General resources

www.disability.gov Managed by the US Department of Labor, together with 21 other federal agencies, this is a very helpful and wide-ranging website covering many of the topics throughout this book, including lists of groups offering support and information on specific disabilities.

www.heath.gwu.edu The Heath Resource Center of George Washington University has a wealth of information on everything from summer programs to financial aid.

www.ccdanet.org/ecp The Western New York Collegiate Consortium and Disability Advocates has an online guide to Effective College Planning with helpful information and links.

Support for specific disabilities

The listing of disability organizations on **www.disability.gov** is extensive, but by no means complete. Some other organizations that provide support for young people with specific disabilities are:

www.ccfa.org Crohn's and Colitis Foundation of America.

www.interdys.org The International Dyslexia Association.

www.chadd.org Children and Adults with Attention Deficit/ Hyperactivity Disorder.

www.tsa-usa.org National Tourette Syndrome Association.

Books for young people about learning disorders

There are numerous books for adults about learning disabilities. There are far fewer books aimed at young people. We have found the following books by Mel Levine (also available on tape) to be helpful:

For elementary age students: *All Kinds of Minds: A Young Student's Book About Learning Abilities and Learning Disorders* (1992) Cambridge, MA: Educators Publishing Service, Inc.

For middle school students: *Keeping a Head in School: A Student's Book About Learning Abilities and Learning Disorders* (1990) Cambridge, MA: Educators Publishing Service, Inc.

For older students and adults: *A Mind at a Time* (2002) New York: Simon & Schuster.

Training programs for parents

www.taalliance.org/ptidirectory/pclist.asp Has a state-by-state listing of Parent Training and Information Centers which work with families of young people (up to age 26) with all kinds of disabilities.

www.wrightslaw.com Offers programs at various locations to train parents in advocacy skills and legal issues; focus is on younger students.

State and local bar associations also hold occasional programs on legal issues. See the link to these groups in the resources for Chapter 1.

Chapter 4: Creating a Paper Trail

Where to go for private educational testing

Contacting a local college or asking your primary care physician for referrals are generally the best ways to go about finding a reputable person or organization to provide educational testing. National organizations also have websites that can help you find a local member. These include:

http://locator.apa.org/ The American Psychological Association.

www.yellowpagesforkids.com State-by-state listings are included in the "Yellow Pages for Kids" feature on the Wrightslaw website, but listings for educational evaluators are mixed in with other services and there is no vetting of these professionals.

www.centerforlearningdifferences.org/evaluations.php Includes a discussion of how to select an evaluator.

Chapter 5: College Admissions Tests

Testing organizations

http://sat.collegeboard.com/home The website for the SAT exam. It also has a link to the PSAT exam for tenth graders, the pre-test to the SAT. Use the search term "ssd" to find Services for Students with Disabilities.

www.ets.org The website for the ETS (formerly Educational Testing Service), which develops the SAT exam for the College Board. This site contains research studies and lists of conferences relating to the SAT and related exams, all done under the auspices of ETS.

www.act.org/aap The website for the ACT tests; also contains a link to Services for Students with Disabilities.

www.act.org/plan Information on the PLAN test for tenth graders, the pre-test for the ACT.

Test preparation

http://sat.collegeboard.com/practice Contains information on preparation materials provided for free or for sale by the College Board.

www.actstudent.org/testprep This is the site for preparation materials for the ACT.

The two largest national test preparation companies offer both courses and materials. These are:

www.princetonreview.com The Princeton Review

www.kaptest.com Kaplan Test Prep

There are innumerable other test preparation organizations and individuals operating regionally and locally. Guidance counselors can be good resources for information about these.

Chapter 6: Selecting a College

College search engines

www.collegeboard.com Asks you to indicate your preference for college location, size, majors, and more, and then generates a list of colleges that match your criteria.

www.anycollege.com This resource also matches preferences with a list of colleges. This site also offers a look at colleges via an online video.

www.collegenet.com Also has a college search option. In addition, this site allows you to create forums and post your questions and ideas on topics related to college.

www.petersons.com Allows you to search colleges and offers a comprehensive narrative description of a particular school, highlighting its distinct characteristics.

College readiness survey

www.lansingcatholic.org/images/pdf/College%20Readiness%20Survey%20Results%20and%20Tips.pdf This survey was created by Frank Bernier, Ph.D., who is a high school guidance counselor based in Michigan.

http://impactpublications.com/collegesurvivalandsuccessscalecsss.aspx The College Survival and Success Scale charges a fee for its services, which are designed to help students determine whether they are ready for college.

Diversity on campus

These books may be helpful on the subject of evaluating college campuses for their acceptance of lesbian, gay, bisexual, and transgender (LGBT) students. They are comprehensive guides that feature information gathered from numerous interviews with students, faculty, and administrators from colleges across the country.

Windmeyer, S.L. (2006) *The Advocate College Guide for LGBT Students*. New York: Alyson Publications, Inc.

Baez, J. and The Princeton Review staff (2007) *The Gay and Lesbian Guide to College Life*. Massachusetts: Princeton Review.

Chapter 8: The Campus Visit

See the Campus Visit Form on the last page of this section.

Chapter 9: It's Off to Work We Go...

Finding your state's Vocational Rehabilitation Program

www.rehabnetwork.org/directors_contact.htm The website for the Council of State Administrators of Vocational Rehabilitation contains links to the Vocational Rehabilitation Offices in each state. A similar listing can be found at **http://wdcrobcolp01.ed.gov/Programs/EROD/org_list.cfm?category_ID=SVR**.

www.napas.org/aboutus/PA_CAP.htm Also mentioned as a legal resource, this site contains links and information about Client Assistance Programs in each state that help individuals obtain Vocational Rehabilitation Services.

Other state programs

www.ncsab.org/ncsab_directory.htm The website of the National Council of State Agencies for the Blind, contains links to the agency in each state with responsibility for individuals who are visually impaired.

http://wdcrobcolp01.ed.gov/Programs/EROD/org_list.cfm?category_cd=SCH Contains a list of state agencies with responsibility for children and youth with special health care needs.

Services for veterans

www.va.gov The clearinghouse website for the US Department of Veterans Affairs. There are links to Vocational Rehabilitation Services, educational benefits, and educational benefits for children of disabled veterans.

Employment discrimination claims

www.ada.gov This website has information on filing claims for employment discrimination. You can also find an attorney who practices employment disability law through your state or local bar association. See *Finding an attorney* under the Resources for Chapter 1.

Chapter 11: Keys to Competence

Driving

www.aaany.com/pdf_files/safety/Teen_Guide.pdf From the American Automobile Association, contains information helpful for all teen drivers.

www.cartalk.com/content/features/Special-Needs/index.html Includes information and links to resources compiled by the hosts of the radio show *Car Talk*.

Time-management tools

The success of any time-management tool rests with your comfort in using it. So tech-savvy students will want to use the most up-to-date services for their computers, smart phones, and other devices, including:

www.google.com/calendar

www.effexis.com One of numerous websites that sells organizing software. This company offers a free 30-day trial so you can see if their product is useful for you.

Organizing papers and other belongings

Goldberg, D. with Zwiebel, J. (2005) *The Organized Student*. New York: Fireside Books. A decidedly low-tech approach to organizing school materials, this book was written for parents to help organize their students in elementary and secondary school. The tips and techniques are fundamental to students of all ages, and can easily be adapted by college students.

Finding social skills groups

Social skills groups are local in nature. We have experience with groups run by psychologists, social workers, and (usually within secondary schools) guidance counselors. We have also found that local social service agencies—community centers, agencies serving individuals with disabilities, and groups focusing on employment skills—often have social skills groups for older adolescents or young adults. Parents often need to do a bit of detective work to locate these groups, since young people are often reluctant to seek them out. When a group is not available or where a student does not want to participate in group activities, there are books with lessons that help build social skills. These include:

Cooper, B. (2008) *The Social Success Workbook for Teens: Skill-building Activities for Teens With Nonverbal Learning Disorder, Asperger's Disorder, and Other Social-skill Problems*. Oakland, CA: New Harbinger Publications.

Parents or teachers who are interested in forming a social skills group may want to consult Kiker Painter, K. (2008) *Social Skills Groups for Children and Adolescents with Asperger's Syndrome: A Step-by-Step Program*. London: Jessica Kingsley Publishers.

Chapter 12: Pulling it All Together

Accommodation letter to the professor

Although each college has its own accommodation form, the following are typical of what you can expect at most schools:

www.umw.edu/disability/resources/instructor/documents/SampleAccommodationForm7-17-07.pdf From the University of Mary Washington.

www.wcu.edu/WebFiles/PDFs/disabilityservices_Accommodations.pdf From Western Carolina University.

Chapter 13: Money Matters

Scholarships

www.heath.gwu.edu The Heath Resources Center at George Washington University has a section of its website devoted to financial aid information and scholarships for students with disabilities.

www.disability.gov Has its own listings of scholarships plus links to other websites with additional listings.

Websites for organizations offering information and support for specific disabilities often have information about scholarships for students with the specific disability on which they focus.

Calculating college costs

http://cgi.money.cnn.com/tools/collegecost/collegecost.jsp This site from CNN will provide the cost of tuition, fees, and room and board for any US college.

www.collegeboard.com/student/pay The College Board offers both calculators for college expenses and information on scholarships and student loans.

Loans and financial aid

www.fafsa.ed.gov The website of the Free Application for Federal Student Aid has links under "Student Aid on the Web" to financial calculators, as well as information on the federal student loan programs. And, of course, the main website has the FAFSA form itself—the key to financial aid from most colleges, as well as to federal student loans.

http://studentaid.ed.gov/PORTALSWebApp/students/english/Glossary.jsp#halftime Explains the requirements for part-time students to receive federal loans. Note, however, that individual colleges can have stricter definitions as to which students will be eligible for loans.

Government benefits

www.socialsecurity.gov This is the portal to information about both disability benefits (including benefits for disabled young adults whose parents are retired) and Supplemental Security Income (SSI), which pays benefits to disabled individuals who meet strict income and asset limits.

www.socialsecurity.gov/disabilityresearch/wi/medicaid.htm Offers information about Medicaid, which is jointly funded by the federal and state governments.

Finding an attorney to prepare a trust

See the listings under Chapter 1 for state and local bar associations. You will want to work with someone who is experienced in trusts and wills or in disability law. Make sure to ask specifically whether they regularly set up special needs trusts. And don't be shy about asking in advance how much they charge. It's a perfectly appropriate question and reputable attorneys shouldn't be offended.

CAMPUS VISIT FORM

Institution Name ______________________________

State _____ *Date of Visit* _____________

Admissions Personnel Contact __________________________

SAT/ACT required? Average accepted scores? _________________

Average accepted GPA? _________

Weight of other factors? _________

FL required for admission? _________

FL required for graduation? How many semesters? _________________

Does college consider disability in admission decision? _________

Office of Disability Services Personnel Contact ______________________

How many registered students with disabilities (SWD)? _________

How many staff? Role? __________________

Technology available? ______________________________________

Academic coaches? _________

What accommodations available? ______________________________

FL substitution or waiver process? _________

FL class for SWD only? _________

Additional Contacts (Learning Disability/ADHD Program, Asperger's Program, Counseling Center, Health Services, etc.) __________________________

____

General Impressions ______________________________________

____

____

Notes

Chapter 1

1 20 U.S.C. §1400 *et seq.*

2 Pub. L. No. 94–142, 89 Stat. 773 (1975).

3 347 U.S. 483 (1954).

4 Mills v. Bd. of Educ., 348 F. Supp. 866 (D.D.C. 1972).

5 S. Rep. 94–168, at 8 (1975), quoted in Honig v. Doe, 484 U.S. 305, 309 (1988).

6 Education of the Handicapped Amendments of 1990, Pub. L. No. 101–476, 104 Stat. 825 (1990).

7 Individuals with Disabilities Education Improvement Act of 2004, Pub. L. No. 108–446, 118 Stat. 2647 (2004).

8 Bd. of Educ. v. Rowley, 458 U.S. 176 (1982).

9 42 U.S.C.A. § 12101 *et seq.*

10 See note 8 above.

11 Rowley, at 203.

12 See, for example, Kule-Korgood, M., (2009) *The Anachronism of Rowley—Using a Chisel and Stone Tablet in the Digital Age*, Compendium of Materials, Council of Parent Attorneys and Advocates, Inc., 11th Annual Conference, 326 (2009).

13 20 U.S.C. § 1415(i)(3).

14 See, for example, Florence County School Dist. Four v. Carter, 510 U.S. 7 (1993); Forest Grove School Dist. v. T.A., 129 S. Ct. 2484 (2009).

15 Rehabilitation Act of 1973, Pub. L. No. 93–112, § 504, 87 Stat. 355 (1973) (codified as amended at 29 U.S.C. § 794). All students with disabilities are also protected by the Americans with Disabilities Act, passed in 1990, but since the protections are virtually the same as Section 504's (passed in 1973), people still tend to use the language of Section 504.

16 ADA Amendments Act of 2008, Pub. L. No. 110–325, § 7, 122 Stat. 3553 (2008).

17 42 U.S.C.A. § 12101 *et seq.*

18 42 U.S.C.A. § 12102(1)(A).

19 42 U.S.C.A § 12101(2)(A).

20 42 U.S.C.A. § 12102(2)(B).

21 42 U.S.C. § 12133.

22 Sutton v. United Airlines, Inc., 527 U.S. 471 (1999). See also Murphy v. UPS, Inc., 527 U.S. 516 (1999) and Albertson's, Inc. v. Kirkingburg, 527 U.S. 555 (1999).

23 527 U.S. 471 (1991) at 482.

24 Toyota Motor Mfg. v. Williams, 534 U.S. 184 (2002).

25 Littleton v. Wal-Mart Stores, Inc., 231 Fed. Appx. 879 (11th Cir. 2007).

26 154 Cong. Rec. S. 8840–01 (daily ed. September 16, 2008) (statement of Managers-S. 3460).

27 34 C.F.R. § 104.44(a); 34 C.F.R. § 104.44(d); 28 C.F.R. § 35.104.

28 20 U.S.C. § 1232(g).

29 Health Insurance Portability and Accountability Act, Pub. L. No. 104–191, 110 Stat. 1936 (1996).

Chapter 2

1 Yankton School District v. Schramm, 93 F.3rd 1369 (8th Circuit, 1996).

2 20 U.S.C. §1400(c)(14).

3 20 U.S.C. §1400(c)(14).

4 20 U.S.C. §1414(d)(1)(B), 34 C.F.R. §300.321(b).

5 20 U.S.C. §1401(34)(B).

6 See, for example, Yankton and Brett v. Goshen Community School Corporation, 161 F.Supp. 2nd 930 (N.D. Indiana), citing Zobrest, 509 U.S. 1 (1993).

7 20 U.S.C §1401(34)(C).

8 20 U.S.C §1401(34)(C).

9 20 U.S.C. §1414(c)(5)(B).

10 20 U.S.C. §1414(d)(1)(B)(vii).

Chapter 3

1 US Department of Education, Office of Civil Rights, (March, 2007), *Transition of Students With Disabilities To Postsecondary Education: A Guide for High School Educators*, available at www.ed.gov/about/offices/list/ocr/transitionguide.html, accessed on January 15, 2010.

2 US Department of Education, Office of Civil Rights, (March, 2007), *Transition of Students With Disabilities To Postsecondary Education: A Guide for High School Educators*, available at www.ed.gov/about/offices/list/ocr/transitionguide.html, accessed on January 15, 2010.

3 42 U.S.C. §1202(3)(B).

Chapter 4

1 Website of Association on Higher Education and Disability (AHEAD), available at www.ahead.org/about, accessed on December 28, 2009.

2 Website of Association on Higher Education and Disability (AHEAD), available at www.ahead.org/sigs/ld-adhd, accessed on December 28, 2009.

3 Website of Association on Higher Education and Disability (AHEAD), available at www.ahead.org/resources/best-practices-resources/principles, accessed on December 28, 2009.

4 Website of Association on Higher Education and Disability (AHEAD), available at www.ahead.org/resources/best-practices-resources/elements, accessed on December 28, 2009.

5 Website of Association of Higher Education and Disability (AHEAD), available at www.ahead.org/resources/best-practices-resources/principles, accessed on December 30, 2009.

Chapter 5

1 Lemann, N. (1999) *The Big Test—The Secret History of the American Aristocracy*. New York: Farrar, Straus and Giroux.

2 Lemann (1999), p.86.

3 The College Board, August 25, 2008 Press Release: *SAT® Scores Stable as Record Numbers Take Test*, available on the College Board Website at www.collegeboard.com/press/releases/197846.html, accessed on December 1, 2009 and ACT, August 13, 2008 Press Release: *College Readiness Stable for 2008 U.S. High School Grads Even as Number of Students Taking ACT® Test Climbs to New Heights*, available on the ACT website at www.act.org/news/releases/2008/crr.html, accessed on December 1, 2009.

4 Breimhorst v. Educational Testing Service, 2000 WL 34510621 (N.D.Cal).

5 The College Board, July 17, 2002 Press Release: *The College Board and Disabilities Rights Advocates Announce Agreement to Drop Flagging from Standardized Tests*, available on the College Board Website at www.collegeboard.com/press/releases/11360.html, accessed on December 1, 2009.

6 Breimhorst, M., *Biography*, available at http://breimhorst.net/bio.html, accessed on December 1, 2009.

7 Written Comment from Jo Anne Simon, Esq., December 28, 2009.

8 The College Board, *Examples of Accommodations Available on College Board Tests*. Available at http://professionals.collegeboard.com/testing/ssd/accommodations/other, accessed on December 1, 2009 and The ACT, *ACT Test Accommodations for Students with Disabilities 2009–2010*, available at www.act.org/aap/disab/chart.html, accessed on December 30, 2009.

9 The ACT, *ACT Policy for Documentation to Support Requests for Test Accommodations on the ACT (No Writing) or ACT Plus Writing*, available at www.act.org/aap/disab/policy.html#reco, accessed on December 1, 2009.

10 The ACT, *Services for Students with Disabilities*, available at www.act.org/aap/disab/index.html, accessed on December 2, 2009.

11 Rooney, C. with Schaeffer, B. and the Staff of FairTest (September, 1998) *Test Scores Do Not Equal Merit: Enhancing Equity and Excellence in College Admissions by Deemphasizing SAT and ACT Results*. Cambridge, MA: The National Center for Fair and Open Testing, available at www.fairtest.org/files/optrept.pdf, accessed on December 1, 2009.

Chapter 6

1 Streichler, R. (2005) *Graduate Teaching Assistant Handbook*. California: University of California, available at http://ctd.ucsd.edu/resources/tahandbook.pdf, accessed on November 9, 2009.

2 Active Minds website available at www.activeminds.org/index.php?option=com-content&task=view&id=13&Itemid=42, accessed on November 9, 2009.

Chapter 7

1 The Common Application (2009), available at www.commonapp.org/CommonApp/mission.aspx, accessed on November 2, 2009.

2 Universal College Application (2009), available at www.universalcollegeapp.com/index.cfm?ACT=Display&APP=APPONLINE&DSP=CollegeMembership, accessed on November 2, 2009.

3 Universal College Application (2009), available at www.universalcollegeapp.com/index.cfm?ACT=Display&APP=APPONLINE&DSP=CollegeMembership, accessed on November 2, 2009.

4 US News and World Report (2009) Colleges Where Applying Early Decision Helps. New York: US News and World Report, available at www.usnews.com/articles/education/2009/09/30/colleges-where-applying-early-decision-helps.html, accessed on January 2, 2010.

5 Thrower, R.H., Healy, S.J., Margolis, G.J., Lynch, M., Stafford, D. and Taylor, W. (2008) Overview of the Virginia Tech Tragedy and Implications of Campus Safety—The IACLEA Blueprint for Safer Campuses. West Hartford: The International Association of Campus Law Enforcement Administrators, available at www.iaclea.org/visitors/PDFs/VT-taskforce-report_Virginia-Tech.pdf, accessed on November 15, 2009.

6 Rasmussen, C. and Johnson, G. (2008) The Ripple Effect of Virginia Tech: Assessing the Nationwide Impact on Campus Safety and Security Policy and Practice. Minneapolis: Midwestern Higher Education Compact, available at www.mhec.org/policyresearch/052308mhecsafetyrpt_lr.pdf, accessed on November 29, 2009.

7 Hawkins, D.A. and Clinedist, M.E. (2007) The State of College Admission. Arlington: National Association for College Admission Counseling, available at http:bulletin.nacacnet.org/NR/rdonlyres/2AD53442-8CC7-4EA6-8263-1B1568DEE736/0/07soca.pdf, accessed on November 30, 2009.

8 National Association for College Admission Counseling (2009) Responses: Advice for Wait Listed Student. Arlington: National Association for College Admission Counseling, available at http://peach.ease.lsoft.com/scripts/wa.exe?A0=NACAC, accessed on April 6, 2009.

Chapter 9

1 A study by the US Department of Labor found that of the 3.2 million students who graduated from high school in spring of 2008, some 2.2 million (71.5% of women and 65.9% of men) were enrolled college by that fall. US Department of Labor, Bureau of Labor Statistics, Report (April 28, 2009): *College Enrollment and Work Activity of 2008 High School Graduates*, available at www.bls.gov/news.release/hsgec.nr0.htm, accessed on November 14, 2009.

2 Day, J.C. and Neuburger, E.C. (July, 2002) *The Big Payoff: Educational Attainment and Synthetic Estimates of Work-Life Earnings*, US Census Bureau Current Population Reports, available at www.census.gov/prod/2002pubs/p23—210.pdf, accessed on October 10, 2009.

3 29 U.S.C. §705(2)(b)(2).

4 29 U.S.C. §705(20).

5 29 U.S.C. §705(21)(A).

6 29 U.S.C. §705 (21)(B).

7 US Department of Labor, *ADA and Rehabilitation Act*, available at www.dol.gov/asp/programs/drugs/workingpartners/regs/ada.asp, accessed on November 24, 2009.

8 Maurer, M. (2009) *The Mythology of Discrimination*, talk delivered at the University of Notre Dame on March 6, 2009, as reported in *The Braille Reporter* (May, 2009) available at www.nfb.org/images/nfb/Publications/bm/bm09/bm0905/bm090505.htm, accessed on December 1, 2009.

9 Department of Defense (December 15, 2000) *Department of Defense Directive Number 6130.3*, available at http://biotech.law.lsu.edu/blaw/dodd/corres/html2/d61303x.htm, accessed on December 1, 2009.

10 50 U.S.C. §454.

11 US Army (December 14, 2007, Revised September 10, 2008) *Regulation 40–501, Standards of Medical Fitness*, available at www.army.mil/usapa/epubs/pdf/r40_501.pdf, accessed on December 26, 2009.

12 Osten, F.M. and Noveck, C. (1996) survey reported in *Beyond Threshold* (2006). Cambridge, MA: The Threshold Program at Lesley University.

13 The US Equal Employment Opportunity Commission (March 25, 1997) *EEOC Enforcement Guidance on the Americans with Disabilities Act and Psychiatric Disabilities, Number 915.002*, available at www.eeoc.gov/policy/docs/psych.html, accessed on November 20, 2009.

14 Dixon, K.A. with Kruse, D., Ph.D. and Van Horn, C.E., Ph.D. (March, 2003) *Americans' Attitudes About Work, Employers and Government: Work Trends; Restricted Access: A Survey of Employers About People with Disabilities and Lowering Barriers to Work*. John J. Heldrich Center for Workforce Development, New Brunswick, New Jersey, available at www.heldrich.rutgers.edu/uploadedFiles/Publications/Restricted%20Access.pdf, accessed on November 20, 2009.

15 The President's Committee's Job Accommodation Network (January 15, 2009), study reported by US Department of Labor Employment and Training Administration, *Myths and Facts About Workers with Disabilities*, available at www.doleta.gov/disability/htmldocs/myths.cfm, accessed on November 20, 2009.

Chapter 11

1 SleepEducation.com website, from the American Academy of Sleep Medicine, available at www.sleepeducation.com/Hygiene.aspx, accessed on December 18, 2009.

2 Van Dongen, H.P., Maislin, G., Mullington, J.M., Dinges, D.F. (March 15, 2003) "The cumulative cost of additional wakefulness: dose-response effects on neurobehavioral functions and sleep physiology from chronic sleep restriction and total sleep deprivation," *Sleep*, Official Publication of the Associated Professional Sleep Societies, LLC, a joint venture of the American Academy of Sleep Medicine and the Sleep Research Society, available at www.ncbi.nlm.nih.gov/pubmed/12683469, accessed on December 18, 2009.

3 Faedda, G.L. and Austin, N.B. (2006) *Parenting a Biopolar Child: What to Do and Why*. Oakland, CA: New Harbinger Publications.

4 28 C.F.R. Part 35 Nondiscrimination on the Basis of Disability in State and Local Government Services, available at www.ed.gov/policy/rights/reg/ocr/28cfr35.pdf, accessed on December 15, 2009.

5 Mooney, J. (2007) *The Short Bus: A Journey Beyond Normal*. New York: Henry Holt and Company.

6 23 U.S.C. § 158.

7 Bailey v. Ga. Pac. Corp., 306 F.3rd 1162 (1st Cir. 2002).

8 Website of Alcoholics Anonymous at www.aa.org, accessed on November 14, 2009.

9 Website of Al-Anon/Alateen at www.al-anon.alateen.org, accessed on November 14, 2009.

10 Transcript of interview with Dr. Jay Giedd, aired on PBS program *Frontline*, January 31, 2002, available at www.pbs.org/wgbh/pages/frontline/shows/teenbrain/etc/script.html, accessed on December 18, 2009.

Chapter 12

1 Website of National Technical Institute for the Deaf, a college of Rochester Institute of Technology, available at www.ntid.rit.edu/research/cprint_home.php, accessed on December 22, 2009.

2 Website of Communication Access Resource Center (CART), available at www.chr.ucla.edu/chr/comp/webdocs/ClassSpecAlpha_files/pdfclassspecs/captionist.pdf, accessed on December 22, 2009.

Chapter 13

1 Higher Education Opportunity Act, Pub. L. No. 110–315, 122 Stat. 3078 (2008).

2 Heller, D. (November 26, 2008) *Need Blind but "Gapping"*, Report prepared for National Association for College Admission Counseling, available in summary form at www.insidehighered.com/news/2008/11/26/aid, accessed on December 1, 2009.

3 Credit Card Accountability Responsibility and Disclosure Act of 2009, Title III, 15 U.S.C. 1637(c).

Index